KINGDOMS *of the* CELTS

KINGDOMS
of the
CELTS

A History and a Guide

JOHN KING

BLANDFORD

Rag ow myrgh Emmeline, elvenn golowder y'n tewlessa nos.

For my daughter Emmeline, a spark of brightness in the darkest night.

First published in the United Kingdom in 2000 by Blandford

Previously published in hardback in 1998 by Blandford

Text copyright © 1998 and 2000 John King
Design and layout copyright © 1998 Cassell & Co.

The moral right of John King to be identified as the author of this work has been asserted by him in accordance with the Copyright, Designs and Patents Act 1988.

A CIP catalogue record for this book is available from the British Library.

ISBN 0-7137-2692-X (hardback)
ISBN 0-7137-2693-8 (paperback)

Designed by Chris Bell

Printed and bound in Great Britain by Mackays of Chatham plc, Chatham, Kent

Blandford
Cassell & Co.
The Orion Publishing Group
Wellington House
125 Strand
London WC2R 0BB

CONTENTS

ACKNOWLEDGEMENTS

I am grateful, as always, to my wife, Mary Jane, for reading this book in manuscript and making helpful suggestions for improvements; and to the woman or man who invented the accordion file for helping me make sense of my research notes.

INTRODUCTION

HE best thing I ever did was to meet my wife. That happened many years ago in Cill Airne (Killarney), Ireland, where, fortuitously, we were both attending the annual Feile Pan Cheilteach, an international Celtic festival of song, dance, talk and merrymaking. Night after night was filled with music, as we sang our heads off in Cornish, Welsh or Irish, or listened to the playing of the *piobaireachd* ('pibroch') in the piping competition, or watched those Irish girls in the embroidered dresses and green satin cloaks, with their faces set in concentration and their upper bodies stiff as trees, and their heels and toes clacking like little hammers. I have heard a Scots traditional singer, Mary-Ann Kennedy, sing *Eilean a Cheo* ('Misty Isle') with such simplicity and grace that it was impossible not to weep at the beauty of it. I have seen Brenda Wootton, a dear friend now departed, follow one of Dick Gendall's haunting Cornish songs with a belly-shaking rendition of *Tishomingo Blues*. I remember, on one occasion, that the ferry back from Brittany was delayed and we had to spend a night sitting in the waiting room at Roscoff, while a lone Scots piper, swaying gently from the few drams he had taken to sustain himself, walked up and down the tiled floor playing *Scotland the Brave* (or something quite like it) without pause for five and a half hours. I remember a night in Lorient, Brittany, when my small male-voice choir, *An Tryskell*, arrived at a village sports centre to give a concert, advertised for seven o'clock. At around nine o'clock, when we had just about given up hope, a bereted, Gauloise-smoking caretaker, accompanied by a small spotted dog, came to unlock the building. By about ten o'clock, a couple of hundred people had sauntered over, after finishing their long dinners and bottles of *vin de table*. By three in the morning, we were really singing. By five in the morning, we had discovered that not only are Cornish and Breton very close sister languages, but that if you wait long enough, and slake your thirst sufficiently while you are waiting, they become one and the same language; indeed, that any language in the world at all is quite intelligible.

After such experiences, I think I can be forgiven for having developed an enduring enthusiasm for the vigour of Celtic culture. The Celts adore merriment, and they adore sadness; what they cannot abide is the dullness of the in-between. They are happy enough with the bustle of cities – talk to the lads and lasses who work the little passenger ferries in Boston Harbour – but they have a deeply ingrained passion for the quietness of wild places, the lonely moor, the long and narrow road winding down to the sea, the heather-drenched glens, the little islands where the black cattle come down to the beach and stand in the shallow waves. They revel in change, flux, movement. They like the weather that is coming, not the weather that is here, the fresh dampness in the wind, or seeing the rain as it comes, what the Irish call 'smoke on the mountain', or the first nip of frost, or the early morning dew curling into little wisps of steam in the strong sunlight of spring. They like loneliness and sorrow; they like company, and the *craic* (lively conversation), and singing through the night until you fall asleep in your chair.

All this culture comes from somewhere. It has nothing to do with race because there is no such thing as a Celtic race. Anyone who starts talking about 'the Celtic blood' is talking dangerous nonsense. It does have a lot to do with history, with language, with religiosity if not actually with religion, and with a sense of place and the numinous. This book attempts to explore one aspect of Celtic culture, namely the Celtic pursuit, in many different forms, of governance by a king or queen. It is not intended as any kind of polemic in favour of royalty or the monarchy; if anything, my personal political views tend towards republicanism and disestablishmentarianism. There is a very broad spectrum of experience to be found within this apparently narrow topic. There is a great deal of difference between a brutish, petty king of the Arverni tribe in pre-conquest Gaul and an effete, kilted, feather-capped lord of the nineteenth-century Scottish Highlands, yet they do have some things in common. In this volume, I hope to discover at least in part what were the enduring qualities and characteristics which made the Celtic kingdoms, in their many different forms, such significant contributors to the world.

ONE

❋

WHO WERE THE CELTS?

THE CELTIC IDENTITY

OR more than two thousand years, the Celts have established a clear and recognizable identity on the world stage, yet, paradoxically, there is no convincing evidence of how, when or even where the Celts first appeared, nor has there ever been a single, unifying characteristic (apart, perhaps, from language) which unequivocally defines what it is actually to be a Celt. Whatever their origins, the Celts emerged in prehistory – Gerhard Herm calls them, poetically, 'the people who came from the darkness'[1] – as a group of peoples which shared many common bonds of social customs, art, religious practices and, especially, of language, across a vast area of Europe, and which remains to this day, particularly on the Atlantic seaboard, a sufficiently distinctive group to merit recognition as separate Celtic nations. There are traces of the Celtic heritage not just in Britain and Ireland, Brittany and Galicia, where Celtic culture and political identity are still actively pursued, but also broadly across France, Spain, southern Germany, Austria, the Czech Republic, northern Italy, the Balkans and even Turkey. Celtic art, which has flourished for two millennia, is still in production and sold across the world. Many Celtic social and legal ideas, including individual combat and fair play and the huge complexity of ideas which constitutes the chivalric code generated through the Arthurian legends and the Matter of Britain, have become deeply embedded in western culture. The Celts changed the world, and continue to do so.

Yet even the origin of the name 'Celt' is unclear. It is highly likely that almost all of the early tribes which we now group together under the title Celt never used the words Celts or Celtic to describe themselves. The Latin term *Celtae* was used by Caesar and others, and the name *Celtici*, used widely in south-western Spain, seems also to be a Romanization of an originally Celtic word. Caèsar tells us that the tribes he met used the word *Celtae* to describe themselves, even though they also had individual tribal names. The Greeks used *Keltoi*, which was simply their version of the same word. The Greek and classical Latin spellings do indicate, however, that the name 'Celt' should always be pronounced with a hard |k| sound, the Boston Celtics notwithstanding. The two other generic terms found in classical writing are *Galli*, 'the people of Gaul', and *Galatae*, a term more frequently used by Greek writers. The Galatians, to whom St. Paul's Epistle is addressed, are these same *Galatae*. The word *Gael*, now used to describe the northern Celts, is obviously related to *Galatae*. A large bronze tablet, found at Contrebia Belaisca (modern Botoritta) near Saragossa in Spain, which appears to be a legal document, contains about two hundred words of a language which has been called *Hispano-Celtic*, but which is known only through similar such tiny fragments. The name *Celt*, ancient though it obviously is, only came into widespread use following the work of sixteenth- and seventeenth-century linguists, in particular George Buchanan (1506–82) and Edward Lhwyd (1660–1709). No classical writer ever used the term to describe tribes or individuals in Britain or Ireland.

No matter how complex it may be to find perfectly accurate and historically attested definitions, it remains true that the single, most persuasive evidence of Celtic identity is evidence of use of a Celtic language. Celtic, or proto-Celtic, divided into two related, but separate, branches at some unknown point in its history. These branches are commonly called *Q Celtic* (sometimes *K Celtic*) or *Goidelic*, and *P Celtic* or *Brythonic*.

The modern Goidelic languages are Irish Gaelic (earlier called Erse), Scots Gaelic, and Manx. During the nineteenth century, Manx virtually died out as a widely spoken language, and the numbers of Scots and Irish Gaelic speakers declined markedly during the eighteenth and nineteenth centuries, but subsequently all three languages have been vigorously maintained (revived, in the case of Manx) and defended. Gaelic is still widely spoken in the west of Ireland, particularly in the area known as the Gaeltacht, the ancient kingdoms of Munster and Connaught, and it would not be unusual to hear Irish spoken anywhere in counties Galway, Cork, Kerry or Clare. Both Scotland and Ireland have realized the importance of the modern broadcast media to language survival, and so Scots and Irish Gaelic now thrive in radio, film and television as well as in the streets and in the schools. The Republic of Ireland requires its children to learn Gaelic and earnestly defends its official status, despite the predominance of spoken English.

The modern Brythonic languages are Welsh, Cornish and Breton. The most obvious characteristic which distinguishes them from the Goidelic group is a consonantal shift: where Goidelic has a |k| sound (developed from the original Indo-European |qᵛ|), Brythonic shifted to a |p| sound. Thus, Goidelic *cenn* ('head') becomes *penn* in Brythonic. Penzance, spelled Pennsans by modern Cornish speakers, means 'holy head'. The well-known Goidelic *mac*, meaning 'son of', becomes *map* or *mab* (and *ap* or *ab* in later

Welsh) in Brythonic. The Irish saint, Cieran, when he sailed on his millstone across the Irish Sea to become the patron saint of Cornwall, changed his name from Cieran to Piran (*cf.* the modern town name Perranporth, 'Piran's harbour'). The strongest of these languages is Welsh, both because it has the largest and longest literary heritage and also because it has a larger population of modern speakers, with even more healthy representation through modern broadcast media than Gaelic. Breton has been in decline for many years, but it is actively defended by a vigorous language movement which has achieved notable successes in recent years. Cornish died as a widely spoken language, but its revival, which began in 1904 with the publication of Dr. Henry Jenner's handbook of the language, has also been remarkably successful.

From the limited evidence available, it seems certain that the Celtic which Julius Caesar heard spoken – Gaulish, in other words – was P Celtic, or Brythonic, in character. It is sometimes called *Gallo-Brittonic* or *Gallo-Brythonic*. As Rome's influence spread throughout Gaul, and then into much of the rest of the Celtic world, so Latin increasingly influenced the Celtic languages. This influence was much stronger in Brythonic than in Goidelic. For example, the modern Cornish *eglos* (Welsh *eglwys*), meaning 'church', is derived from Latin *ecclesia*, and the Cornish *pons* ('bridge'; the Welsh cognate is *pont*) and *fenester* ('window') are clearly directly borrowed from Latin *pons* and *fenestra*. One Celtic word has had a rare history: the English word 'car', now used to describe a motor vehicle, was originally a very ancient Celtic word which the Romans adopted (*currus*) to describe the wheeled chariots which they also adopted from the Celts.

Interpreting linguistic evidence is tricky, however. We know that Sanskrit *raj*, Latin *rex* and Celtic *rix* all mean 'king', and that they all derive from some earlier (proto-Indo-European) word with the same meaning. But how much does that tell us about the practice and significance of kingship in Indian, Roman and Celtic societies, other than the fact that it existed? We know that proto-Indo-European **peku* appears directly related to Latin *pecus* ('cattle'), Greek *pekos* ('pelt'), and the Latin and Greek verbs *pectere* ('to comb') and *pektein* ('to shear'), and we can, therefore, make educated guesses that **peku* must also have referred to sheep, and that combing, shearing, spinning and weaving were activities in those communities – if it doesn't exist, why have a word for it?[2] But making convincing statements about social practice from linguistic evidence alone is very difficult, and has led to much heated argument.

So, we use linguistic evidence to identify the Celts, but this evidence is limited in quantity and frequently open to varying interpretation. Our other sources are documentary evidence, mostly from classical authors, and archaeological evidence.

The Celts are described or mentioned by name by Herodotus, Aristotle, Sotion, Poseidonius, Julius Caesar, Cicero, Polybius, Diodorus of Sicily (Diodorus Siculus) and Timageneus, and, in the Christian era, by Strabo,

Pomponius Mela, Lucian, Pliny, Tacitus, Suetonius, Dion Chrysostom and Clement of Alexandria. All these authors were describing peoples whom they were, in varying degree, keen to characterize as barbaric, alien, uncivilized or threatening. All their accounts, therefore, are unreliable to some extent. For example, both Caesar and Strabo describe a Celtic method of execution or human sacrifice, supervised by druids, in which victims were burned alive in a huge wickerwork structure: Strabo uses the Greek word *kolosson* ('giant'), Caesar writes of *immani magnitudine simulacra* ('a huge dummy'). Two authors, writing in different places at different times, give the same description: that sounds convincing. Yet Strabo also describes Celtic executions involving bows and arrows, and we are virtually certain from archaeological evidence that the early tribal Celts never used bows and arrows – indeed, the very words for bows and arrows are late loan words in all the Celtic languages – so our conviction tends to evaporate. Strabo, an Asiatic Greek (his name is actually a nickname, meaning 'squint-eyed') who lived from *c.*64 BC to AD 21, spent all his time in the great library at Alexandria (perhaps poring over the books made him squint-eyed). He did meet Poseidonius personally, but apart from that meeting, all his descriptions of Britain, Gaul, Spain, Italy and Galatia came from other authors' manuscripts. It is perfectly possible, for example, that he borrowed Caesar's description of the wickerwork giant to add colour and local authenticity to his own writing. Classical historians were not at all scrupulous about acknowledging their sources, nor avoiding florid invention when it suited their purposes, so we have to read their accounts with cautious scepticism.

Of these authors, the most noted for descriptions of the Celts are Polybius, Poseidonius and Diodorus Siculus. Polybius, a Greek politician who lived from *c.*200 to sometime after 118 BC, published in about 150 BC a popular account of Rome's rise to power, from Hannibal and the Punic Wars to the Battle of Pydna in 168 BC which marked the Roman conquest of Greece (and which led to Polybius's own exile to Rome). He tells us a great deal about the early tribal Celts of Gaul. Poseidonius (his name derives from Poseidon, god of the sea) was a Syrian, the teacher of Cicero. He lived from about 135 to 50 BC, and he travelled extensively in the western Mediterranean, so it may be that he actually met and spoke with Gauls and Hispano-Gallic tribes. Unfortunately, only fragments of his writings survive and most of what he wrote comes to us through later authors who either quote him directly or borrow his descriptions, with or without acknowledgment. Diodorus Siculus ('the Sicilian') wrote a world history between 60 and 30 BC which included extensive descriptions of Britain and Gaul, but what knowledge, if any, was first hand is no longer ascertainable. Nevertheless, his vivid descriptions of the Celts' physical and social characteristics have been very widely quoted and used by later authors.

Some classical authors were more directly acquainted with the Celts, most notably Caesar and Tacitus. Julius Caesar (100–44 BC), a man of extraordinary ambition and achievements, was the last leader of the Roman republic; indeed, it was the internecine wars following his assassination which led to the restoration of rule by the emperors. He conquered Gaul and invaded Britain, and wrote a detailed account of his exploits. This account, properly known as *The Commentaries*, but more widely known as *The Gallic War*, is a work of propaganda written to justify what was, in fact, an illegal series of campaigns, so it is heavily biased in political terms. Nevertheless, it contains much convincing detail, and it is still a rich source of information for historians of the early Celts.

Caius Cornelius Tacitus ('the silent one'), who lived from AD 55 to 100, never visited Britain, but his father-in-law, Agricola, was Roman governor of Britain for many years, so there is good reason to believe that much of his material came from first-hand accounts. His Latin prose style is unusual – dense, poetic, sometimes elliptical – but, in general, he is considered a fairly reliable witness. He gives us some very vivid pictures of the British Celtic tribes.

The archaeological evidence describing the Celts has greatly increased in quantity over the past century and, for good reason, is viewed as of vital importance. Real artefacts or real inscriptions, which can be subjected to all kinds of testing, are obviously convincing. The difficulty with archaeological evidence lies always in interpretation. We know that this urn was found in such-and-such a place, but how did it get there? Are we certain about what it was used for? Much of the evidence is 'text-free', to use archaeological jargon; in other words, it is not accompanied by writing which would unarguably define or describe its function or purpose. While a good deal of the archaeological evidence is not seriously disputed, there are also some classic enigmas (for example, the souterrains known as *fogous*) which still provide rallying points for vigorous argument.

PHYSICAL DESCRIPTIONS

Herodotus, the Greek 'father of history' who lived from *c*.484 to 425 BC, tells us that the Celts came originally from the area of the Danube.[3] He describes Iberians, Celts and Scythians together, and some of the material in the descriptions has led to conjecture that there was certainly cultural influence from one group to another, and possibly even some common genetic inheritance. Take, for example, Herodotus's account of head-hunting among the Scythians, which is strikingly similar to what we know about head-hunting among the Celts:

> Each of them cuts off an enemy's head and takes it back home.
> He then skewers it on a long wooden stave and sets this up so that
> the head sticks far above the house, often above the chimney. They
> maintain that the head is put there as guardian of the whole house. . . .

With the heads of their worst enemies they proceed as follows: once they have sawn off everything below the eyebrows, they carefully clean out the head. If the owner is poor he will merely stretch calf-leather round it and use it thus. But if he is rich, he will also line the inside with gold and use it as a drinking vessel.[4]

There is frequent confusion between Germans and Celts in the classical texts. For example, the three tribes which most plagued Rome during the first century BC, namely the Cimbri, Teutones and Ambrones, are described in most encyclopedias as Germanic tribes and their place of origin is usually given as Jutland. We still use 'Teutonic' as a euphemism for Germanic. Yet the name Cimbri is convincingly similar to the *cymbr element which we find in Cymru (Welsh for Wales) and, a little transmogrified, in the Cumber- of Cumberland. Even more convincingly, the leader of the Cimbri was Boiorix, and that name is indisputably Celtic; we even know what it means – 'king of the Boii'. Similarly, Plutarch includes in his account of the Battle of Aquae Sextae descriptions of the Ambrones using their individual tribal names as rallying calls, a distinctly Celtic practice. Strabo differentiated between the Celts, who lived on the west bank of the Rhine, and the Germans, who lived on the east bank and were 'even taller, more savage and blond'. But remember that Strabo, who even promised, 'I shall . . . describe, in part what I myself have seen in my travels over land and sea . . .', was an Alexandrian bookworm, who may well have never once laid foot outside his library. The only certainty which emerges is that the distinctions between Celts, Germans and Scythians in classical texts are not always trustworthy.

There are some very early, fragmentary references to the Celts. Xenophon, a pupil of Socrates, mentions Celtic mercenaries in the wars of Athens and Sparta against Thebes. Plato includes the Celts in his list of tribes inclined to drunkenness. The world picture of these earliest Greek commentators included three great groups of barbarians: the Scythians, wild horsemen and archers from somewhere in the north-east; the Iberians and the Celts, possibly related, hirsute savages from the north-west; and the Hyperboreans, a mysterious people so little known that their only description was that they came from beyond ('hyper') the home of the personification of the north wind, the *Boreas*.

In much the same way that Geoffrey of Monmouth, many centuries later, felt the need to create historical individuals to personify events affecting whole peoples, so Diodorus Siculus felt the need to find an individual founder of the tribes of the Celts. His founder, the equivalent of Geoffrey's Brutus as father of all the Britons, is Herakles. He spins a yarn in which Herakles, travelling in what is now France, finds himself among the Mandubii, falls in love with their princess, and sires a 'little Heraklid', a child-hero called Galates, from whom the Galatai, or Galli, and the nation of Gallia itself, all took their names. This is fun, but it is also hokum. Diodorus saw in the Celts a replication of the ancient Achaean warrior society, after whose vigour and directness the softer Greeks sometimes hankered. Diodorus relishes his descriptions of Celtic feasts:

> They squat, not on couches, but on the ground, with wolf or dog-skins as cushions. . . . Nearby are the fires, stoked up with charcoal and well-furnished with kettles and spits full of large pieces of meat. Brave warriors are rewarded with the choicest pieces. . .[5]

With that predisposition in mind, we note Diodorus's famous physical description of the early Celts:

> The Gauls are tall of body, with rippling muscles, and white of skin, and their hair is blond, and not only naturally so, but they also make it their practice by artificial means to increase the distinguishing colour which nature has given it. For they are always washing their hair in lime-water, and they pull it back from the forehead to the top of the head and back to the nape of the neck, with the result that their appearance is like that of Satyrs and Pans, since the treatment of their hair makes it so heavy and coarse that it differs in no respect from the manes of horses. Some of them shave the beard, but others let it grow a little; and the nobles shave their cheeks, but they let the moustache grow until it covers the mouth. Consequently, when they are eating, their moustaches become entangled in the food, and when they are drinking, the beverage passes, as it were, through a kind of strainer . . .[6]

Diodorus also informs us that the men wore brightly coloured and embroidered shirts, and a garment unknown to the Romans for which he uses the word *bracae*, which some have related to the word breeches, since the description is clearly of what would nowadays be called trousers in English, or pants in American English. Over the shirt the men wore a cloak, fastened at the shoulder with a brooch, and the material of the cloak was striped or checkered, suggesting a pattern like tartan or plaid.

These small, but easily visualized, details are helpful when we try to clarify the distinctions in classical descriptions between Celtic and non-Celtic barbarians. For example, Tacitus gives us the following description of the classical ancient German physique, but in so doing reveals that the extent to which these distinctions were agreed was open to dispute even in his own time:

> For myself, I accept the view that the peoples of Germany have never contaminated themselves by intermarriage with foreigners but remain of pure blood, distinct and unlike any other nation. One result of this is that their physical characteristics, in so far as one can generalize about such a large population, are always the same: fierce-looking blue

eyes, reddish hair, and big frames – which, however, can exert their strength only by means of violent effort. They are less able to endure toil or fatiguing tasks and cannot bear thirst or heat, though their climate has inured them to cold spells and the poverty of their soil to hunger.[7]

Despite Tacitus's claim, his description of Germans is strikingly similar to many descriptions of the Celtic physical type, or at least one of them. Similarly, Herodotus describes the Scythians of Eastern Europe:

The Euxine Pontus, against which Darius made his campaign, contains – except for the Scythians – the stupidest nations in the world. For within this country of Pontus we cannot put forward any nation for its cleverness, nor do we know from there of any learned man; the exceptions are, among nations, the Scythians, and, of men, Anacharsis. For the Scythian nation has made the most clever discovery among all the people we know, and of the one thing that is greatest in human affairs – though for the rest I do not admire them much. This greatest thing that they have discovered is how no invader who comes against them can ever escape and how none can catch them if they do not wish to be caught. For this people has no cities or settled forts; they carry their houses with them and shoot with bows from horseback; they live off herds of cattle, not from tillage, and their dwellings are on their wagons. How then can they fail to be invincible and inaccessible for others?[8]

The firing of arrows from horseback is unequivocally Scythian and not Celtic, but some of the other attributes are not so distinctive. Later Celts were certainly farmers and tillers, but many of the early Celtic tribes led a wandering existence within more or less defined territories, taking their cattle with them.

Nobody can now confirm whether Tacitus knew the difference between a Celt and a German, or Herodotus the difference between a Celt and a Scythian, there runs throughout all the classical descriptions a thread of recurring doubt about accuracy. This is particularly true of the accounts of the Punic wars and the other engagements which shaped the emergence of Rome as a dominating power.

Tacitus, in many ways the most reliable and credible of all the classical historians, notes that among the Celts there were, indeed, many different physical types, just as there are to this day:

Who the first inhabitants of Britain were, whether natives or immigrants, is open to question: one must remember we are dealing with barbarians. But their physical characteristics vary, and the variation is suggestive. The reddish hair and large limbs of the

Caledonians proclaim a German origin; the swarthy faces of the
Silures, the tendency of their hair to curl, and the fact that Spain lies
opposite, all lead one to believe that Spaniards crossed in ancient times
and occupied that part of the country. The peoples nearest to the Gauls
likewise resemble them . . .[9]

The Silures came from what is now Wales, so the small, swarthy, curly-haired
type is familiar, but it is worth pointing out that Tacitus's geography is suspect, since he places Spain 'opposite' Wales. Nevertheless, he correctly recognizes, at a very early date, an important truth about the Celtic identity,
namely that physical appearance alone is by no means a reliable or adequate
indicator.

Diodorus gives us mode and style of speech as a distinguishing characteristic:

The Gauls are terrifying in aspect and their voices are deep and
altogether harsh; when they meet together they converse with few
words and in riddles, hinting darkly at things for the most part and
using one word when they mean another; and they like to talk in
superlatives, to the end that they might extol themselves and depreciate
all other men. They are also boasters and threateners and are fond of
pompous language, and yet they have sharp wits and are not without
cleverness at learning.[10]

Diodorus's preoccupation with Celtic similarities to the heroic Achaeans
perhaps also influenced his description of their women, and of their sexual
practices:

The Celtic women are not only as tall as their men, but as
courageous. . . . But, despite their charm, the men will have nothing
to do with them. They long instead for the embrace of one of their
own sex, lying on animal skins and tumbling around with a lover
on either side . . .[11]

Strabo also describes homosexual practices among the young men of Gaul,
who are 'shamelessly generous with their boyish charms', but both Strabo's
and Diodorus's descriptions may be heavily influenced by the cult of the male
body which permeated early Greek society, as evidenced by the famous
devotions of Achilles to Petroclus, or Alexander to Hephaestion. Queen
Cartimandua's elopement and alleged sexual promiscuity, described more
fully in Chapter Seven, scandalized Roman society, and was long cited as an
exemplar to Roman matrons of the misery awaiting them if they succumbed
to barbarian patterns of lasciviousness.

Ammianus Marcellinus, writing many years after Diodorus and Strabo,
continues the description of the Achaean warrior type:

Almost all Gauls are tall and fair-skinned, with reddish hair. Their
savage eyes make them fearful objects; they are eager to quarrel and
excessively truculent. When, in the course of a dispute, any of them
calls in his wife, a creature with gleaming eyes much stronger than her
husband, they are more than a match for a whole group of foreigners;
especially when the woman, with swollen neck and gnashing teeth,
swings her great white arms and begins to deliver a rain of punches
mixed with kicks, like missiles launched by the twisted strings of a
catapult. The voices of most sound alarming and menacing, whether
they are angry or the reverse, but all alike are clean and neat, and
throughout the whole region, and especially in Aquitaine, you will
hardly find a man or woman, however poor, who is dirty and in rags,
as you would elsewhere. . . . They are fit for service in war at any age;
old men embark upon a campaign with as much spirit as those in their
prime; their limbs are hardened by the cold and by incessant toil, and
there is no danger that they are not ready to defy. No one here ever
cuts off his thumb to escape military service, as happens in Italy, where
they have a special name for such malingerers. As a race they are given
to drink, and are fond of a number of liquors that resemble wine; some
of the baser sort wander about aimlessly in a fuddled state of perpetual
intoxication . . . [12]

The liquors that resembled wine certainly included mead, a potent wine fer-
mented from honey which is still widely available in Celtic countries, particularly Cornwall, and beer brewed from barley to a high strength and clarity,
similar to the barley wines now commercially available in Britain, but less
well known in other European countries or America.

Fine hair was the first and most significant attribute of Celtic beauty.
Both men and women wore their hair long, frequently lime-washed, dyed and
braided. In the Irish epic, the *Tain Bo Cuailnge* ('Cattle Raid of Cooley'),
Queen Medb's supporters are identified by their 'flowing hair, fair-yellow
golden streaming manes'. The warrior-hero of the *Tain*, Cu Chulainn, whose
exploits are described much more fully in Chapter Eleven, has hair of three
shades, black at the roots, red in the middle and blond at the tips:

His hair curled about his head like branches of red hawthorn used to
refence the gap in a hedge. Though a noble apple tree weighed down
with fruit had been shaken about his hair, scarcely one apple would
have reached the ground through it, but an apple would have stayed
impaled on each single hair, because of the fierce bristling of his hair
above him. [13]

Dio Cassius describes Boudica, Queen of the Iceni, as having 'a great mass of
bright red hair' which fell to her knees. In the *Tain*, the Druidess Fedelm has
'long, fair-yellow, golden hair; three tresses of her hair wound round her

head, another tress falling behind, which touched the calves of her legs'. The elaborate shape of the hair was as important as the colour, and it seems likely that the Celts used grease, animal fat probably, as well as lime-washing, to style their coiffures; a later passage in the *Tain* tells us that Cu Chulainn's hair looks 'as if a cow had licked it'. One of the reasons why so few Celtic battle helmets have been found may be that hair was so important that helmets were rarely worn.

Both men and women may have used cosmetics. The Irish texts describe a herb called 'ruam' which was used to redden cheeks; brows were blackened with berry juice. Deirdre, in the Irish tales, is so consumed by sorrow that, as she says, 'I do not redden my finger-nails.' The Roman poet Propertius reviles his mistress for wearing *belgicus color* and 'making up like the Celts'.

The Celts were unusually clean among ancient peoples. They did not use oil, like the Romans, but soap and water, the soap made from fat and ashes, probably scented with herbs. The Romans introduced more elaborate bathing rituals, including the use of body oils, into Gaul after the occupation. Men shaved regularly, typically shaving the chin and throat, but leaving side whiskers and long, droopy moustaches. Many mirrors and razors have been found among archaeological artefacts.

Strabo tells us that Celtic men were typically slim of figure: 'They try not to become stout and fat-bellied, and any young man who exceeds the standard length of the girdle is fined.' Other descriptions in the vernacular texts confirm the notion that physical beauty and moral and political superiority were very closely identified, and this idea is of special importance when we

Back of a Celtic mirror found at Birdlip, Gloucestershire,
dating to the first century AD.

consider the significance of kingship. Any royal figure, king or queen, had to be impeccably, strikingly handsome or beautiful, without physical blemish of any kind; the smallest physical deficiency would invalidate the royal status.

Bracae, or breeches, have already been mentioned as distinctively Celtic. The other instantly recognizable item of dress is the Celtic woollen cloak, usually woven in a plaid or tartan pattern. These were so highly valued for their quality that they were significant items of import to Rome. They were of two types: a light, finely woven cloak for summer, and a heavier version for winter. The length and weight of the cloak, and the elaborateness of the brooch or clasp which fastened it, appear to have been important indicators of wealth and social status. Beneath the cloak was sometimes worn a short tunic of linen, shaped at the waist by a girdle or belt, often highly decorated. Strabo uses the Latin word *sagus* (plural *sagi*) to describe these garments, but tells us that the Celtic word for them was *laenae*. The modern Irish and Scottish Celtic word for a shirt is still *leine*.

The Greek word *peplos* is sometimes used to describe the longer tunic-dress worn by women, although this kind of dress, made from two rectangles of fabric fastened at the sides, is also found among non-Celtic tribes. A wrap-around skirt, which may or may not have been Celtic, despite its bold check patterns, was found in Denmark. The number of anklets found suggests that skirt length may have been no longer than to mid-calf.

A golden torc, one of several found at Snettisham,
Norfolk, England.

Shoes and sandals were made from leather, or sometimes from linen uppers sewn to leather soles. There is some evidence that the Celts also made wooden shoes, or clogs: alder, a workable but highly water-resistant timber, may have been used.

Abundant finds of jewellery confirm the classical descriptions of Celtic love of adornment. Strabo tells us:

> To the frankness and high-spiritedness of their temperament must be added the traits of childish boastfulness and love of decoration. They wear ornaments of gold, torques on their necks, and bracelets on their arms and wrists, while people of high rank wear dyed garments besprinkled with gold. It is this vanity which makes them unbearable in victory and so completely downcast in defeat.[14]

The torques, or torcs, mentioned by Strabo were distinctive Celtic neck-rings. They were fashioned from heavy silver or gold threads or chains, twisted and bent around the neck so that an opening remained in the front. They indicated high status, and appear so frequently in depictions of gods and heroes that they may also have had a religious significance, perhaps associated with the cult of the human head. A torc found at Tayac in the Gironde, deliberately snapped in three, was buried with a treasure of five hundred coins. At Mailly in Champagne, a torc was inscribed with Greek letters which indicate that it was part of an offering made to the gods by the tribe of Nitrobriges of southwestern Gaul.[15] The Romans later adopted the torc as a form of military decoration, and cheaper versions, made from iron or copper alloy, have been found.

OUTLINE HISTORY

We shall be examining the history of the Celts much more extensively in later chapters, but a brief outline may be helpful at this stage, while we are still pursuing a description of the Celtic identity.

We have already seen that the origins of the Celts are shrouded in the mist of prehistory. The first identifiable Celtic period dates from around 700 BC, and is named after Hallstatt, a town near Salzburg in the Salzkammergut area of Austria, where an ancient salt mine and a vast prehistoric cemetery were discovered during the nineteenth century. The finds at Hallstatt provide evidence of a people in transition from the use of bronze to the use of iron. Remains of clothing, of jewellery, of cultivated foods like barley, beans, millet and apple, of fragments of domestic pottery, and traces of wooden huts, as well as traces of imported materials like amber, combine to give us a limited but fascinating picture of early Celtic tribal society. It appears to have been an aristocratic society, with richly adorned tombs reserved for the chieftains and royal families. There seems to have been some trade with Mediterranean peoples, notably the Greek colony of Massalia (modern Marseilles).

Sometime around 500 BC, a separate Celtic culture becomes discernible: it is usually called La Tène, after a site discovered near Lake Neuchâtel in Switzerland in 1858. A distinguishing feature is that, whereas the Hallstatt tribes had buried their dead (certainly the richest and most important of them) under four-wheeled carts, the La Tène burials were accompanied by a new, lighter, two-wheeled chariot, drawn by two horses yoked to a central pole. The La Tène art style is more abstract and complex, although distinguishing Celtic themes, such as the transformation of one form into another, human into plant, plant into abstract design, recur. Decorated wine jars indicate frequent trade with Etruria and the Mediterranean regions. To establish a wider context, it is worth noting that at about the same time as the La Tène Celts were flourishing, the first Greek alphabet was just beginning to emerge, iron was being used for the first time in Egypt, and the Chinese classical age had not yet begun. Pythagoras, from whom so much of early Greek achievement appears to be traceable, died sometime around 500 BC.

The Celts did not reach the British Isles until around 900 BC at the very earliest, and probably a good deal later than that. This means that the common assumption that Stonehenge, which was finished around 1500 BC, and other henges like Avebury, are the work of the Celts in general, and Celtic druids in particular, is quite false. Whoever the long-headed people who built the cairns, henges and barrows were, they were not Celts.

The first encounter with Celts mentioned in the classical texts is the Battle of Clusium in 390 BC, described in detail three hundred years later by Livy, which we shall examine in detail in Chapter Three. Hannibal's march from Carthage, in which Celtic mercenaries were involved, took place in 219 BC. At roughly the same time – sometime between 500 BC and 250 BC – the La Tène culture appears to have gained predominance in Britain and Ireland. An expansion in the other direction, eastward, brought Celtic tribes into the Balkans, Greece and central Turkey – these were the *Keltoi* or *Galatae*, the Galatians. The sacking of the oracle at Delphi in 279 BC is attributed to them.

Rome's expansion through the subsequent centuries obliterated the Galatians and brought the tribes of modern Italy, Spain and France under Roman control. The conquest of Gaul was completed about halfway through the first century BC.

The next classical encounter, this one much more fully and widely acknowledged and documented, is Julius Caesar's invasion of Britain in 55 BC. Caesar's initial conquest was consolidated by the emperor Claudius (of Robert Graves's *I, Claudius*) in AD 43. For the next four hundred years, the whole Celtic world (apart from Ireland, which the Romans never reached) was subject to Rome, and there was much cultural assimilation, particularly in matters of religion. When the Romans left Britain in 436, the nation they left behind was culturally as much Roman as it was British.

The Germanic invasions of Britain which followed over several centuries, led by the Angles, Saxons and Jutes, drove the Celts further westward and northward, where they became increasingly culturally and politically marginalized, a process which has continued until comparatively recent historical times, and which, according to some, continues to the present day. During this period, a substantial group of Celts from southwestern Britain fled across the English Channel to what was then called Armorica, and which is now called, after them, Bretagne or Brittany. It was during this time, from the sixth to the ninth centuries, that the linguistic separations described earlier (see page 10) took place.

There was a powerful Celtic resurgence against the Germanic invasion, led notably by Arturus (or Ar Dhu, or Arthur), who, in time, became the King Arthur of legend. The Celtic Church maintained Christianity in Britain and Ireland against the Thor- and Odin-worshipping invaders, and many of the earliest Celtic saints and martyrs belong to this period. Ireland experienced a golden age from the sixth to eighth centuries until it, too, was invaded, this time by tribes from further north – the Vikings. Some Irish seafarers, known as Scotti, founded a kingdom in western Caledonia, and gave their name to the mediaeval kingdom of Scotland. There is an old joke that the Hibernians, who were Scots, founded Ireland, and the Caledonians, who were Irish, founded Scotland.

During the twelfth, thirteenth and fourteenth centuries, the first vernacular Celtic texts appeared. Often dense, elliptical, and clearly intended for a highly trained body of intellectual *literati*, the vernacular texts often create as many problems as they appear to solve. They were written down almost exclusively by Christian monks, but are based on centuries-old oral traditions and frequently deal with very ancient pagan mythological stories and themes, so there is much garbling and intercalation of inappropriate commentary. Nevertheless, the best of them, notably the Irish and Welsh sagas, not only provide us with much valuable information about the Celts, but also stand as outstanding works of literature in their own right.

Wales lost her independence during the thirteenth century; remote and hardy Cornwall gradually succumbed to increasing English influence – the Cornish army's unsuccessful march in 1497, led by Myghal Josef an Gov and Tomas Flamank, was, in fact, the last invasion of London by a foreign power; Brittany was subsumed by France in 1532; Ireland fell under English rule during the reign of Elizabeth, and her death in 1603 triggered the union of Scotland with England, which became formal in 1707; the defeat of the rebellions of 1715 and 1745 effectively destroyed the traditional Scottish clan system; and Ireland was deemed part of the United Kingdom in 1801, until the rising of 1916 challenged that annexation, and Irish statehood was, at least partially, re-established in 1921.

The following time-line summary also includes the dates of the classical authors on whose writings we depend for much of our evidence about the early Celts:

TIME LINE SUMMARY

753 BC	Traditional date of foundation of Rome by Romulus.
c.700	Hallstatt period.
c.600	First Celtic tribes in Ireland.
507	Deposition of last Roman king, Tarquinius Superbus, and foundation of Roman Republic.
c.500	Separation of Goidelic (Q) and Brythonic (P) Celts in Britain.
497	Death of Pythagoras.
484–425	Life dates of Herodotus, Greek 'father of history', who describes Celts, Iberians and Scythians; tells us that the Celts came originally from the area of the Danube.
c.460–400	Thucydides, Greek historian.
454–429	Age of Pericles at Athens.
c.450	First Celtic invasions of Italy, first Celtic incursions into Iberian peninsula.
c.428–354	Xenophon, Greek historian.
390	Battle of Clusium; Celts sack all Rome except Capitol.
387	Celts defeat Romans on River Allia.
c.380	Plato's *Republic*.
c.300	Beginning of the La Tene period in Ireland; creation of the first heroic and royal sagas.
c.280	Celtic tribes advance into Galatia in Asia Minor.
264–241	First Punic (Carthaginian) Wars.
c.250	La Tène culture gains predominance in Britain.
225	Battle of Telemon; all Celtic tribes south of River Po destroyed; Roman expansion begins.
218–201	Second Punic Wars, Celtic tribes employed as mercenaries.
202	Hannibal defeated by Scipio; extensive Romanization of Celtic tribes begins.
c.200–c.118	Polybius, Greek historian and politician, writes popular account of Rome's rise, including many descriptions of early Celts.
149–146	Third Punic Wars.
135–50	Poseidonius, Syrian historian, travels extensively, probably meets Celtic tribes first-hand.
133	Galatia is bequeathed to Rome as a semi-autonomous Celtic province.
121	Roman annexation of Gallia Narbonensis (southern Gaul).
c.75	Belgic tribes cross the Channel into Britain.
c.60–c.30	Diodorus Siculus writes his world history, which includes vivid descriptions of the Celts.
c.60 BC – c.AD 15	Life dates of Livy, Roman historian, whose *Early History of Rome* includes descriptions of Celtic battle tactics.

58–51	Julius Caesar's victories in Gallic and Civil Wars.
55	Caesar leads first Roman invasion of Britain.
54	Second Roman invasion of Britain; King Cassivellaunus subjugated and required to pay tribute.
53–50	Caesar defeats Vercingetorix and pacifies Gaul.
51	Queen Cartimandua allies with Rome.
46	Vercingetorix is executed.
44	Caesar is assassinated.
After 22 BC	Diodorus Siculus dies.
AD 5	Cunobelinus (Cymbeline) recognized by Rome as King of Britain.
43	Claudian invasion; permanent Roman occupation of Britain begins.
60	Agricola, Tacitus's future father-in-law, takes his first command in Britain.
61	Suetonius Paulinus defeats Boudica, Queen of the Iceni.
77	Tacitus marries Agricola's daughter.
98	Tacitus publishes a biography of his father-in-law, Agricola, which includes detailed descriptions of Britain and British Celtic tribes.
c.122	Emperor Hadrian erects a defensive wall in northern Britain.
c.230	fl. Dio Cassius, Roman historian.
285	Diocletian partitions Roman Empire.
296	Roman rule in Britain restored.
330–395	Life dates of Roman historian Ammianus Marcellinus.
395–405	Irish raids on northern and western British coasts.
410	Emperor Honorius abandons Britain; troops withdraw.
c.450	Partition of Ireland into northern and southern kingdoms; Christianity spreads.
c.450–850	Successive waves of invasion of Britain by Angles, Saxons and Jutes.
c.500	St. Patrick arrives in Ireland.
c.540–550	St. David converts Wales to Christianity.
c.540–550	King Arthur, British military leader, killed at the Battle of Camlann.
597	St. Augustine lands in Kent to begin conversion of Angles, Saxons and Jutes (the 'English') to Christianity.
793, 795	Celtic monasteries at Lindisfarne and Iona are destroyed by Vikings.
c.1000	Irish Christianity is restored; the Book of Kells and the Book of Durrow are produced.
1066	Norman invasion of Britain led by William the Conqueror.
c.1110–1300	Earliest written texts of Celtic literature.

CELTIC SOCIAL STRUCTURE

From the earliest archaeological evidence, dating from around 1200 BC, through the classical descriptions of the first and second centuries BC and AD, and on to the most recent of the traditional Celtic vernacular texts, dating from around AD 1400, there emerges a remarkably consistent picture of Celtic society. Tribes were led by a warrior aristocracy which, in turn, was headed by a royal figure, king or queen (since matriarchal succession was common), who at the very least was held to represent some semi-divine attributes, but who may also have been held to be actually divine.

The earliest evidence of the aristocratic hierarchy is to be found in the elaborate graves of the Hallstatt era. We know that there was Celtic commerce in salt from at least 1000 BC, and in iron from around 800 BC, and somewhere around the time of this transition from Late Bronze Age to Early Iron Age there begin to appear more elaborate and affluent Celtic graves, some with iron swords buried with the warrior, and a small number with four-wheeled waggons. Between 800 BC and 600 BC, sometimes called the Hallstatt C period, this kind of elaborate burial chamber appears with markedly greater frequency north of the Alps, usually within or close by hilltop fortified sites, the earliest Celtic 'palaces'.

From c.600 to 475 BC, the Hallstatt D period, these graves are found further to the west, in eastern France and southwestern Germany, and clustered even more obviously around specific hillfort sites, suggesting a further intensification of the aristocratic social structure. It may be that the western movement was influenced by the Greek settlement at Massalia (modern Marseilles) in about 600 BC. There is some evidence that Greek artisans may have been involved in the production of some of the funerary goods, and Greek imports have been found among the treasures of Hallstatt D period graves. The most famous of these sites is at Heuneberg on the Upper Danube; others of note are at Britzgyberg between the Rhône and the Rhine, Asperg near Stuttgart in Germany, and Mont Lassois near the headwaters of the Seine in France.

The body buried at Mont Lassois belonged to a woman – we can use the word 'queen' with some confidence – who was about 35 years old when she died. She was laid out on a four-wheeled waggon, from which the wheels had been removed and placed in a row along one side wall of the burial chamber, which was about 3 metres (10 ft) square. Found with the skull was a gold torc, weighing 454 grams (1 lb), worked in filigree with figures of a winged horse, presumably Pegasus; the torc is clearly northern and Celtic in origin, but the style and technique of the artwork are Greek. Also in the chamber were found valuable drinking vessels and flagons, one at least from Etruria. A huge bronze krater, or cauldron, standing 1.64 metres (5 ft 4 in) high, was decorated with chariots, gorgons, and what appear to be Greek, rather than Celtic, warriors.

These finds strongly suggest that the Celtic kingdoms of the Hallstatt D period achieved their wealth and power at least in part through trade with the Mediterranean, and there are enough finds of wine jars and clay vessels from the period to suggest that one of the chief commodities moving from south to north was wine; there is no evidence that the vine was yet cultivated anywhere north of the Alps. The southbound trade probably included amber from the Baltic, tin from Britain, perhaps honey, and probably salt.

The presence of Greek pots, Etruscan flagons and, later, Roman *amphorae* suggests that wine trade with the Mediterranean continued through many centuries, although in the Hallstatt D period the evidence is localized, and there are settlements which show the same presumed levels of wealth and aristocratic status in their burials, but none of the evidence of trade. Conversely, there are also sites which show frequent Mediterranean trade, but no evidence of major centres or luxurious burials.

In the late 1970s, an unusually rich and complete burial chamber, replete with spectacular funerary goods which had survived without being looted, was discovered at Hochdorf in the Baden-Württemberg region of Germany. The king buried here had died at about 40 years old, probably around 530 BC, and had stood 1.87 metres (6 ft 2 in) tall, a spectacular and very imposing height at the time. He wore a gold belt clasp, and a dagger encased in gold. Beads of gold and amber and bronze brooches found close to the body were presumably originally laid on his chest or attached to his clothing. As well as his hat, his gold-decorated boots, his iron razor and his wooden comb, there lay nearby a bag of fish-hooks and a quiver of iron-tipped spears, presumably intended for him to use for hunting in the afterworld. The body was laid out on a bronze couch at one side of the chamber, and a four-wheeled funerary waggon stood on the other side. There were nine large drinking horns hanging from hooks on the south wall.

Sometime after 500 BC, the La Tène culture began to predominate over the Hallstatt culture. New Celtic kingdoms began to emerge, generally further north than the Hallstatt D period centres, although there was also a significant migration across the Alps into the Po Valley region. The archaeological evidence is, unusually, supported by some written history, although the historian, Livy, has a tendency to personalize and to attribute historical trends to the wills of individuals, rather than wider social forces. Here is Livy's account of what he calls the 'Gallic migration'. Note that he says that this is an account which has 'come down to us'; in other words, an account heavily influenced by folklore. Although it is a little long and laborious, Livy's account does contain enough names of individuals and of specific tribes to make it noteworthy:

> The following account has come down to us of the Gallic migration. During the reign of Tarquinius Priscus in Rome, the Celts, one of the three Gallic peoples, were dominated by the Bituriges, and their king was consequently a member of that tribe . . . indeed, under his rule, Gaul became so rich and populous that the effective control of such large numbers was a matter of serious difficulty. The king

[Ambitgatus], therefore, being now an old man and wishing to relieve his kingdom of the burdensome excess of the population, announced his intentions of sending his two nephews, Bellovesus and Segovesus, both of them adventurous young men, out into the world to find such new homes as the gods by signs from heaven might point the way to. . . . The gods were duly consulted, with the result that to Segovesus were assigned the Hercynian uplands in South Germany while Bellovesus was granted the much pleasanter road into Italy; where-upon collecting the surplus population – Bituriges, Arverni, Senones, Aedui, Ambarri, Carnutes, Aulerci – he set out with a vast host, some mounted, some on foot, and reached the territory of the Tricastini at the foot of the Alps.[16]

Livy informs us that Bellovesus crossed the Alps – one of the first historical figures to do so, since only Herakles had done it before – and, with his army of ragbag Celtic tribes, founded the settlement of Mediolanium, modern Milan. Livy continues:

Later, another wave, this time of the Cenomanni, followed in their footsteps, and crossing, under the leadership of Etitovius, by the same pass and without opposition from Bellovesus, settled near where the towns of Brixia and Verona are today. After them came the Libui, then the Salluvii who settled on the Ticinus, near the ancient tribe of the Laevi Ligures. Then the Boii and Lingones came over by the Poenine pass, and finding all the country between the Alps and the Po already occupied, crossed the river on rafts and expelled not the Etruscans only but the Umbrians as well; they did not, however, pass south of the Apennines.[17]

While Livy's account may be more legendary than factual, the central idea that overpopulation was the driving force behind the expansion may have some historical truth. The archaeological evidence of the shift from the Hallstatt culture to the La Tène culture shows continuing interaction with the influences of the Mediterranean, but a distinctive change in art style. The simpler geometric patterns of the Hallstatt era – the chevrons, circles and stripes – become, in the art of the La Tène period, something much more elaborate, fluid and complex. Plant motifs, notably of acanthus and lotus, become more common, and there appears throughout the La Tène period a remarkable freedom of artistic expression, in which forms are allowed to wander into other forms without restraint: leaves become faces, animals become plants, figurative representations melt into abstract swirls, whorls and trefoils. The geometry of these designs is extremely complex, and suggests a sophistica-tion, social as well as aesthetic, quite at odds with the traditional picture of early Celtic society as crude, belligerent and brutish. The decorative chasing and inlays of coral and glass indicate a level of sensitivity and complexity which certainly took the classical world by surprise, and which continues to astonish to this day.

Much of the La Tène art is concentrated in articles of personal adornment. The Romans and Greeks decorated their buildings, but the Celts decorated themselves. Almost all of the finest works of La Tène art are portable artefacts – mirrors, swords, scabbards, helmets, brooches, clasps. Interestingly, when Rome later occupied Gaul, the Celtic masterpieces disappeared within a generation, and shoddy Celtic copies of Greek and Roman statuary rapidly replaced them as the predominant art form. Celtic art and culture were emasculated in less than a century, in much the same way that Scottish Highland art and culture were sanitized and emasculated by English victories, many centuries later.

The La Tène culture reached Britain around 250 BC, and the British Celtic aristocrats and royal houses continued their traditions long after Gaulish princes and warrior-chieftains had become Romanized tavern-keepers, booksellers and grocers. The traditional Celtic warrior-king societies survived longest of all in Ireland, to which Rome's grasp never extended.

At the head of the tribe was the king or queen, whose role the bulk of this book is intended to examine. Inheritance of the royal status (the Celts did not use actual crowns, so the metaphorical 'crown' seems inappropriate) was both patrilinear and matrilinear; the overriding principle appears to have been the fitness or appropriateness of the candidate, in keeping with the general religious principle of the 'fitness of things', which we shall examine shortly. The vernacular tales reveal a common theme of unusual birth: the king, queen, god, goddess, hero or heroine is born of an adulterous or incestuous relationship (cf. Arthur's siring by Uther Pendragon in the guise of Gorlois), or is born in an unusual setting. Fosterage, which was a common Celtic practice, also appears frequently in the tales of royal childhood. The king or queen is physically unblemished, an acknowledged warrior of perfect and absolute courage.

Fierce personal loyalty to the tribe, to its king or queen, to its nobles and chieftains, and to its tutelary gods appears to have been the most important binder of the Celtic social fabric. There are Celtic laws – indeed, many of them are older than Greek or Roman law in origin – but the politics of statecraft in Celtic society was based in two linked societal patterns: the universal reverence for a common set of religious beliefs, which Caesar and other classical commentators describe in some detail, and an equally universal system of tribal allegiances.

There were, then, three main classes in early Celtic tribal societies: the aristocracy, headed by the king or queen; the priestly class, led by the druids; and everyone else. As in many warrior societies, exceptional valour or battle achievement was frequently rewarded with exceptional social status, even kingship in some instances. Very different to most other early warrior societies is the high status also given to the priestly class. Caesar specifically states that the druids had the rank of *equites*, a word which literally means 'horse riders', but is usually translated as 'knights'. These were not knights in shining armour; rather, it means that druids were equivalent to senior members of the royal family, and there are, indeed, examples in the classical and vernacular texts of druids being described as if they were of equal rank to kings, since they frequently gave judgment on kings. The druids, and their retinues of ovates (prophets, or interpreters of omens) and bards (poets, chroniclers, writers of eulogies and satires), sometimes even kept their own small armies, and kings and queens whom the druids served were expected to feed and house them.

There must also have been a higher rank among the lowest class, peopled by artisans with particular skills, notably the jewellers, weaponsmiths, chariot-builders, and so on. However, all the evidence suggests that membership of the clan or tribe, and the concomitant right of protection from the tutelary aristocratic family, was the most important indicator of status, and that even the humblest farmer with one pig and one plough was a somebody if his tribe had standing. This pattern of tribal allegiance was eroded very rapidly in Gaul after the Roman occupation, but remained strong in Britain and Ireland for many centuries, and, to some extent, still survives in the Scottish clan allegiances, although a lot of that modern clannish identity has more to do with revival than with survival.

Another distinguishing feature of early Celtic tribal society is the high status accorded to women. Indeed, apart from the followers of the school of Pythagoras, who encouraged women to be leaders, there are very few examples of early societies which routinely gave positions of high rank, status and wealth to women, as the Celts did. We know that many tribes were led by queens rather than by kings. We also know that Celtic women fought in battle alongside their menfolk. Caesar mentions an unusual custom relating to the marriage dowry which gives further evidence of equal status between men and women:

> The men, after due reckoning, take from their own goods a sum of money equal to the dowry they have received from their wives and place it with the dowry. An account is kept of each sum, and the profits are saved. Whichever of the two survives receives the portion of both, together with the profits from previous years.[18]

However, in the same passage, Caesar goes on to tell us how, if a Celtic nobleman died, his wife and family were interrogated under torture if there were suspicious circumstances surrounding the death, and he states specifically that 'men have the power of life and death over their wives', which seems inconsistent with the earlier description.

Miranda Green points out the fact that women and men are usually portrayed as being the same size in Celtic art, which is strongly indicative of a symbolic relationship.[19] Marriages ranged from highly formal affairs between high-status partners, in which kin groups were significant contributors to the pact (called marriage 'by gift of kin' in the Welsh laws), to the Teiltown fair marriages of Ireland, where partners who met at the fair could exchange vows good for one year, then return the following year to disavow the marriage if they so chose. We shall look more closely at wooing and marriage customs, among kings and queens and gods and goddesses as well as mortals, in later chapters.

Fosterage was an important bonding agent in the fabric of Celtic life. The traditional practice, mentioned by classical authors and very frequently described in the vernacular texts, was for the son or sons of a particular noble family to be raised by a different family. The foster-parents would teach the child the arts of war and statesmanship. The advantage to the foster-parents was that they could ally themselves to a powerful royal or noble house, with all the advantages of status and political power afforded by such an alliance. The advantage to the natural parents was that strong ties could be established with the foster family, so that in times of war it would be very easy to call on that family for material and military support, and so pull together large and effective fighting forces. One of the results of the fosterage system was the development of a profound sense of honour, which permeated Celtic society, which was even further intensified in the mediaeval code of chivalry, and which still has a deep influence on western society. The word of a foster or client family was its bond. The speaking of truth, and with it the importance of correct utterance, also became a fundamental tenet of druidism. A promise given was sacred, and debts of honour were inviolable. The reader may be familiar with the story of King Arthur, whose natural father was King Uther Pendragon, being fostered by Merlin to Sir Ector, whose natural son was Kay; the foster-brother bond which developed between Kay and Arthur, despite their mutual antagonism as young boys, became a powerful political alliance in adulthood. Fosterage encouraged this kind of bonding throughout Celtic society.

A critical time for the tribe was the onset of winter, when a store of harvested grains (principally oats and barley) and of salted meat became an urgent necessity for survival. There were frequent cattle raids before the main slaughter and meat-salting in late autumn – one of these raids, or at least a highly dramatized variant of one, is the central theme of the *Tain Bo Cualgne* or *Cattle Raid of Cooley*, one of the great Irish vernacular texts. Links of fosterage often helped to temper the ferocity of such predations and skirmishes.

Another powerful bond between tribes was the accepted significance of religion, and the universally acknowledged power of the druidic priesthood. Several classical commentators comment on the religiosity of the Celts, sometimes respectfully, sometimes disparagingly. The druids functioned as a kind of judiciary, since they were of high rank, sometimes even equal to kings, but they were also often independent of territorial or tribal obligations. A visiting druid could command bed and board for his retinue under the accepted rules of hospitality. As a consequence, many political and military disputes were settled by the priesthood, without recourse to bloodshed. A correct and true utterance of judgment was binding. Cowards and wrongdoers could be punished by the composition and declamation of satires or lampoons, which were thought sufficiently powerful to raise boils, sores and cankers, even to bring on death.

The classical descriptions repeatedly tell us what a disordered shambles the Celts were, at least by comparison with the measured and orderly might of Rome. Livy, for example, describes the Celtic warriors after the Battle of Clusium:

> They are big men – brave men, too, at a pinch – but unsteady. Always they bring more smoke than fire – much terror but little strength. See what happened at Rome: the city lay wide open, and
> they walked in – but now a handful of men in the Citadel are holding them. Already they are sick of the siege, and are off – anywhere, everywhere – roaming the countryside; crammed with food and soused in drink they lie at night like animals on the bank of some stream – unprotected, unguarded, no watches set – and a taste of success has now made them more reckless than ever.[20]

But Celtic social and military structure was not quite so disordered as Livy's comments suggest. There is a good correlation between sources to demonstrate otherwise: comments from other classical authors, the vernacular texts (and, in particular, the Irish law tracts) and archaeological evidence tend to agree in their descriptions. The king or queen was the head and shaping influence of the social structure (with one notable exception: by the time Caesar had completed his conquest of Gaul, some of the Gallic Celts had, to a large extent, replaced traditional kingship with rule by elected chief magistrates, called *vergobretos*, who ruled alongside aristocratic families). Below the king or queen came the chief nobles, heads of families or clans. In Gaul, the priests always came from this class, and there is good reason to believe that the same pattern obtained in Britain and in Ireland. Below the aristocratic families came the freeborn gentry, landowners and farmers, and chief artisans, especially metalsmiths and jewellers. Alwyn and Brinley Rees identify specific groups of trade or craft specialists, similar to the *sudra* caste in ancient India, which included carpenters, wheelwrights, potters, dog-leaders, huntsmen, jugglers, entertainers and musicians.[21]

The lowest of the common people were, according to Caesar, 'nearly regarded as slaves'. Celtic revivalists had a hard time accepting that slavery was a part of traditional Celtic society, but the evidence is irrefutable: slave chains and manacles for working gangs of slaves have been found at La Tène on the continental mainland, in the lake at Llyn Cerrig Bach in Anglesey in Britain, and elsewhere. Diodorus Siculus tells us the value of a slave: 'For one jar of wine they receive in return a slave – a servant in exchange for a drink.' British slaves were a common sight in Rome and in the provinces, after the conquest. There is the famous story of Pope Gregory I, who lived from

AD 540 to 604, who saw British child slaves in the market and is reputed to have described them as 'Non Angli, sed angeli' ('not Angles, but angels') because they were so pretty. Although Gregory's servant called them Angles, these may well have been slaves of Celtic stock.[22]

The early Celtic tribal societal pattern is very similar to that which survived into the eighteenth century in the clans of highland Scotland, which retained the traditions both of fosterage, already described, and of ceilsine, or clientship. With ceilsine, one freeman would voluntarily enter into a contract of clientship or vassalage to another, more powerful freeman or noble, usually by borrowing money or land which was to be repaid with interest. For both parties, useful opportunities for advancement were thus created in a society which might otherwise become dangerously static.

As well as laws governing fosterage, clientship, rank, marriage and inheritance, there was a wealth of common law. The Celtic tradition was oral, so what remains with us from written sources is a mere fragment of what must have once existed. Nevertheless, the fragments are sufficiently impressive to confirm that Celtic society was deeply attuned to the idea of law. Two principles are consistently enunciated, in a variety of settings and ways. The first is 'the fitness of things', the notion that there is a universal natural order, and that good law springs from observation of what is natural, fitting, appropriate and connected. The second is fir fer, or 'fair play', a concept which has become so firmly entrenched in western value systems that we take it for granted: big should fight with big, little with little; a hero offering individual combat should be met by individual combat; the punishment should fit the crime; reparations should match the severity of losses. These laws were later written down in a number of texts, notably the Lebor Gabala Erenn (the Book of Invasions of Ireland), which places the laws of administration, war, games, races, assemblies, domestic dispute and so on, in a mythological and historical context; the Brehon law books of Ireland, probably written in the seventh century but undoubtedly composed orally much earlier, codifications of civil law and precedents (the Irish word breitheamh means 'judge') which are written in such arcane and difficult language that their precise meaning is frequently disputed; and the Welsh triads, a mixture, also often obscure, of philosophical and mystic law as well as more mundane customs and observances. There were very specific laws concerning the inauguration of kings and queens, which we shall examine in detail in later chapters.

WARFARE AND HEAD-HUNTING

Feasting and fighting were major Celtic preoccupations, with elaborate boasting a frequent cause of bloodshed. For example, in the Irish tale of Mac Da Tho's pig, the hero, Cet Mag Magach, takes his knife at the feast to cut the champion's portion of the pig and invites any Ulsterman to challenge his right to it. A succession of challengers receive Cet's insults: one has been blinded, another emasculated, and a third, the king's son, is nicknamed the 'Stammerer of Macha' because Cet had wounded him in the throat. Finally, the Ulster hero Conall steps down and challenges Cet. When Cet retaliates by saying that his champion Auluan would wipe Conall out on the spot, Conall pulls out Auluan's head from under his tunic and flings it at Cet 'so that a rush of blood broke over his lips'.

The classical accounts provide some very detailed descriptions of Celtic methods of warfare, including the weapons they used. Here, for example, Tacitus explains how a group of Batavian and Tungrian mercenaries hired for the British campaigns were able to defeat the British Celts:

> The fighting began with exchange of missiles, and the Britons showed both steadiness and skill in parrying our spears with their huge swords or catching them on their little shields, while they themselves rained volleys on us. At last Agricola called on four cohorts of Batavians and two of Tungrians to close and fight it out at the sword's point. These old soldiers had been well-drilled in sword-fighting, while the enemy were awkward at it, with their small shields and unwieldy swords, especially as the latter, having no points, were quite unsuitable for a cut-and-thrust struggle at close quarters. The Batavians, raining blow after blow, striking them with the bosses of their shields, and stabbing them in the face, felled the Britons posted on the plain and pushed on up the hillsides.[23]

Celtic warriors from the Gundestrup cauldron. The three warriors on the right are blowing carnyxes or battle-horns.

A typically Celtic fortification was the hillfort, built on a natural elevation and surrounded by ramparts and ditches. The tribe would live a semi-nomadic existence, leading its herds from pasture to pasture, with more permanent settlements on land cleared, ploughed and seeded, but with retreat to the safety of the hillfort an ever-present option. One of the best examples of a Celtic hillfort is Danebury in Hampshire, England. The site, which was occupied from about 650 to 100 BC, has been extensively excavated and has revealed much useful information about the early British Celtic way of life. One of the most dramatic hillforts is that at South Cadbury in Somerset, which some have claimed to be the stronghold of the historical Arthur, in other words the real and original Camelot; the site offers a commanding view across the Glastonbury plain, and I can attest from personal experience that its atmosphere is very imposing. The Hibernian Celts built circular towers of unmortared stone, now called *brochs*, on their hillfort sites, the remains of which can still be found in the Highlands and Islands, notably at Dun Telve in Gleann Beage and Clickhimin in Shetland.

Spears, swords and shields were traditional Celtic weapons, but not bows and arrows. The swords of the La Tène era were short, but the swords of the second and first centuries BC were long, heavy swords used for hacking and slashing, and Tacitus's description, given earlier, suggests that they continued in use in Britain well into the first century AD. Spears were of two kinds, a long one for throwing and a short one for thrusting in hand-to-hand combat. The Irish texts mention a special spear called the *ga bulga*, which tore out entrails as it was withdrawn, which suggests that it might be either spiral in shape or fitted with some kind of hooks. Helmets have been found, but their comparative scarcity, and the often elaborate nature of their design, suggests that they may have been as much decorative as functional.

Several of the classical authors tell us that Celtic battles were noisy. Diodorus tells us about their battle trumpets which were 'of a peculiarly barbaric type' and produced 'a harsh sound which suits the tumult of war'. War trumpets are depicted on the famous cauldron from Gundestrup, in Denmark. We also know that battle cries, ululation from the women and the hurling of insults from the men, and perhaps war drums, pipes and rattles, may have contributed to the battle din. Add to that picture the spectacle of warriors charging into battle completely naked, the intended effect being to show the enemy how little death mattered, and the classical depictions of the Celts as awe-inspiring, even terrifying foes make good sense. Tacitus tells us that the legionaries who confronted the druids and their retinues at Anglesey in AD 61 were so shocked by the insults, battle cries and ululations of the druidic priestesses that they were badly shaken and had to be whipped back into the ranks.

The most distinctively Celtic weapon was actually a vehicle. It was the chariot, a small and very light wickerwork structure mounted on an axled frame, usually drawn by a pair of swift-turning, sure-footed ponies. As was mentioned earlier, the modern word 'car' is derived from *currus*, the Roman version of the original Celtic name for this unique transport. The chariot was usually driven by two riders, often kinsmen. One would drive the horses, while the other threw spears. The usual practice against the Romans was to hurl the chariot at high speed into the slow-moving ranks of infantry, fire off a rapid volley of spears, leap down to engage in swift hand-to-hand combat while the chariot spun quickly to change direction, then leap aboard again to retreat to safety and prepare the next assault. It was a highly efficient and effective battle tactic, and the Romans quickly adopted and adapted chariots to their own use, as anyone who has seen *Ben Hur* will know. (The Celtic war chariots were actually much lighter and quicker than the later Roman versions.) Among the Gauls and Celtiberians, military horsemanship replaced chariot warfare and a more traditional style of cavalry fighting emerged. Early Celtic saddles had tall pommels to help the rider remain seated, but there were no stirrups, which were not introduced until the post-Roman period.

A Celtic shield dating from the first century AD, thrown into the River Thames at Battersea, London as a votive offering.

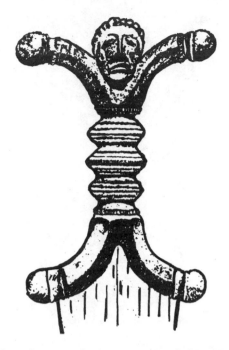

A sword hilt found at North Grimston, Yorkshire, England. Weapons were often given individual names and personal attributes.

When large armies of Celts fought together against a common enemy, the clan structure led to frequent confusion and competition for supremacy of command, with the notable exceptions of the one or two Celtic kings like Vercingetorix or Ambiorix who managed to inspire confidence among many tribes or clans simultaneously. The Celts also frequently fought as mercenaries, the best recorded examples being those given in the classical descriptions of the Punic Wars, which included Hannibal's crossing of the Alps. One group was called *Gaesaetae*, which Polybius translated as 'mercenaries', but actually means 'spearmen'. Accounts of the Battle of Telamon tell us that they fought naked there, while the Cisalpine Gauls (those who lived on the Italian side of the Alps) wore breeches and cloaks. Celtic mercenaries served in Anatolia, Macedonia and Egypt, and later, of course, after prolonged Roman domination, as soldiers and even citizens of the Empire.

As Caesar discovered, the Celts could fight at sea, as well as on land. The Veneti, from the region of Gaul which is now Brittany, battled the Roman quinqueremes with heavy, squat ships; the Gaulish vessels had high foredecks and afterdecks which thwarted the Roman archers and stone-throwers, and 'for the same reason it was still less easy to seize them with grappling-hooks'. The Celtic ships used leather sails, which were presumably more resistant to Atlantic storms than cloth ones.

A stone door-post with a skull niche, found at Roquepertuse,
Bouches-du-Rhône, France, probably dating from the
third century BC.

The Celtic warrior was reputed to hold death in contempt. Caesar tells us
that Celts would arrange to meet and pay back cash debts in the next world
if they happened to fall in battle, so absolute was their belief in a real and
immediate afterlife. The defeated King Catuvolcus of the Eburones hanged
himself from a yew tree rather than submit to Roman rule. Unfortunately, the
same high pride and dismissal of danger which made Celtic armies so intim-
idating also made them vulnerable; the fighting was as much a matter of personal, individual pride as of achieving any joint objective, and quests for
death and glory often thwarted broader military objectives.

The Celts collected heads, but nobody is certain why. There may have
been a straightforward coup-counting purpose, each head being a tally of the
number of the enemy killed, but the evidence suggests that it was not that
simple. Heads of defeated enemies were displayed in specially constructed
wall niches, and greatly prized heads were preserved in oil and possibly
mounted as trophies, like game in a later age. The Celts held that the spirit
resided in the head, and there seems to have been a mystic or religious element in the practice, as well as whatever purposes of battle glory were met.
The Welsh tale of the *Assembly of the Wondrous Head*, in which the severed
head of Bendigeidfran ('Bran the Blessed') stays alive for many years, before
finally being buried at White Hill in London, seems related to the religious or

mystic aspects of head-hunting. White Hill is the site of the Tower of London, and the legend that if the ravens ever leave the Tower, then London, and eventually all of Britain, will fall to a foreign enemy derives from the earlier, Celtic myth. The name Bran, an important Celtic father-god, means 'raven' – *bran* is still the modern Celtic word for 'crow' or 'raven'.

So important was religion to the Celts, and so deeply connected with the patterns and traditions of Celtic kingship, that the topic merits a chapter to itself, and to that subject we now turn.

Notes

1   Gerhard Herm, *The Celts,* p. 1.
2   Gerhard Herm, above, p. 73.
3   *The Histories* II.35 and IV.48.
4   Quoted in *The Celts*, p. 37.
5   Diodorus Siculus, V.28 and V.31, trans. C.H. Oldfather, quoted in Michael Grant, *Readings in the Classical Historians*, pp. 261–262.
6   Diodorus Siculus, V.31.
7   Tacitus, *Germania*, 4, *The Agricola and the Germania*, trans. H. Mattingly, revised S.A. Handford, 1948 and 1970, Penguin Classics, p. 104.
8   Herodotus, IV.46, trans. D. Grene, *Readings in the Classical Historians*, p. 47.
9   Tacitus, *Agricola*, 11.
10 Diodorus Siculus, V.31.
11 Diodorus Siculus, V.33.
12 Ammianus Marcellinus, XV.12, trans. W. Hamilton, *Readings in the Classical Historians*, pp. 604–605.
13 *Tain Bo Cualnge*, trans. C. O'Rahilly, p. 202.
14 J.J. Tierney, The Celtic Ethnography of Posidonius, *Proceedings of the Royal Irish Academy*, Vol. 60, Section C, No. 5 (1960), p. 269.
15 Miranda J. Green, *Dictionary of Celtic Myth and Legend*, p. 211.
16 Livy, *The Early History of Rome*, V.34, trans. Aubrey de Selincourt, Penguin Classics, pp. 379–380.
17 Livy, V.34.
18 Caesar, *The Commentaries*, 6.19.
19 Miranda J. Green, *Dictionary of Celtic Myth and Legend*, p. 117.
20 Livy, V.44.
21 Alwyn Rees and Brinley Rees, *Celtic Heritage*, 1961, pp. 112–113.
22 The quotation, which is found in Bede's *Ecclesiastical History*, II, i, should actually be, *Responsum est, quod Angli vocarentur. At ille: 'Bene,' inquit, 'nam et angelicam habent faciem, et tales angelorum in caelis decet esse coherides.'* (The reply was that they were called Angles. 'It is well,' said he, 'for they have the faces of angels, and such should be the co-heirs of the angels in heaven.')
23 Tacitus, *The Agricola and The Germania*, p. 87.

TWO

CELTIC
RELIGION

THE CELTIC PANTHEON

THE names of many of the Celtic gods are known to us only because they survive in Latin (and occasionally Greek) inscriptions. That the gods are, indeed, indigenous Celtic gods is indisputable, but the Celtic tradition was an oral one, so it is only after the Romanization of the Celts, and the subsequent identification of Celtic gods with Roman ones, that the inscriptions begin to appear from which we first learn of the Celtic deities' existence. The historian, Tacitus, coined the phrase *interpretatio Romana* ('Roman translation') to describe the process by which native or local gods became identified or paired with Roman equivalents, reflecting the general Roman policy of tolerating, absorbing and assimilating the religious practices of conquered peoples during the pre-Christian era.

Apollo, originally a Greek god who was never fully Romanized, was identified most closely in the Celtic pantheon with Bel or Belenus, who gave his name to Beltane, the important spring festival celebrated on the first day of May. The name Beltane means 'Bel's fire'. The name may be related to the biblical Ba'al, which means 'master', a Phoenician name later widely used in Syria and Arabia. Bel, whose variant names appear as Beli, Belinus and Beli Mawr ('great Bel'), was a sun god. He was associated with horses, and several clay votive figurines of horses have been found at shrine sites. It was a widely spread cult, mentioned by the classical authors Ausonius, Herodian and Tertullian. Cunomaglus, whose name means 'hound lord', was honoured by inscriptions found at Nettleton Shrub, Wiltshire, England. He also was identified with Apollo, but the name suggests a connection with hunting. Grannus was a sun-god (*cf.* the Irish word *grainne* for a sun room), but also a god of healing. His name is frequently found in dual inscriptions with the goddess Sirona (Sarana, Tsirona), a goddess of healing springs. Cassius Dio mentions Grannus as a god of healing. The variant title Apollo Grannos was found in an inscription at Musselburgh in Scotland, and the compound name Apollo Grannus Mogounus appears at a shrine in Horburg, Germany. Another Apollo-type healing god, also with a divine consort, was Apollo Moritasgus, to whom a large temple complex at Alesia, France was dedicated. Dedications include references to a bathing pool, and surgeons' instruments were found at the site. His consort, Damona, was widely worshipped in the Burgundy region. She is paired with the healing god Abilus at Arnay-le-Duc, and an inscription at Bourbonne-Lancy refers to healing through incubation, where the goddess is invited to enter the supplicant's dreams while sleeping. Apollo Vindonnus, also a god of healing, appears, from the number of dedications on bronze plaques with eyes drawn on them, to have specialized in diseases of the eye. He had a temple at Essarois, near Châtillon-sur-Seine. Apollo Virotutis, worshipped in Gaul, was probably also a healing god. His name means 'benefactor to humanity'.

The cult of Jupiter spread very widely in the Roman Empire, particularly after Augustus Caesar's many temple dedications to him as father of all the gods. The Romanized Celts applied the name to many local gods of the same type. Jupiter Beissirissa, also known as Jupiter Optimus Maximus ('the greatest') Beissirissa, was worshipped at Cadeac in the Pyrénées. Jupiter Brixianus gave his name to Brixia, modern Brescia, in northern Italy. Jupiter Cernenus (a variant of the stag-god Cernunnos) is known from a Gallic dedicatory inscription. The names Tanarus and Taranus, with many variant spellings, identify Jupiter as the thunder-god (*taran* is the modern Welsh and Cornish word for thunder). This figure was an exact counterpart of the Jupiter Tonans ('Jupiter the Thunderer') commemorated in the temple which Augustus had built on the Capitoline Hill after he was almost struck by lightning in 26 BC. Jupiter Parthinus, whose dedicatory inscriptions are found in northeast Dalmatia, appears to have been the eponymous god of the Partheni tribe. Jupiter Poeninus was worshipped in the Alps in the region of the Great St. Bernard Pass, where a sanctuary established in the Iron Age continued to be used well into the Roman period. The name Poeninus appears as Poininus – almost certainly the same god – in a dedication in Turnovo in Bulgaria. Jupiter Uxellinus was a god of the high mountains, worshipped in Austria.

There were other Celtic gods of the father-thunderer type, although not all had the name Jupiter appended. Mogons ('the great one') appears in inscriptions in northern England, along Hadrian's Wall, but also in Germany and eastern France. There are many variant spellings of the name, including Mogtus, Mogunus and Mountus. Mogons Vitiris is attested in a single inscription found at Netherby, Cumbria, in northern England. The name Vitiris alone (with many variant spellings, such as Hvitiris, Veteris, Veteres) is found in fifty-four dedicatory inscriptions, all of them in northern England, which suggests that he was a Jupiter- or Mars-type god popular with the soldiers stationed on and around Hadrian's Wall. There is, however, one dedication to Vitiris at Great Chesters on Hadrian's Wall which clearly comes from a female supplicant. Dedications to the god as thunder are very widespread: Tanarus is found at Chester in England, and at Orgon in France; Taran is found at Tours, France; Taranis is found at altars in Britain, Germany, France and Dalmatia, and is mentioned by name in the Roman poet Lucan's *Pharsalia*, specifically in connection with human sacrifice.

Mars, as the god of war, naturally found many counterparts in the warrior societies of the early Celts. Mars Alator is recorded in two dedications, one on an altar in South Shields in northern England, the other on a silver-gilt votive plaque found at Barkway, Hertfordshire, in southern England. Mars Albiorix ('king of the Albi, or fair people') was worshipped as a mountain god by the Albici, a tribe of southern France. Mars Barrex or Barrecis is recorded at Carlisle in England, and Mars Belatucadrus ('fair shining') appears in twenty-eight inscriptions found in the region of Hadrian's Wall. The simplicity of the altars dedicated to him, and the frequent variety in the spelling of his name, have led to suggestions that Belatucadrus was the favourite god of humble, uneducated people. The name Mars Braciaca is found in only one inscription, at Bakewell in northern England. Camulos, frequently recorded as Mars Camulos, was worshipped much more widely throughout Britain and Gaul – he gave his name to Camulodunum ('fort of Camulos'), the Roman name for modern Colchester, in England. It has been suggested that King Arthur's court, Camelot, derives its name from this god. Mars Caturix was worshipped in Gaul, presumably as the eponymous god of the Caturiges tribe. Condatis, although a god of sacred waters and healing in the Tyne-Tees region of northern England, is recorded as Mars Condatis in inscriptions found at Piercebridge, Bowes and Chester-le-Street, all near Hadrian's Wall. Similarly, Cocidius, a Celtic god of the woodland and hunting, is recorded as Mars Cocidius in the militarized areas of north and west Cumbria. Mars Corotiacus has only one dedicatory inscription, at Martlesham, Suffolk, England, in Iceni territory. Two important Celtic gods, Lenus and Loucetius, were strongly identified with Mars during the Roman occupation of Gaul and Britain. Lenus was a god of healing, associated with the large and influential Treveri tribe who gave their name to modern Trier in Germany, although dedications to the god are also found in Britain – one, at Caerwent in Wales, associates Mars Lenus with Ocelos Vellaunus, another variation of the Mars type. Loucetius, an epithet meaning 'bright shining', is recorded as Loucetius Mars (the significance of the name order probably being that Loucetius is the older-established deity) at Bath, England, as the divine consort of the goddess Nemetona. Mars Loucetius or Loucetius Mars appears in several other dedications across Europe, including one at Mainz, Germany.

Other Celtic gods of war, some of them specifically associated with Mars by name, appear in dedicatory altars and shrines all across Europe and even into Asia Minor. The hammer-god, frequently known as Sucellus in Gaul, appears in many dedicatory inscriptions with his consort Nantosuelta, the

*Sucellus, the hammer-god, and his consort Nantosuelta ('Winding Valley'),
from a stone relief found at Sarrebourg, near Metz, France.*

goddess whose name means 'winding valley' or 'meandering river'. He is usually pictured as mature, bearded, and carrying a long-handled hammer. She
usually carries a model of a house on a long pole. Their images are often
accompanied by barrels, pots and domestic animals, which suggests that they
were widely worshipped as archetypes of domestic order and prosperity. The
warrior hero, Hercules, originally Greek Herakles, is Celticized as Hercules
Ilunnus in southern France, as Hercules Magusanus in eleven dedications
found in northeastern Gaul, and as Hercules Saegon (a variant of Segomo,
'the victorious one') at Silchester in England. Mullo, which means 'mule', is
the name of the god whose cult centre was in northern and western Gaul,

near modern Rennes in Brittany. At Allones, in the Sarthe area of France, Mars Mullo was worshipped as a healer of eye afflictions. Mars Nabelcus was worshipped in the mountain regions of southern France, particularly the Vaucluse mountains of Provence. Mars Olloudius, known from an image and inscription found at Custom Scrubs, Gloucestershire, England, carries a double cornucopia, symbolizing abundance and fertility, and a *patera* or libation bowl, accoutrements not usually associated with a god of war. The Celtic name element *rix* or *rig*, which means 'king', is found in Mars Rigas, known from a single dedication found at Malton, North Yorkshire, England, in Mars Rigonemetis ('king of the *nemeton* or sacred grove'), found in an inscription at Nettleham, Lincolnshire, England, and in Mars Rigisamus ('very kingly'), to whom dedications are found at Bourges, France and West Coker, Somerset, England. Mars Rudianus, worshipped in southern Gaul, simply means 'Mars the Red'. Teutates, also called Totatis and Toutiorix, and immortalized in the Asterix comics as the Toutatis of the oath, 'By Toutatis!', is commemorated both in Gallic inscriptions and by an inscription found at Barkway, Hertfordshire, England, and probably by the letters TOT on a silver ring found at York. There are dedications to Mars Nodens, a Celtic god of healing found only in Britain, at Lydney in Gloucestershire and near Lancaster in Lancashire, but Nodens, frequently associated with representations of a dog, is a complex and important deity whose Martial attributes are only marginally important. Mars Vorocius, depicted as a Celtic warrior, was worshipped at the medicinal springs at Vichy, Allier, France.

In the Celtic pantheon there were goddesses as well as gods of war, since women could also be warriors. Apart from the great female war deities such as the Morrigan, whose significance will be discussed in greater detail in later chapters, there were many goddesses whose main attribute was their warlike strength and ferocity. Andarte, also known as Andarta, Andate and Andraste, was a goddess of victory, similar to the Greek winged victory, Nike, and having some of the character of the great goddess Athene. She was worshipped by the Vocontii in Gaul, and inscriptions dedicated to her have been found in the valley of the Drome in southern France, and in the Roman town known as Dea Augusta, modern Die. The rite of *taurobolium* or bull sacrifice appears to have been conducted in her name there. The Roman historian Dio Cassius associates Andraste with the British Iceni in his description of Boudica's revolt of AD 61, and specifically claims that human sacrifices were made to the goddess in sacred groves. Brigantia, the eponymous goddess of the important Brigantes tribe in northern Britain, was also a war goddess. In a sculptured relief found at Birrens, a fort north of Hadrian's Wall, she is depicted wearing a crown and wings, and she carries a spear, shield and *aegis*, the breastplate traditionally associated with classical Athene or Minerva. At Slack, West Yorkshire, England, there is a single dedication to a god, Bregans, who is presumably a male counterpart or consort with Brigantia. Tutela Boudiga ('protectress of victory'), whose name is clearly related to the Icenian queen, Boudica, is a war goddess known from an inscription found in

Bordeaux, France, although there is a British connection. The altar, which was dedicated in AD 237, was erected by Marcus Aurelius Lunaris, an envoy who was expressing thanks to the goddess (presuming Boudica or Boudiga was a British, rather than Gallic name) for his safe return from Britain after a difficult and dangerous voyage.

Mercury, the divine messenger who came into the Roman pantheon originally as the Greek Hermes, also has direct counterparts in the Celtic pantheon. Artaios, whose name means 'the bear', was worshipped as Mercurius Artaios at Beaucroissant, France. The name Artaios may be related to the name Arturus, or Arthur. Mercurius Arvernus was worshipped in the Rhineland, although the name strongly suggests that he was the particular god of the Arverni tribe, who lived in the territory now known as the Auvergne, in central France. Mercurius Cissonius was also known in Germany, specifically near modern Cologne, and across France. Mercurius Gebrinius is commemorated at Bonn in Germany; Mercurius or Lenus Iovatucarus at Trier; and Mercurius Moccus ('the pig'), at Langres, in France. The name Moccus (the modern Celtic equivalent is *mogh*), meaning 'pig' or 'boar', was an epithet of great distinction, indicating exceptional valour.

Even though most of these names of deities have survived because they appear in inscriptions made in the Roman era, almost entirely written in Latin, many of the gods and goddesses honoured are purely Celtic and have no obvious classical counterparts.

This is particularly true of the mother cult goddesses, and especially of the Triple Goddess, whose names and titles are many. Alauina was worshipped at Manderscheid, Germany, and Aveta at Trier; both goddesses are represented by figurines carrying baskets of fruit, or holding children in their arms or lap. The mother-goddess, Caiva, had an altar dedicated to her at Pelm, Germany, on 5 October AD 124, by Marcus Victorius Pollentius, who bequeathed 100 000 sesterces (a very large sum) for the maintenance of her temple after his death. The inscribed sculpture to the goddess, Cuda found at Cirencester, England also contains three small, hooded standing figures. These figures, called *genii cucullati* or 'hooded spirits' by the Romans, appear very frequently in company with the mother goddess, usually in groups of three in Britain, but singly, as a giant or dwarf, in mainland Europe. They often carry objects, including eggs, coins and paper scrolls, and they are sometimes shaped into lamp fittings, with the enlarged phallus forming the lampholder, all of which suggest roles complementary to the central fertility role of the mother goddess.

The Triple Goddess, whose presence is almost absolute evidence of a region's Celtic identity, is commemorated very widely, although many of the names by which she is known are later Roman coinages. She was portrayed as three deities in one, the young virgin, the middle-aged mother and the elderly crone. Her complex religious significance is explored in intense detail in Robert Graves's famous study, *The White Goddess*. The figures representing her often carry cornucopiae, flowers, bread, birds, snakes or other

Three genii cucullati *('hooded spirits'), from a relief statue at Housesteads on Hadrian's Wall.*

animals. Her name in inscriptions was very frequently prefixed by Matres ('mothers') or Matrones ('matrons'). The Matrones Aufaniae were Celto-Germanic goddesses worshipped in the Rhineland. The Matres Comedovae, worshipped at the very important healing centre of Aix-les-Bains, France, were tutelary goddesses of the hot springs, as were the Matres Griselicae at the medicinal springs of Gréoux, in southern France. It is clear that the Triple Goddess cult made wide inroads into the Roman imperial culture, as evidenced by the more than one hundred and sixty altars dedicated to the Matronae Vacallinehae at Pech, near Zulpich, Germany, set up by the soldiers of Legion XXX Ulpia. She came into Romano-Gallic and Romano-British domestic life, too. She appears in British dedications at Chichester, York, Stanwix and Burgh-by-Sands, under the name Matres Domesticae ('mothers of the home'). In Gaul, she was the Matres Nemausicae, and her associated consort, Nemausus, gave his name to the healing spring, and subsequently the town, now known as Nîmes, France. The Suleviae, also called Matres Suleviae, were worshipped in Britain, Gaul, Germany, Hungary and in Rome itself. They were often identified with Matres Iunones (the name comes from the great mother goddess Juno), and sometimes called Suleviae Iunones. An altar dedicated to them was included in the religious complex of Sulis Minerva at Bath, England.

There were many fertility couples in the Celtic pantheon, attested by double inscriptions and altar dedications. Ancamna, who was a significant goddess of the powerful Treveri in Germany, was the consort of Mars Lenus or Mars Smertrius. Bergusia and Ucuetis are recorded in two inscriptions at Alesia, France, and a portrait, possibly of the divine couple, suggests that they may have been tutelary deities of craftspeople and metalworkers. Inciona and Veraudinus are recorded at only one location – that is, Widdenberg, Luxembourg – which may mean that they were very local deities. The great goddess Rosmerta, whose name means 'provider of plenty', and who was very widely venerated across Celtic Europe, was often portrayed with the Roman god Mercury as her consort, sometimes carrying purses of money. A carving of Rosmerta from Mannheim, Germany, shows a sacred serpent laying its head on her purse. In Britain, she is portrayed with a bucket, and in one carving with a sceptre and a ladle held over the bucket, as if about to dispense her favours.

There were many Celtic gods and goddesses of hunting and the forest. Abnoba, a Celtic goddess worshipped in the Black Forest in Germany, was sometimes associated with the Roman goddess of the chase, Diana. Nemetona takes her name from the Greek word *nemeton*, which signified the sacred grove in which religious ceremonies were conducted, and to which all classical commentators on Celtic druidism attached particular significance. She represents the numen, or divinely charged ambiance of the wild grove. She was often paired with a Celtic variant of Mars. A dedication to her, made by a citizen of Trier, Germany, was found at the temple of Sulis Minerva in Bath, England.

The male gods of the forest find their counterpart to some extent in the Roman, Silvanus, although he is a fairly weak and feeble character by comparison. Callirius, known from an inscription at Colchester, England, had his name carved on a bronze plaque thrown in a pit, in which was also found a small bronze figurine of a stag. The name Callirius has two elements: the first (which would be *kelli* in modern Cornish or Welsh) means 'hazel wood', and the second is a variant of *rix* or *rig*, the ancient Celtic word for a king. So Callirius is 'king of the hazel wood'. The name Silvanus Cocidius is found in two inscription at Housesteads fort on Hadrian's Wall, while at Risingham, a fort a short way to the north of the wall, the god is portrayed in sculptural relief as a hunter dressed in a short tunic, accompanied by a stag and a dog, and carrying a bow and arrow. The bow and arrow reveal that this is a late dedication during the Roman occupation, since bows and arrows were unknown to the pre-Roman tribal Celts, and only came into use in the Roman army towards the end of the imperial era, following centuries of integration of Scythian archers into the legions. Another woodland god is Fagus, god of the beech tree. He was worshipped in the Pyrénées, but his name, not immediately recognizable, also survives in the place name Fowey in Cornwall, Britain. Fowey is derived from the Cornish word for beech trees, *fawith*. Contrebis, whose name means 'with the people', was another god of the woodland and is commemorated in two inscriptions in Lancashire, England: one at Overborough, the other at

Lancaster. The Celtic veneration of the oak is well known, but other trees were also highly regarded: hazelnuts imparted wisdom; the willow yielded an effective painkiller, and was associated with a variety of goddesses; alder timber, which is especially resistant to water, was widely used for bridges and house supports, and was associated with the god Bran in the Brythonic tradition.

Arduinna, a goddess worshipped in the Ardennes forest, was one of several deities associated with specific animals – in her case, it was the boar, the hunting of which was very significant in Celtic tribal culture. Baco, a god known from an inscription found at Chalon-sur-Saône, France, was also a boar god. The Greek myth of the Calydonian boar hunt, which appears in Ovid's *Metamorphoses*, was widely known in the classical world, and would have had particular resonance for the Celts. Tacitus tells us (*Germania*, 35) that the tribe of the Aestii wore boar amulets for protection in battle. The most famous boar in Celtic mythology is Twrch Trwyth, a former evil king who was transmogrified into the shape of a giant, enchanted boar, but this story has no happy Beauty and the Beast ending – this boar is killed by Culhwch, the hero in the Welsh legend of Culhwch and Olwen. There is a similar beast in Norse mythology, called Saehrimir, on whose flesh the gods and heroes of Valhalla continuously feast, but who nevertheless remains alive and willing to be pursued in the hunt.

Artio, worshipped at Muri near Berne, Switzerland and at Bollendorf, Trier, Germany, was a bear goddess – her name probably means 'bear', like the name Artorius or Arturius, better known as Arthur. The god Matunus, worshipped at Risingham, England, was a bear god. Jet talismans of bears have been found at Malton, Bootle and York in northern England.

Atepomarus, identified with Apollo in an inscription found at Mauvières, France, is associated with horses. Far better known, and much more widely venerated, was Epona, the mare goddess. The cult of Epona was strong in eastern Gaul, but she was also worshipped in Britain, Dalmatia and Africa, and she even had a festival dedicated to her (on 18 December) in Rome, which was highly unusual for a Celtic deity. She is always portrayed on or with horses, but she also frequently carries corn or fruit, symbolizing fertility. A shrine at Hagondange, Germany depicts her in triplicate, like a mother goddess. There was a major shrine to her at Alesia in Burgundy, which is of particular interest to us because this was the last bastion of the Celtic king Vercingetorix, whose story we shall examine more fully in Chapter Six. There is evidence from cart or chariot burials found at King's Barrow, East Yorkshire, Mildenhall in Suffolk and Fordington near Dorchester, in Dorset, that horses were slain and buried along with the dead noble and his or her belongings. A ritual shaft at Bekesbourne in Kent contained a flat stone on which a circle of horse teeth had been carefully arranged. The stylized white horse carved into the chalk at Uffington, in Oxfordshire, some 110 metres (360 ft) in length, is very similar in design to the horses found on many Celtic coins.

There are two inscriptions, one found at Paris, France, the other at Trier, Germany, to a deity whose name is a compound of different creatures: Tarvostrigaranus is the bull (*tarvos*) with three (*tri*) cranes (*garanus*). The sculptures which accompany the inscriptions depict a willow tree, a bull and three cranes, as well as other gods – Esus, a woodcutter god associated with willow trees, on the Paris monument, and Rosmerta and Mercury, the divine couple, on the Trier monument.

There are many images of Cernunnos, whose name means 'the horned one', both in Gaul and in Britain, but only one, that dedicated by sailors from the Parisi tribe during the reign of Tiberius, identifies the name with the god's distinctive image. In the Parisi sculpture, the god is portrayed as a balding old man with the ears and horns of a stag. From each of his antlers hangs a torc, or neck-ring. In many images of Cernunnos, notably the famous image on the Gundestrup cauldron found in Denmark, the god holds a serpent in his hand, often a ram-horned serpent. Stag images are widely found on Celtic coins and other artefacts, and stag antlers have been found in burial pits.

Other animal images and totems abound in Celtic archaeological finds, and there are references in the classical texts to specific animal taboos or rituals. Caesar tells us that the cockerel, the goose and the hare were sacred to the Britons, and were never eaten by them. Dio Cassius tells us that Boudica released a hare as an act of augury before engaging, successfully, in battle with Suetonius Paulinus, in AD 61. The bull, also widely venerated in many other cultures, appears very frequently in Celtic iconography. Pliny gives us a detailed account of a Celtic bull sacrifice (see page 56). The salmon, although it appears very little in iconographic representations, was associated with wisdom, and appears frequently in the vernacular tales. *The Salmon of Llyn Llyw*, who appears in the legend of Culhwch and Olwen mentioned earlier, is described as one of the oldest (and, therefore, wisest) animals living. Like

The stag-horned god Cernunnos ('the Horned One'), from the Gundestrup cauldron.

the boar legends, there are legends of salmon which remain alive and eager for the hunt, no matter how much of their flesh has been eaten. In the Irish legends, the salmon of all the world, the source of all wisdom, lives in the River Boyne and receives his wisdom from eating the nuts of the nine sacred hazel trees which grow along the river's banks. Dolphins, more frequently associated with classical legends, appear in some Celtic tales. The British goddess Coventina was invoked on an altar decorated with dolphins, and one of the depictions of the Matronae, or Triple Goddess, at Cirencester in Gloucestershire has the swirls of the goddess's robes transmuting into dolphins. There was a dog cult associated with the god Nodens, and even the humble goat, whose attributes certainly include virility and aggression, is commemorated in many icons.

Apart from the goose, already mentioned as being described by Caesar as a totemic animal, there were several other birds which held special religious significance for the Celts. First and foremost among these was the swan, which, particularly in the Irish tales, appears again and again as a representative, symbol or harbinger of the otherworld. Swans appear frequently in funerary imagery – sometimes they are depicted pulling the funeral waggons. In the Irish tale, *The Dream of Oenghus*, the young heroine, Caer Ibormeith (Yew Berry), takes on the form of a swan. From Wagner's *Lohengrin* to Tchaikovsky's *Swan Lake*, the story's imagery seems to have had a wide appeal across Europe through many ages. The owl was venerated by the Celts, as were the duck, the crane and the eagle. One of the most persistent bird totems is the crow or raven. The Celtic word for crow is *bran*, which is also the name of the god Bran, whose story was mentioned at the end of the previous chapter. The Irish war-goddess, Macha, was also represented by the crow or raven. The Morrigan (Great Queen) is often given the epithet 'battle-crow' in the vernacular literature. There are many tales, both in the classical and in the vernacular texts, of birds being used for divination. The Romans loved such tales; for example, the famous story of the eagle dropping a bloody lamb into the arms of the young, stuttering Claudius, who was thereby destined to become emperor and rescue Rome from the clutches of her would-be destroyers. According to Justinian, it was a flight of birds that guided the Celts on their advance south into the Po Valley. A Celtic king of Galatia is supposed to have retreated from imminent disaster because an eagle's erratic flight warned him of the potential debacle.

Water sites – springs, lakes, rivers, holy wells, even marshes – were venerated by the Celts, and so there are many goddesses of water (and a few gods, mostly Apollo variants), almost all of them associated with healing. The goddesses include Apadeva (Cologne, Germany); Arnemetia ('she who rules the nemeton or sacred grove', Buxton, England); Coventina (Carrawburgh near Hadrian's Wall, England and Narbonne, France); Ianuaria (Beire-le-Châtel, France); Icovellauna (Metz in northeastern France, and Trier, Germany); Laha (Pyrénées region, France); Latis, goddess of bogs and marshy places (Cumbria, England); Meduna and Vercana (the healing springs of Bad

Relief of the water-goddess Coventina, set up at Carrawburgh on Hadrian's Wall.

Bertrich, Germany); Nehalennia, a goddess of sailors and seafaring (Domburg and Colijnsplaat, the Netherlands); Ritona or Pritona, a goddess of fords and water crossings (Trier and Pachten, Germany); Telo, the goddess of the sacred spring who gave her name to Toulon, France; and Verbeia, personification of the Wharfe River (Ilkley, North Yorkshire, England). The best known of the water goddesses are Boann, who gave her name to the River Boyne in Ireland; Sequana, who gave her name to the River Seine in France and whose Celtic sanctuary at the source of the river (a little north of Dijon) was extended by the Romans with the addition of two temples; and Sulis, later Sulis Minerva, whose sacred thermal springs at Bath, England were developed into a large religious complex during the first century.

Many of the deities have no known attributes or associations, or appear to be local gods. Of note among these are Antenociticus (Anociticus, Antocidicus), whose life-size cult statue was found at Benwell, on Hadrian's Wall, England; Arausio, who gave his name to the classical town of Arausio (now Orange) in France; Deiotarus ('divine bull'), worshipped in ancient Galatia, now in northern Turkey; Ogmios (Ogham), described by the Greek author Lucian, who travelled in Gaul in the second century, as a bald old man with a golden chain from his tongue linked to the ears of his followers, and presumably a symbol of eloquent speech in general, and of the Ogham alphabet and Ogham script (see page 62) in particular; and the Deae Quadruviae, or 'goddesses of the crossroads', to whom there are many dedications in Germany.

THE PRIESTLY CLASS

Caesar gives us the first detailed account of the status and function of the now famous Celtic priestly class, which was led by the druids (and ultimately, according to Caesar, by a single archdruid, whose political status and influence must have been considerable). The following quotations, interspersed with my comments, are taken from Caesar's *Commentaries*, better known as *The Gallic War*:[1]

> Throughout Gaul there are only two classes of men who are of any
> account or importance . . . the druids and the knights. The druids are
> in charge of religion. They have control over public and private
> sacrifices, and give rulings on all religious questions. Large numbers of
> young men go to them for instruction, and they are greatly honoured
> by the people.

Caesar's mention of both public and private sacrifices is suspect. The distinction is never defined, and it is difficult to imagine how a sacrifice at which a druid and his or her retinue presided could be a private affair. There is also evidence that young women as well as young men were trained in the priesthood. The vernacular texts use the word druidess as well as druid, but the generic term priestess is also widely used, which leads to confusion about function. There are two rather obscure references in the classical literature, both from Vopiscus, a historian from Syracuse, who flourished c.AD 300. In one, Vopiscus tells the story of a druidess prophesying to Diocletian that he will one day be emperor; in the second, the druidess foretells the illustrious fate of the descendants of Claudius. In both references, the function is actually that of a vate or seer (see page 54), but Vopiscus unmistakably uses the title druidess. Many women held positions of high status in Celtic society, and Caesar's suggestion that only young men received priestly training may reflect Roman practice, rather than Celtic. Caesar continues:

> In most disputes, between communities or between individuals, the
> druids act as judges. If a crime is committed, if there is a murder, or if
> there is a dispute about an inheritance or a boundary, they are the ones
> who give a verdict and decide on the punishment or compensation
> appropriate in each case. Any individual or community not abiding by
> their verdict is banned from the sacrifices, and this is regarded among
> the Gauls as the most severe punishment. Those who are banned in
> this way are reckoned as sacrilegious criminals. Everyone shuns them;
> no one will go near or speak to them for fear of being contaminated
> in some way by contact with them. If they make any petitions there
> is no justice for them, and they are excluded from any position of
> importance.

(Everything Caesar describes about the power of the druids is in accord with what we learn from the vernacular texts, but they go even further: they describe how druids can inflict physical injury, even cause death, by uttering ritual curses and shame-inducing satires.)

> There is one druid who is above all the rest, with supreme authority
> over them. When he dies, he is succeeded by whichever of the others is
> most distinguished. If there are several of equal distinction, the druids
> decide by vote, though sometimes they even fight to decide who will be
> their leader.

The modern Welsh Gorsedd (the word *gorsedd* means literally 'great sitting', and is used in the vernacular texts to refer to events, assemblies and, by inference, to the sites of famous events or assemblies) is indeed led by the *Archderwydd*, but there is not a single instance in any of the texts, nor any mention by any other classical writer, of druids actually fighting each other for precedence. There is some evidence that Caesar may have picked up this idea from Poseidonius of Apamea, who wrote a century earlier. Caesar's account continues:

> On a fixed date each year, they assemble in a consecrated place in the
> territory of the Carnutes; that area is supposed to be the centre of the
> whole country of Gaul. People who have disputes to settle assemble
> there from all over the country and accept the rulings and judgments
> of the druids.

(The Carnutes lived a little to the south and west of where Paris now stands. As we shall see shortly, it is almost certain that the druids presided over at least eight major festivals per year, not just one.)

> It is thought that the doctrine of the druids was invented in Britain and
> was brought from there into Gaul; even today, those who want to
> study the doctrine in greater detail usually go to Britain to learn there.

Discussions of the origins of druidism have produced some magnificent flights of speculation. The druids have been linked to the Persians (and more specifically the Magi); the Egyptians; the Brahmins of India; the tribes of Israel; the Phoenicians; the Greeks; the lost civilization of Atlantis. There is even one author who tells us that the druids came from the Moon (the far side, naturally). There are more genuinely persuasive arguments for suggesting a link between early Greek Pythagoreanism and the tenets of druidism, but all of these suggestions are speculative. However, the vernacular texts, and to some extent the observed patterns in archaeological finds of religious objects, tend to confirm Caesar's description of the importance of Britain as a seat of druidic learning. He continues:

> The druids are exempt from military service and do not pay taxes like
> the rest. Such significant privileges attract many students, some of
> whom come of their own accord to be taught, while others are sent by
> parents and relatives.

(This would make fine sense if there was good evidence that the Celts had
military service in the Roman sense, or paid taxes to a central source, but
there is no such evidence.)

> It is said that during their training they learn by heart a great many
> verses, so many that some people spend twenty years studying the
> doctrine. They do not think it right to commit their teachings to
> writing, although for almost all other purposes, for example for public
> and private accounts, they use the Greek alphabet.

(There is plenty of supporting evidence for the description of the learning of
magnum numerum versuum, but the Greek inscriptions are scarce, although
some do exist.)

> The druids attach particular importance to the belief that the soul does
> not perish but passes after death from one body to another; they think
> that this belief is the most effective way to encourage bravery because
> it removes the fear of death.

Caesar seems to be suggesting that the druids deliberately fostered a religious
viewpoint to further a political end; this is a very cynical, Roman interpretation, for which there is no other evidence at all. The direct transmigration of
the soul, which was a central tenet of Pythagoreanism dating from at least
500 BC, was ridiculed in Rome for many years before Caesar's time.

There were at least two other groups who made up the priestly class,
namely the bards and the vates (sometimes called ovates). The Irish had a
term *fili* (plural *filid*), often translated as 'seer', which seems to describe a
similar function to that of the vates, although the Irish term *ollam*, often
translated as 'poet', was reserved for senior or very important poets, and does
not seem to be exactly equivalent (at least in terms of rank) to the Brythonic
term *bardh* or bard, which appears to have been a more humdrum position.
Diodorus Siculus gives us an account of these lesser priestly functions:

> Among them are also to be found lyric poets whom they call bards.
> These men sing to the accompaniment of instruments which are like
> lyres, and their songs may be either of praise or of obloquy.
> Philosophers, as we may call them, and men learned in religious affairs
> are unusually honoured among them and are called by them druids.
> The Gauls likewise make use of diviners, accounting them worthy of
> high approbation, and these men foretell the future by means of the

flight or cries of birds and of the slaughter of sacred animals, and they have all the multitude subservient to them. They also observe a custom which is especially astonishing and incredible, in case they are taking thought to matters of great concern; for in such cases they devote to death a human being and plunge a dagger into him in the region above the diaphragm, and when the stricken victim has fallen they read the future from the manner of his fall and from the twitching of his limbs, as well as from the gushing of the blood . . . [2]

As was mentioned in Chapter One, there has been much heated debate about whether the Celts did or did not indulge in human sacrifice. Such barbarity was too painful for the Victorian Celtic revivalists to contemplate, so there was much woeful denial, which turned out to be rather ineffective, since almost the first thing the modern proverbial man in the street would tell you if you asked him about druids is that they sacrificed humans on the altar at Stonehenge, which (he will also tell you with equal confidence) they built for that very purpose. Well, the druids did not build Stonehenge, nor is there any evidence that they sacrificed any person (or even any animal, for that matter) at that place. There may well have been Celtic human sacrifice, the victims almost certainly having been condemned criminals, and, in that light, the so-called civilized modern states which continue to allow capital punishment are merely continuing the same time-honoured tradition (although they may be trying to appease different gods). The Romans themselves continued making human sacrifices until 96 BC, when the practice was outlawed by the Senate. Even so, when Caesar himself had two rebellious soldiers executed in the Regia in 56 BC, he dedicated their deaths to the god Mars, which comes as close to human sacrifice as makes no difference.

The Irish traditions make Tara the seat of kingship, but Uisneach (in Meath) the centre of druidism. This is a very important distinction. A druid could be wiser than a king, richer than a king, have more retainers than a king, even have a greater army than a king, but a druid could not be a king. Druidism is said to have come to Uisneach in the form of Mide, the first druid (his name means 'Evil', and is the source of the name Meath), who lit the first fire in Ireland. The fire blazed untended for seven years, and could be seen over the four quarters of the land. Early Celtic law enshrines many traditions concerning the sanctity of fire. The Welsh laws refer to *datanhud*, which lit-erally means 'the right to uncover the fire', but which actually signified the right to enter and occupy land which one's father had occupied until his death.[3] The fire of Mide or Meath is almost certainly associated with the fires of the spring festival of Beltane (see page 57). While there were many sym-bols of kingship, fire was the symbol of religious, rather than territorial, authority. The Pythagoreans also depicted fire at the centre of the universe. According to the early Irish poems known as *dinnseanchas* (a difficult word to translate but 'poems of place' conveys a partial meaning), whenever the King of Ireland (i.e. the king at Tara) celebrated a feast, the king of Meath must also celebrate likewise on the hill of Slemain Mide, or terrible calamity would befall the whole of Ireland. Symbolically, the relationship being described is that which obtained between the ruler wedded to the land, the king or queen (Tara), and the judge who spoke the truth of the universe, the druid or druidess (Uisneach). Religion, then, was not merely an opiate to send warriors happy to their deaths, as Caesar cynically suggests, but an essential, deeply permeating force in the everyday life of the tribal Celts, perceived as integrally linked to kingship and stewardship of the land. Kingship or queen-ship was a marriage to the land and nation, with abundant potency and fer-tility as the essential royal qualifications, and the druid was the priest who officiated at the ceremonies, both of symbolic marriage and of symbolic dis-solution. That symbolic power explains why the priestly class held such high status in Celtic society.

PATTERNS OF WORSHIP

There is strong evidence that the Celts worshipped in the open air. Although there may have been buildings used as temples or altar sites, there are clear indications that specific lakes, pools, springs, rivers, rocks, headlands and clearings were important sites of religious activity. The Irish word *nemed*, which appears as *nemeton* in many place-name elements, and which may be derived from an earlier Greek term, is frequently translated as 'grove' or 'sanctuary', although in some cases it may equally well have been describing a promontory or even a hillfort. Drunemeton, which is recorded as the wor-ship site of the Galatians, means 'Oak Sanctuary'. In Britain there was a Medionemeton, meaning 'Central Sanctuary'. Nemetodurum, meaning 'Sanctuary of the Oak', was the original name of modern Nanterre, and there is a site in Galicia, Spain called Nemetobriga, which means 'Shining Grove' or 'Bright Sanctuary'. At Buxton in Derbyshire, the local sacred spring was Romanized as Aquae Arnemetiae, 'the waters of (the goddess) Arnemetia', the name Arnemetia also deriving from *nemed* or *nemeton*.

The common opinion of which ceremonies may have taken place within these sacred groves has been heavily coloured by a single description in the classical texts, that of Pliny describing the ceremony of the cutting of the mistletoe:

> They call the mistletoe by a name meaning the all-healing. Having
> made preparation for sacrifice and a banquet beneath the trees, they
> bring thither two white bulls, whose horns are bound then for the first
> time. Clad in a white robe, the priest ascends the tree and cuts the
> mistletoe with a golden sickle, and it is received by another in a white
> cloak. Then they kill the victims, praying that God will render this gift
> of his propitious to those to whom he had granted it. They believe that

the mistletoe, taken in drink, imparts fertility to barren animals, and that it is an antidote to all poisons. Such are the religious feelings that are entertained towards trifling things by many peoples.[4]

A little of this description makes some sense, but much of it must be hokum. Some of the Celts did, indeed, call mistletoe by a name meaning 'all-healing': the Irish is *uil-ioc*. The Brythonic name, however, is *uchelwydd* (Welsh, 'high tree') or *ughelvarr* (Cornish and Breton, 'high branch'). The English name, incidentally, is from Old English *mistiltan*, meaning missel twig, missel being the name of a bird, the mistle-thrush as it is now called. However, mistletoe does not grow on oaks – the timber is too hard. It is more commonly found on apple or pear trees. A knife made from gold would not cut mistletoe. White bulls (unless they were painted white) would have been such rare commodities that the ceremony could only have been conducted once in a large number of years. The white robe for the druid (now firmly established as the druidic uniform by the revived institutions of the Welsh Gorsedd and Eisteddfod, and by the English druidic order which used to meet until recently at Stonehenge) is a Romanization – the Roman priesthood wore white robes, but the Celts never wore white, and the whole concept of innocence, purity and sanctity which Roman and Christian practice have brought into association with the colour white would have been utterly alien and incomprehensible to the early Celtic druidic priesthood. A multicoloured robe, probably with an antlered helmet or totemic animal mask, would have been much more likely.

We know that there were regular religious festivals, and that they were held at fixed stations of the year. Indeed, some of the fairs associated with the festivals still take place, and the festival names have survived intact through many centuries. In *The Celtic Druids' Year*, I give detailed reasons for believing that the Celts measured the year from midsummer to midsummer.[5] There are eight major festivals and, although there is a question about how precisely the festival dates would have been calculated and indicated in early tribal times, there is no dispute about the order in which they occur, nor about the precise seasons of the annual cycle to which they relate.

Beltane, dedicated to the god Bel, takes its name from the god and from the word *tan*, meaning 'fire'. It is the spring festival, during which the tribal herds were driven between two ceremonial fires as a rite of purification following the darkness of winter. Bel is the archtypal Achaean-style warrior hero, the epitome of the golden sun. Modern neopagans celebrate Beltane on 1 May.

Beltane is followed by Midsummer, another fire festival. To this day, Midsummer Eve bonfires are lit throughout Cornwall, although they are now dedicated to St. John, whose feast is set on the following day. There is evidence to suggest that the druids calculated the year as 364 days, with the longest day at midsummer standing outside the named months – the formulaic phrase 'a year and a day' may describe this practice.

The August festival is Lughnasa or Lughnasad, dedicated to the god Lugh, who is a father god of the Hercules type. Lugh is a Goidelic name. The Brythonic equivalent, Lleu, looks like a simple variant, but in fact it is a completely different word, an epithet meaning 'lion' (derived from Latin *leo*) and the full name is Lleu Llaw Gyffes, 'the Lion with the Steady Hand'. The Gauls used the Romanized form Lugus, from which was derived Lugodunum (the fort of Lugus), which is now Lyons, France. The modern towns of Laon and Leyden also take their names from the god, as does Carlisle, England (originally Caer Lugubalion, the hillfort of Lugh). The -nasa element of the name is found in Irish *nasadh*, which means 'commemoration', perhaps of the passing of the old king and the arrival of the new. The symbolic transition from Beltane to Lughnasa is from the young, warrior-hero son to the old, harvest-laden father. Solemnizations of kingship may have taken place at Lughnasa. Centuries after the hegemony of the Celtic tribes in Britain, when the Anglish, Saxon and Jutish tribes not only had established their rule but also had been converted from their Norse paganism to Christianity, a new harvest celebration was introduced and superimposed over the old Celtic Lughnasa festival: they called this feast *hlafmas*, the Mass of the *hlaf* or loaf (of bread). This name became corrupted to Lammas, which is how it still stands in the Christian calendar.

The autumnal equinox, which, for calendrical reasons, must have been marked, is not clearly associated with any particular god or goddess. Nor is the vernal equinox. The midsummer and midwinter festivals are much more clearly associated with specific folk traditions, some of which almost certainly reflect ancient ceremonial practices, but they, too, are not associated with a particular god or goddess. The pattern which emerges, as we shall see shortly, is of two four-arm crosses laid across the year: the north–south–east–west cross marks the equinoxes and the longest and shortest days, which are of great calendrical significance, but none of the dedications are to individual gods, while the diagonal cross which begins with Beltane is very clearly dedicated to specific deities or seasonal stereotypes.

Samhain, which is the modern Irish word for November, is the name of the festival which many people, Christian and humanist as well as neopagan, now celebrate in one form or another on 31 October, or Hallowe'en. The name, also spelled Samain, is pronounced 'sowan', not, as is sometimes heard, 'Sam Hayne'. The Irish call Hallowe'en *Oiche Shamnhna* (ee-uh shown-uh), the Eve of Samhain. Hallowe'en celebrates the dead – it is founded on the Christian festivals of All Hallows, also called All Saints and Hallowmass (1 November) and All Souls (2 November). Before the Christian festivals were established, the same date was dedicated by the Romans to Pomona, goddess of fruit and the harvest – in fact, the Hallowe'en tradition of bobbing for apples is derived from the earlier, Roman celebration. This festival has become so cluttered with traditions from a variety of sources that it is difficult to be certain which, if any, of the traditions are authentically Celtic in origin. The vernacular texts, probably our most reliable source, associate Samhain with the mating of the Dagda ('Good God'), the tribal father-god of all Ireland, and the Morrigan ('Great Queen'), a war-goddess. There was always an assembly at Tara, seat of the Irish kings, at Samhain, and Samhain was the traditional time for the triple killing of the king (by wounding, burning and drowning) so that a new king might take his place. The festival is also associated with tales of shape-shifting and of transports from this world to the afterworld and back again. For these and other reasons, Samhain has come to be thought of as a time of special danger and opportunity, when spirits may be more freely abroad. Many neopagans celebrate Samhain as the beginning of the new Celtic year, although there is no evidence to suggest that the original tribal Celts did this.

The midwinter solstice marks the occasion of a very deep mystery: the point at which the sun begins to fight back, and the dwindling days creep forward to their greater length again. The ancient Romans called their midwinter festival *Dies Natalis Invictis Solis*, the Day of Birth of the Unconquered Sun; the feast was subsequently dedicated to Saturn and became known as the Saturnalia, a week-long celebration which began on 19 December, with special cakes and sweetmeats, the exchanging of gifts, and so on. The Christian festival of the Christ Mass, or Christmas, was later deliberately imposed on 25 December to subsume these pagan festivities. The midwinter traditions of the Yule Log and the Yule Candle are almost certainly Celtic in origin, despite the Nordic provenance of the word Yule. There is a Cornish tradition of chalking the figure of a man on the Yule Log before it is burned, which may hark back to some very ancient sacrifice ritual. The 'first tree in the green wood', namely the holly, was the wood of Saturn's magic club, and the ivy, with which midwinter holly is traditionally paired, was the tree of Saturn's sacred bird, the gold-crested wren.

Imbolc, also known as *Oimelg* in Goidelic, is the feast which took place at the time of the first lambing, around 1 February. It was dedicated to the mother-goddess, Brigit, who was later Christianized into St. Brigid or Bridget. The name Brigit means 'the Shining One', and it is not surprising to see the Roman festival of Lupercalia, which was a festival of lights, and the later Christian festival of Candlemas, commemorating the purification of the Christian holy mother, superimposed on or about the original Celtic feast date (Lupercalia was held in mid-February, Candlemas is on 2 February). At Tailtiu, or Teltown, in County Meath, a special kind of trial marriage was available at Imbolc, and survived until comparatively recent times: a bride and groom could walk towards each other, kiss, and thus be wed, with the option of dissolving the marriage by returning one year later and walking away from each other to effect the divorce.

After the vernal equinox came Beltane, and so the cycle continued. That the dates were properly calculated in a systematic calendar is confirmed by the find at Coligny, near Bourg-en-Bresse in France, of a bronze tablet, originally measuring approximately 1 metre by 1.5 metres (3 ft by 5 ft), but now greatly fragmented, on which was engraved a calendar of sixty-two lunar months and two additional, or intercalary, months. The language is the Brythonic Celtic of Gaul, but the lettering is Roman. Each month is divided into two halves, the propitious half (of the waxing moon) indicated by MAT (meaning 'good') and the unpropitious half by ANM, which presumably represents ANMAT, meaning 'ungood', therefore, 'bad'. There has been much debate about the validity (not the genuineness) of the Coligny calendar. While it does provide indisputable evidence that the early Celts had calendrical skills, its adherence to lunar months of twenty-nine and a half days, rather than the more likely Celtic unit of twenty-eight days, and its use of Roman letters and Roman numerals, have suggested to many commentators that it is more Roman than Celtic, an artefact produced by subjugated Celts to please new masters.

The religious festivals played an important part in unifying Celtic tribal society, divided as it was into several small clans or kingdoms, each of which could easily find itself in armed dispute with its neighbour on the slightest pretext. Of the feast of Lughnasa at Tara, the ancient Irish *dinnseanchas* tell

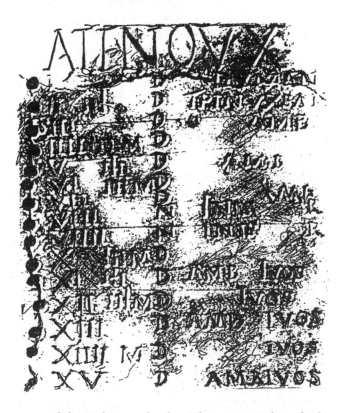

A fragment of the Coligny calendar. The text is Celtic, the lettering and numbers Roman. The holes on the left were probably used for pegs to mark feast days.

us: 'Here too is the reason the feast of Tara was made at all: the body of the law which all Ireland enacted then, during the interval between that and their next convention at the year's end none might dare transgress, and he that perchance did so was outlawed from the men of Ireland.' The same source tells us that the Imbolc feast at Tailtiu was to be conducted 'without wounding or robbing of any man, without trouble, without dispute . . . without challenge of property, without suing, without law sessions, without evasion, without arrest'. It seems that the feasts allowed for insults and other wrongs committed during the year to be redressed without penalty or prolonged legal or military action, and that would have provided a very useful safety valve for a society which valued military courage and proud boasting so highly. It is also clear that the festivals were great fun: there were feasts, fairs, games, horse races and horse markets, chariot races, poets, fiddlers, dancers, mummers, bread, cakes, beer, mead, wine from the Mediterranean, and all the jollities which simple societies have enjoyed throughout the centuries.

Celtic religion was essentially a nature religion. The land itself, with its springs, rocks, lakes and mountains, was a living and sacred thing, and its gods and goddesses were manifest and omnipresent. The famous Giant of Cerne Abbas, with his erect phallus and knotted club, is one manifestation of the god of the land. The hills called Da Chich Anann, or the Paps of Anu, in County Kerry, are the breasts of Mother Earth, Danu or Ana, the ancestral mother of the Tuatha de Danaan. In every place where the Celts have lived or live still, the names of their gods and goddesses ring out in the place names. The River Marne is the river of the three Matronae ('mothers'), the Seine is Sequana, the goddess of its source. The names of the German rivers Rhine, Neckar, Main, Lahn, Ruhr and Lippe are all Celtic. The Severn in Britain is the goddess Sabrina, the Clyde in Scotland is Clota, the death-goddess who, as in the tale of Cu Chulainn, is found washing the hero's blood-stained clothes at a ford of the river.

As was mentioned earlier, there is only limited evidence of buildings set aside for religious purposes. Rectilinear earthworks called *viereckschanzen* ('square enclosures') have been found with accompanying burial shafts, notably at Holzhausen in Bavaria. Many offering- and burial-shafts have been found in Britain, some with remains and artefacts. A shaft at Wilsford in Wiltshire has been radio-carbon dated to the fourteenth century BC, which suggests very strongly that the British Celts learned the practice of shaft burial and votive offering from the people whom they overthrew when they occupied Britain, which happened almost certainly around 900 BC at the very earliest, and probably much later than that.

Although the Celtic religious and cultural tradition was an oral one and, therefore, much of what may have once existed no longer does, we have every reason to believe that early Celtic society was extremely sophisticated in many ways, and that learning and erudition, and in particular learned and correct utterance, were very highly praised. To this day, skill in speech is very greatly respected in Celtic traditions – in any Irish pub, especially in the rural southwest, you will easily find a companion who will maintain the liveliest of conversations, the 'crack', for three or four hours at a stretch and think nothing of it.

Eloquence equalled strength for the early tribal Celts. Ogmios, the bald-headed god mentioned briefly earlier, was described by Lucian of Samosota, a Greek historian of the second century AD. The gold chains which link Ogmios's tongue to the ears of his happy followers are, of course, chains of eloquence. The Irish counterpart of the Romano-Celtic Ogmios is Oghma, depicted in the vernacular texts, like Ogmios, as a strong man, a Hercules type. Eloquence is strength, and it is a strength which grows greater with age. Both gods are representations of the secret alphabet used by the druidic priesthood, now known as Ogham. Ogham was a system of writing which used horizontal or slanting notches cut on stone or wood to indicate letters. Each letter could also be indicated by using joints of the fingers, like a modern signing alphabet for the deaf. In addition, each letter was named for a particular tree, and a vast lore of religious and mythological knowledge could be encoded in cryptic verses, as in the early mediaeval Welsh *Battle of the Trees*, which is really about battles of words, wit and wisdom, not trees at all. Loss of speech was equated with death. In the Welsh tale of Branwen, dead warriors are resurrected by immersion in the magic Cauldron of Rebirth, but they cannot speak, because they are really still dead.

The rules of kingship were deeply intertwined with religious tradition and precedent in Celtic society. We return now to the emergence of the Celts, their sudden spread from Gaul to Galatia and their impact on the classical world, to look more closely at how these patterns and rules which governed the early Celtic clan and tribal system affected and were affected by contact with other cultures.

Notes

1   Book VI, sections 13–14 and 16, trans. A. Wiseman and P. Wiseman, in Michael Grant's *Readings in the Classical Historians*, pp. 201–202.
2   Diodorus Siculus, V, 31.
3   *Ancient Laws of Wales*, London, 1841, quoted in Alwyn Rees and Brinley Rees, *Celtic Heritage*, p. 157.
4   Quoted in T.D. Kendrick, *The Druids*, London, 1928, p. 59.
5   *The Celtic Druids' Year*, Blandford Press, London, 1994.

THREE

✳

FROM GAUL TO GALATIA – THE FIRST KINGDOMS

MIGRATIONS

THE first clearly identifiable Celtic migration is that of the tribes who moved westward from Bohemia and southern Germany, across what was later called Gaul, and into the Iberian peninsula, which they reached sometime before 450 BC. At about the same time, other Celts moved southwards over the Alps, occupying the Po river valley. There is evidence that some tribes reached as far as Rome, and even as far south as Sicily. Archaeologists, careful to avoid the controversies surrounding the Celtic identity, sometimes refer to the bronze-using peoples who made these migrations as the 'Northern Alpine Urnfield' culture. There were many tribes among them, principal of which appears to have been the Insubres, who sacked Etruria and reached Mediolanum, modern Milan, Italy.

Later, Celtic tribes expanded eastwards through Macedonia, invading Greece via Thrace and Thessaly. They attacked the temple at Delphi in 279 BC. Perhaps as many as 25 000 Celts went even further eastwards into Asia Minor and settled the area later known as Galatia.

On the western Atlantic seaboard, there were tribal movements for centuries between the Iberian peninsula, Armorica (later called Brittany), and Scotland and Ireland. As will be described more fully in Chapter Five, the Irish sagas which detail the succeeding waves of invasions form the bedrock of early Irish mythology and literature. The last great migration in pre-classical times was the northward invasion of the Belgae into southern Britain and Ireland around 250 BC.

When we start to examine these migrations in detail, the same problems of identity which were discussed in Chapter One reappear. The essence of the problem is that we are forced to rely on the accounts of classical authors, who had great difficulty distinguishing between Celts, Germans and Scythians.

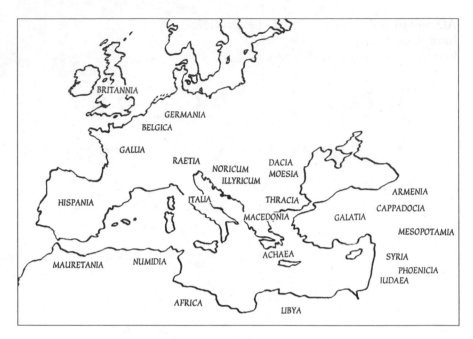

Principal regions of the Roman Empire.

If, as was suggested in Chapter One, we rely on linguistic evidence as the most secure indicator of a Celtic identity, even access to a time machine might not be as helpful as could be imagined. The very name German is actually Latin in origin – it is from *germanus*, meaning 'genuine' or 'authentic', so the Germani were simply 'the real ones' – but the real *what* is not clear. It may well be that the title Germani actually means 'the real *Celts*': that was certainly the interpretation given by the Greek historian, Strabo, who lived and worked in Alexandria. Plutarch, Poseidonius and Strabo recorded what the early Celts (or Germans) did, with greater or lesser dependability according to one's point of view, but nowhere did they report what they said, at least not in their own words or language. Classical writers enlivened their writing by having key players in the story make elaborate and lengthy speeches (this was a favourite device of Tacitus in particular), but, of course, the speeches were in Latin, not in any native tongue. Tacitus does, however, make passing reference to native languages. For example, he identifies the Cotini as a Celtic tribe as follows:

> Close behind the Marcomanni and Quadi are the Marsigni, Cotini, Osi and Buri. Of these, the Marsigni and Buri are exactly like the Suebi in language and mode of life. The Cotini and the Osi are not Germans: that is proved by their languages, Celtic in the one case, Pannonian in the other, and also by the fact that they submit to paying tribute.

> The payments are exacted from them, as foreigners, by the Quadi and
> by the Sarmatians respectively – of which the Cotini have all the more
> reason to be ashamed inasmuch as they work iron mines.[1]

(The meaning of the reference to iron mines is that the Cotini could make
themselves weapons, if they chose.)

Unfortunately, while Tacitus makes the distinction, he gives us no examples of the Cotinic language itself. If we had any authentic samples of tribal language, especially any substantial fragments of written text, there is
enough linguistic expertise available nowadays to reveal a great deal about
the origins and interrelations of these early northern tribes, but such evidence
is, sadly, not available.

We can illustrate the extent of the problem by following the wanderings
of one particular tribe, the Cimbri, over a twelve-year period, namely 113 BC
to 101 BC. The Cimbri originated in the region which is now called Denmark.
Their tribal neighbours were the Teutones, the Harudes and the Ambrones.
Most reference books list all four tribes as Germanic. Teutonic, derived from
Teutones, has come specifically to mean 'relating to the Germanic languages'.
However, the king of the Cimbri during the period in question was Boiorix,
whose name is indisputably Celtic: the *rix* element means 'king', so the name
either means 'King of the Boii' or (far less likely) 'King Boio'. The Boii, who
Cato says were subdivided into one hundred and twelve separate family clans,
were a well known and indisputably Celtic tribe. The tribal name Cimbri is
convincingly similar to the Brythonic term *cymri*, meaning 'companions' or
'tribesmen', from which Cymru, the Welsh name for Wales, is derived.

During the summer of 113 BC, news came to Rome that the Cimbri,
Teutones and Ambrones were moving southward. They passed through the
lands of the Scordisci (modern Serbia and Croatia), then drifted into the territories of the Noricians and the Tauriscian Celts (modern Austria). A Roman
army, led by Papirius Carbo, met them in battle at Noreia, the Norician capital city. According to Plutarch, the northern host was 300 000 strong, which
is probably a considerable exaggeration, but the result of the battle was
abundantly clear – Papirius Carbo's legions were utterly destroyed. Rome
prepared for a second Celtic invasion and feared the worst.

In the event, the invading tribes moved west rather than south, and in
three subsequent battles, the last at Arausio (modern Orange, Provence) in
109 BC, the Romans were again defeated. A young general called Gaius
Marius was then appointed by Rome to deal with the problem. After the
defeat at Arausio, he introduced strict and rigorous training regimes into the
Roman army, which soon proved very effective. He pursued the Teutones and
Ambrones in a series of forced marches towards the Alps, and finally defeated them at the Battle of Aquae Sextiae (modern Aix-en-Provence).

The Cimbri, meanwhile, had advanced further south and east into the
plains of northern Italy. Gaius Marius met them at Vercellae (modern Vercelli
in Piedmont) in the spring of 101 BC. As was the Celtic custom, Boiorix

challenged Gaius Marius to individual combat, and, as was the Roman custom, Gaius Marius declined. Full battle was engaged, and the new Roman tactics prevailed, as they had with the Teutones and Ambrones earlier. Plutarch, the historian who tells us this story, paints a vivid and gory picture of the Cimbri allowing themselves to be slaughtered rather than submit to life as slaves in Rome. He tells us that the tribesmen, severely weakened by heat, thirst and the exhaustion of battle, chained themselves together to await death, so that no individual would be tempted to try to run for his life and thereby bring shame on his people. The women killed their own children and their own menfolk, 'even if they were their husbands, fathers or brothers', and then killed themselves.

So these Cimbri, who spent twelve years wandering from their northern home into Gallia, Germania and Italia, and who were slaughtered in such a spectacular fashion at Vercellae, give every indication of having been Celts – both the tribe and their king had convincingly Celtic names. But the Roman nomenclature seems to have been based very strongly on geographical origin, and followed a very simple scheme: Iberians came from Iberia (modern Spain and Portugal) to the west; Gauls (Celts) came from Gallia or Gaul, to the northwest; Germans ('the genuine ones') came from the north, specifically, according to Strabo, from east of the Rhine, being 'even taller, more savage and blond' than regular Gauls; and the Scythians came from the east. As was mentioned in Chapter One, one convincing detail which suggests that the Cimbri, Teutones and Ambrones were not only Celts, but the 'genuine ones', the most Celtic of the Celts, is Plutarch's description of how the Ligurians, Celtic tribal auxiliaries fighting on the Roman side, called out their tribal names during the Battle of Aquae Sextiae: they heard the Ambrones calling out their individual tribal, or clan names as rallying cries during the battle, and followed suit – 'they too shouted out their old names, for the Ligurians are known after their origins as Ambrones'. In other words, the convincingly Celtic pattern of deep allegiance to the clan or tribal identity emerged even in the heat of battle across opposing armies.

CELTS AND ROMANS

Even the identity of the Romans themselves is not always a straightforward question. Rome was founded after tribal conflict between Latins, Sabines and Etruscans, and the single Roman identity which the Empire created has its origins in murkier waters. In 616 BC, Lucius Tarquinius became the first Etrurian or Etruscan ruler of Rome, and, from that date onwards, the Etruscan influence on Rome was considerable. Livy tells the story of how Tarquin, or Tarquinius, whose original Etruscan name was Lucumo, came to know his destiny. It is another of those 'omen from the sky' stories of which the Romans were so fond:

The pair [Lucumo and his wife, Tanaquil] had reached Janiculum and were sitting together in their carriage, when an eagle dropped gently down and snatched off the cap which Lucumo was wearing. Up went the bird with a great clangour of wings until, a minute later, it swooped down again and, as if it had been sent by heaven for that very purpose, neatly replaced the cap on Lucumo's head, and then vanished into the blue. Tanaquil like most Etruscans was well skilled in celestial prodigies, and joyfully accepted the omen. . . . 'Did it not take the crown, as it were, from a human head, only to restore it by heaven's approval, where it belongs?' Thus dreaming upon future greatness, Lucumo and Tanaquil drove on into Rome, where they bought a house, and Lucumo took the name of Lucius Tarquinius Priscus.[2]

The Latins, the tribe defeated by the Etruscans under Tarquinius, were considerably less advanced than their conquerors. It was the Etruscans who introduced public sewerage and bridges to Rome, and who drained the marsh at the foot of the Palatine hill to create a public space, which eventually housed the Forum. The custom of marking the city boundaries in priest-led rituals was originally Etruscan. The *fasces*, the bundle of rods symbolizing authority which later gave its name to the fascist movement, was an Etruscan device. Even the famous gladiatorial contests and triumphal parades were Etruscan in origin. Livy tells us that many of the Roman festivals of his day were founded on much earlier primitive Etruscan agricultural traditions; for example, the Robigalia, a purification festival concerned with preventing blight in crops, continued to be celebrated centuries later, when Rome was a bustling urban sprawl. Similarly, the cumbersome electoral and legislative procedures introduced by Servius Tullius in about 550 BC remained almost unchanged even in Cicero's time, many centuries later. Even the most famous of Roman legends, that of the twins Romulus and Remus being suckled by a she-wolf, then raised by a shepherd and eventually founding the city of Rome, is actually an adaptation of an earlier myth from Asia Minor, found also in Greece in the legend of Neleus and Pelias, sons of the god Poseidon, who were exposed on the banks of the River Enipeus but saved by being suckled by a wild dog and a wild mare.

So, when the Celts first invaded Italy in about 400 BC, it was Etruscans rather than Romans who were expelled from the Po Valley. The traditional date for the founding of Rome is 753 BC, but even among classical authors there was considerable debate about the accuracy of that date. Livy places the coming of Tarquinius to Rome at about 625 BC.

This early Rome had a king, as each of the Celtic tribes did. He ruled with a senate of elders (called *patres*, meaning 'fathers'), some of whom were blood relatives, in the Celtic style, but some of whom were appointed on merit from other leading families. There was also a consultative assembly, known as the *comitia curiata* ('business committee'), which was constituted on a representative basis from smaller ethnic groups or regions, called *curiae* (often translated as 'parishes', although there is no real religious connotation). It can be seen immediately that this early Roman form of kingship was very different to the Celtic form. Inheritance was strictly patrilinear; promotion rewarded merit as well as rank; there was at least a semblance of democratic representation in the consultative assembly, the *comitia curiata*. When the Etruscans took control of Rome, they introduced more elaborate symbols of monarchy, including distinctive regalia for the king, a central shrine (dedicated to Vesta) near the marketplace, a central palace, and a ceremonial chair or throne, the *sella curulis* (literally 'seat of the chariot'), which was later adopted for use by elected magistrates, and on which the modern notion of a special royal seat or throne is based.

In the same way as the Celts, the Etruscans believed that kingly rule was divinely sanctioned. Livy tells a tale about King Servius which reads almost as though it might have come from one of the Irish or Welsh vernacular texts, with its emphasis on augury and the power of quick thinking and correct utterance. King Servius had built a new temple to Diana in the middle of the city, and to the outskirts of the temple had been brought for sacrifice an extraordinary heifer from the Sabine farmlands. There was a prophecy related to the heifer: whoever sacrificed it, that man's tribe would rule Rome thenceforward. A Sabine saw an opportunity to topple the Etruscan dynasty, but a sharp-witted priest thwarted his plan, as Livy reports:

> Now the Sabine I was speaking of, on the first suitable opportunity,
> drove the heifer to Diana's temple in Rome and led her to the altar.
> The Roman priest in attendance regarded with admiration the great
> beast of which he had heard so much – and, at the same time, he had
> not forgotten the prophecy.
>
> 'Stranger,' he said, 'what can you be thinking of? Surely you do not
> mean to sacrifice to Diana without first performing the act of purification? You must bathe yourself, before the ceremony, in a living stream.
> Down there in the valley the Tiber flows.'
>
> The stranger was a religious man, and the warning went home.
> Unwilling to omit any part of the proper ritual, lest the event should
> fail to correspond with the prophecy, he hurried down to the river.
> During his absence the Roman priest sacrificed the heifer himself.
> All Rome, including the king, was delighted.[3]

Under the influence of several other cultures, most notably that of the Greeks, the Etruscan kings introduced a radically new governmental concept during their period of hegemony: they created three new tribes, the Ramnes, Tities and Luceres (all three names are Etruscan), which, unlike the earlier system of ethnic *curiae* or parishes, were not founded on district or ethnic identity. This change, which predates Romulus and the first purely Roman kings, had a profound impact on the later Roman identity: in the full flowering of the Republic, a person could be a swarthy maize-eater from Ethiopia, or a square-headed onion-eater from Gaul, yet still be as much a Roman citizen as any patrician in the senate.

Sometime around 510 BC, the Etruscan kings were expelled and replaced by elected magistrates, who served two at a time, after the earlier Etruscan fashion. There had been military clashes with Lars Porsenna of Clusium, and the times were generally unsettled, which made major constitutional change more likely. In 494 BC, the ordinary people or *plebs* of Rome also elected representatives called *tribunes* to deal with their grievances, which had been exacerbated by crop failures and widespread disease, notably malaria.

Livy makes a lively story out of the end of the Tarquinian dynasty. The story's hero is Lucius Junius Brutus, whose name means literally 'the stupid one'. Sextus Tarquinius, also known as Tarquin the Proud, the last of the Etruscan kings, had been troubled by a snake which had emerged from a crack in a pillar of the royal palace. He sent Brutus, Titus and Arruns to the world-famous oracle at Delphi in Greece, to seek an interpretation of the omen. Livy's account continues:

> The three young men reached Delphi, and carried out the king's instructions. That done, Titus and Arrans found themselves unable to resist putting a further question to the oracle. Which of them, they asked, would be the next king of Rome? From the depths of the cavern came the mysterious answer: 'He who shall be the first to kiss his mother shall hold in Rome supreme authority.' Titus and Arruns were determined to keep the prophecy absolutely secret. . . . They drew lots to determine which of them, on their return, should kiss his mother first. Brutus, however, interpreted the words of Apollo's priestess in a different way. Pretending to trip, he fell flat on his face, and his lips touched the Earth – the mother of all living things.[4]

Shortly after the envoys' return, Sextus Tarquinius committed his notorious rape of Lucretia, wife of his royal companion and kinsman Collatinus, and Brutus took advantage of the subsequent outrage to throw off his disguise of pretended stupidity, seized control of Rome and thereby brought to an end the dynasty of the Tarquinian kings.

Brutus's kissing of Mother Earth echoes a deeply held Celtic belief, namely that kingship implied a literal bonding with the land. The physical beauty and potency or fertility of the king or queen were directly linked to the beauty and fecundity of the land itself. In Ireland, the bond was conceptualized as a marriage, and the rituals which accompanied the installation of a new king were essentially marriage rituals. The concept of an Earth Mother is common to many cosmogonies, and the ancient Greek personification of Gaia as the real and living spirit of the planet Earth has become widely known more recently through the influence of ecological movements. For the Celts, the seasons maintained their succession and delivered their fruits in the same way that the people of the tribe went through their seasons and delivered their children: because the tribe or clan was bonded to the land in the person of the royal partner, who was always physically without blemish, strong, proud, beautiful, potent or fertile, and vigorous.

There are one or two notable similarities between the earliest Celts and the earliest Romans. Although, as we saw above in the case of King Boiorix challenging Gaius Marius to personal combat, the Celtic notion of represent-ative combat between kings or champions was not reflected in Roman prac-tice generally, Livy tells us, with details of the oaths and ceremonies, how the Romans and Albans agreed to let their battle be settled by three chosen cham-pions in 670 BC. However, the emphasis of the story is to suggest that the practice was romantic and archaic. Similarly, Livy tells us about cattle raids – a very authentic Celtic practice – taking place between the early Romans and Albans.[5]

The notion of the king's divinity is also strongly emphasized in Livy's accounts. He tells us how Romulus, Rome's first real (i.e. non-Etruscan) king, passed from this world:

> Such, then, were the deeds of Romulus, and they will never grow old.
> One day while he was reviewing his troops on the Campus Martius
> near the marsh of Capra, a storm burst, with violent thunder. A cloud
> enveloped him, so thick that it hid him from the eyes of everyone
> present; and from that moment he was never seen again upon earth.[6]

Romulus has been assumed into the pantheon of higher beings, the gods who sanctioned his kingship. Similarly, King Numa, Romulus's successor, who was a Sabine and therefore potentially unpopular, had his succession con-firmed by a series of heavenly signs and omens specifically invoked by a tutel-ary priest.

There were more mundane connections between Celtic and Roman prac-tices, particularly in matters relating to warfare, since it was in battle that Celts and Romans usually first got to meet each other, and therefore to learn from each other. As Rome expanded into Celtic territories in Gaul and fur-ther north, the nature of campaigning changed: instead of fighting through the summer, then returning to their farms and homesteads in Italy for the winter, Roman troops now had to set up permanent *hiberna*, or winter camps. That meant greater and more prolonged contact between each side, with inevitably greater cultural interaction. The Celts observed the effective-ness of the Roman *gladius* or short sword, and the Romans observed the effectiveness of the Celtic chariot, which they adopted and called a *currus*, from which the modern word 'car' is derived. When the Celtic long sword became too effective for comfort, the Romans developed the *pilum*, a spear used for thrusting, unlike the *alia* or javelin, which was thrown. The Celts had long battle horns, for which the term *cornyx* is nowadays used, and the Romans had a shorter *cornu*, or signalling horn. The Celts carried totemic banners, with boars, stags or bulls painted on them, and the Romans carried the imperial eagle (and, before the Empire, probably also carried totemic flags – we know of the existence of at least one type, a dragon flag or banner, because the word for its carrier, the *draconarius*, survived in the Latin vocabulary). Even under the imperial eagle, individual legions carried subsidiary banners with other animal totems, often zodiac creatures associated with special birthdays or famous battle dates in the legion's history.[7]

CELTIC ADVANCES INTO ITALY

The first Celtic raids into the Po Valley were so effective that the tribes not only occupied the region, but also gave their collective name to it: as was mentioned earlier, these fertile plain lands south of the Alps became known as Gallia Cisalpina, 'Gaul this side of the Alps'. Gaul proper, at least before Caesar's conquest of it, was Gallia Transalpina, 'Gaul beyond the Alps'. When the Senones, a Celtic tribe, attacked and destroyed the Etruscan settlement of Clusium in 390 BC, the Romans retaliated, which, in turn, led to the first direct Celtic advance against Rome itself.

The Roman army was defeated at the Battle of Allia, and the Gauls now seized and sacked the city. Livy and other Roman historians tell us that the Capitoline hill was staunchly defended by heroes, but this appears to be fictional propaganda. In real terms, it took Rome over fifty years to recover from the shock of the Celtic invasion. The Gauls had to be bribed to leave the city, and there is a legend that, when the Romans complained at the unjust way in which the ransom money was being weighed out on the scales, the victorious Celtic King Brennus (Bran is probably the Celtic original of the name) threw his sword onto the scale, saying (presumably in perfect Latin), 'Vae victis!' ('Woe to the conquered!'). The Romans coined the term *terror Gallicus* to describe the Celtic threat, and all later classical descriptions of the Celts have to be read in the context of this deep historical animosity.

A few extracts from Livy's account of the Celtic sack of Rome convey a vivid impression of the event, and of the Celtic character as perceived by Rome:

> Rumour had preceded them . . . but in spite of warnings the sheer speed of the Gallic advance was a frightful thing. The Roman army moving with all the haste of a mass emergency levy had covered hardly eleven miles before it met the invaders at the spot where the river Allia descends. . . . The ground in front and on both sides was already swarming with enemy soldiers, and the air was loud with the dreadful din of the fierce war-songs and discordant shouts of a people whose very life is wild adventure. The Roman commanders had taken no precautions. . . . Alas, not good fortune only, but good generalship was on the barbarian side. In the lines of the legionaries – officers and men

The western provinces of the Roman Empire.

alike – there was no trace of the old Roman manhood. They fled in panic. . . . The Gauls could hardly believe their eyes, so easy, so miraculously swift their victory had been. . . . They began to collect the arms and equipment of the dead and to pile them, as their manner is, into heaps. . . . Rome was indeed a city of lamentation. . . . Then news came that the Gauls were at the gates; the anguish of personal bereavement was forgotten in a wave of panic, and all too soon cries like the howling of wolves and barbaric songs could be heard, as the Gallic squadrons rode hither and thither close outside the walls.[8]

Mediolanum (modern Milan, Italy) was the capital city of the Insubres, the largest and most powerful of the invading Celtic tribes. The Cenomani settled Brixia (modern Brescia). The Boii settled Felsina (modern Bologna). The

Senones and Lingones advanced further south, and led the sack of Rome. Rome signed a treaty with the Senones in 332 BC. Further unrest followed, however, complicated by the Roman wars against Carthage, known as the First and Second Punic Wars. In 232 BC, exactly a century after Rome's original treaty with the Senones, Roman troops seized the Senones' territory and installed colonists.

In 225 BC, the Celts were decisively routed at the Battle of Telamon. According to the account of the battle given to us by Polybius, over 40 000 Celts were slain and 10 000 taken prisoner. These were men and women of the Insubres, the Boii, the Taurisci and the Celtic mercenaries known only as *Gasaetae*, or sword-bearers. In effect, it had taken Rome over fifty years to recover from the Celtic invasion, and over a century to exact vengeance for it.

THE ADVANCE INTO GALATIA

Strabo tells us that Alexander the Great met Celtic tribesmen in the Balkans in 335 BC, drank with them, and, when he asked them what they feared most, received the now-famous reply that the only thing they ever feared was the sky falling on their heads – in other words, they were afraid of nothing and no one, other than the gods. Nor was Alexander afraid of them at that particular time – he was about to embark on his great conquest of Persia, and the Celts were an insignificant little group of barbarians away to the north and west.

After Alexander died in 323 BC, however, the break-up of his empire made space for the aggressive Celts to begin moving south and east into Macedonia. They were successfully contained and repulsed until 281 BC, when Celtic tribes seized and beheaded King Ptolemy Ceraunus. The leader of the Celtic force was King Bolgios, whose name may be related to the tribal name Belgae. The invasion of Macedonia was completed in 279 BC. The Celtic force ('army' is too organized a word) then divided into two factions, following the kind of tribal infighting which was endemic in Celtic society. One faction, headed by Leotarios and Leonnorios, set off eastwards, eventually settling in Turkey and establishing a state subsequently known as Galatia, land of the Gauls or Gaels. The other faction, led by Acichorios and Brennus (Bran in Celtic, not the same person as the King Brennus who cried, 'Vae victis!' in Rome), headed south towards Greece, intending to attack and loot the great sacred oracle and shrine at Delphi.

The attack on Delphi was unsuccessful, but it provided yet another opportunity for classical historians to write accounts of the barbarous Celts' savagery. Pausanias, for example, a Greek geographer and historian of the second century AD whom Sir James Frazer described as 'a man made of common stuff and cast in a common mould', wrote in his *Description of Greece* tales of Celtic warriors pulling spears out of their own wounds so that they could throw them back at the enemy and of tribesmen slaughtering women so they could drink the blood and eat the flesh of their babies (baby-eating was always good for spicing up a chapter). Pausanias also tells us that the Celts killed their own wounded as they retreated, that they were so terrified by thunder and lightning which accompanied the battle that they started killing each other, and that King Brennus took his own life by drinking undiluted wine – a fair amount of it, one would have to guess. One suspects that Pausanias got through a flagon or two of undiluted wine himself while writing his account.

Another Celtic force was decisively beaten at Lysimachia by King Antigonos Gonatas of Macedonia in 277 BC, and that defeat effectively ended the Celtic presence in Greece itself. A few small tribal settlements persisted, but they were eventually absorbed into post-Alexandrian Greece.

The Galatian settlement lasted much longer, but there remains in central Turkey little archaeological evidence of the Celtic enclave which existed there. A Galatian state existed from about 270 BC to AD 74, and the use of the Celtic language persisted for many centuries after that: St. Jerome (AD 331–420) recorded that the Galatians still used their own language, which was very similar to that of the Treveri, the Celts of eastern Gaul.

The faction led by Leotarios and Leonnorios originally decided to move eastwards because they were invited there to support King Nicomedes of Bithynia. He was happy to propel these invading barbarians further eastwards to create a buffer state between himself and the Phrygians. The classical accounts tell us that the force consisted of three tribes – the Tectosages, the Trocmii and the Tolistobogii (or Tolistoagii – both variants appear). Strabo tells us that the Tectosages came originally from the region near modern Toulouse, and that they were a sept or clan of a larger tribe called the Volcae. These three tribes rapidly established territorial control and then ruled over the people they had conquered, Phrygians and Cappadocians, for generation after generation. They were feared for their barbarism and cruelty. They conducted cattle raids, but also extended the tribal family business into kidnap for ransom and general dealing in the slave trade.

They adopted a system of government unlike that of any other Celtic society. Each tribe was divided into four units, each of which was ruled by a *tetrarch* (the word, which is Greek, simply means 'ruler of a fourth part'). The classical authors do not tell us whether these tetrarchs were appointed or inherited their titles. There was also a national assembly with 300 delegates. The central Galatian shrine was the *drunemeton*, which means 'sanctuary of the oak'. There is no mention in the classical authors either of traditional kingship or of druidism in Galatia. There is mention of a human sacrifice in 165 BC – the victims were prisoners whose home states refused to pay ransom.

The Galatians of the first century BC allied themselves first with the Greek cause, more specifically with Antiochus III of Seleucia, then later with Rome, after the massacre of Pergamon, in which Mithridates VI of Pontus invited sixty Galatian representatives to his stronghold and murdered all of them and their families, except for three who escaped to tell the tale. The Galatians were on the wrong side in the Roman civil war of 49 BC; they sided with Pompey, who had promoted Deiotarus of the Tolistobogii as sole king of all Galatia. Deiotarus was reprieved from execution by the victorious Caesar, in part owing to the advocacy of Cicero.

In AD 74, Galatia was absorbed into the province of Cappadocia. St. Paul wrote his Epistle to the Galatians after travelling among them, in particular to the settlements of Ancyra (modern Angora or Ankora), Pessinus and Tavium. It is interesting to observe that, even in Paul's time, the settlement at Tavium was distinctly less Celtic in character than those at Ancyra and Pessinus. As noted above, Celtic speech survived in many parts of the region for almost three centuries after the Celtic state of Galatia itself had ceased to exist.

There are many curious anomalies and omissions in the story of the Celts in Galatia. We have no idea why there are so few artefacts yet discovered (all we have so far is three brooches from the La Tène era); the absence of any reference to druidism or to druids is surprising, especially since there is reference to a central place of gathering and worship, the *drunemeton*; the appointment or election of *tetrarchs* is unique in Celtic societies, as is the 'promotion' of a single king as representative of the whole people, as happened with Deiotarus. We can only guess that the Celts who followed Leotarios and Leonnorios were unusually susceptible to outside cultural influence. The tales of savagery remind us of the wild Macedonians, from which stock Alexander himself came, while the accounts of Paul and, indeed, the Epistle he wrote convey a picture of a society which is greatly Hellenized, despite its continuing use of a Celtic language, but whose vices, including boasting, idolatry, sorcery, drunkenness and jealousy, seem to reflect a more distinctively Celtic past.

THE PUNIC WARS – HANNIBAL, ELEPHANTS AND CELTIC MERCENARIES

In addition to Iberians and Gauls from the west and northwest, Germans from the north and Scythians from the east, the Romans also had potential enemies from Africa in the south. Egypt, whose early civilization was a constant source of admiration to the Greek and Roman world even when its political power had long since waned, was always important strategically, as the episode of Antony and Cleopatra indicates. In the third and second centuries BC, the more immediate threat was from Carthago or Carthage in Numidia. Carthage stood where Tunis now stands, only a few nautical miles from Sicily. From 264 to 146 BC a series of wars, known as the Punic Wars, took place between Rome and Carthage. (Punic is a variant form of the adjective Phoenician, and refers to the language spoken in ancient Carthage.)

Of these, the most important for our present purpose is the Second Punic War of 218–201 BC, which brings together the famous story of Hannibal and his elephants and the less well-known story of the Celtic tribes which took part in the campaigns.

Hannibal, born in 247 BC, was the son of the Carthaginian leader Hamilcar Barca. When he was only 9 years old, his father brought him to Spain and trained him in the arts of war, after making him swear an oath of eternal hatred against Rome. Hamilcar was killed by the rebellious Oretani in 229 and succeeded by Hannibal's brother-in-law, Hasdrubal. When Hasdrubal died in 221, Hannibal, at the age of only 25 assumed command of the army and the province of Spain. From 221 until his suicide in 183 BC, Hannibal conducted a relentless and inspired series of military campaigns against Rome.

Livy gives us a vivid description of Hannibal's complex character:

> His time for waking, like his time for sleeping, was never determined
> by daylight or darkness: when his work was done, then, and then only,
> he rested, without need, moreover, of silence or a soft bed to woo
> sleep to his eyes. Often he was seen lying in his cloak on the bare
> ground amongst the common soldiers on sentry or picket duty. His
> accoutrement, like the horses he rode, was always conspicuous, but not
> his clothes, which were like those of any other officer of his rank and
> standing. Mounted or unmounted he was unequalled as a fighting
> man, always the first to attack, the last to leave the field. So much for
> his virtues – and they were great; but no less great were his faults:
> inhuman cruelty, a more than Punic perfidy, a total disregard of truth,
> honour and religion, of the sanctity of an oath and of all that other
> men hold sacred.[9]

We know that Hannibal was holding tactical discussions with Celtic delegates of the Boii as early as 219 BC. They were considering a joint expedition through southern Gaul and into northern Italy, and discussion was necessary since the first part of the expedition would cross Boii territory. King Magalos allied the Boii to Hannibal's cause in 218 BC.

Other Celtic tribes, however, were either indifferent to Hannibal's campaign or actively hostile to it. Only the Boii appear to have supported Hannibal from the start. Ten thousand Celtiberians deserted the expedition before it had even crossed the Pyrénées. Some of them even acted as scouts for the Romans, and sent reports via the Hellenized town of Massilia (modern Marseilles) of Hannibal advancing with gigantic grey pack animals across the mountains. Naturally, the reports used the Greek word for these previously unseen animals: *elephantoi*. The Romans had never seen these animals either, so their consternation was great, since the reports seemed to suggest that each of these monsters had an arm on the front of its head which could lift a man and throw him bodily to the ground, and that they had skins of such tough leather that neither swords nor even lances could pierce them. Livy gives us a detailed account of how Hannibal transported his elephants across rivers by raft, and of how he coped with the panic and confusion when the terrified animals fell off the rafts into the cold, swift-moving water.[10]

The Allobroges, who had been defeated and driven back to the Alps by Rome, might have been expected to join Hannibal, but they did exactly the opposite: they resisted his advance, until a successful night raid scattered their forces. The Ceutrones supplied Hannibal with provisions, but later – presumably because they felt that they had been insufficiently paid, or because some debt of honour had not been properly satisfied – they ambushed the Punic army on a narrow mountain pass. Hannibal suffered some loss of men, but more of horses and elephants. There must have been some rare dinners of elephant steak during those few days and nights, while the Ceutrones nursed their wounds and their grievances. The Taurini, who lived in what is now Piedmont, also showed signs of ambivalent support for Hannibal, but Hannibal had by now lost patience with the treacherous barbarian Celts: he stormed their capital. However, instead of the routine slaughter and burning which usually followed such victories, he showed a remarkable understanding of the Celtic character. He offered each captive member of the Taurini a chance to fight in individual combat against one of his own men, with a horse, weapons and freedom to leave as the prize for the victor. To a man, the Celts accepted his offer, and, after a few deaths had proved that he was in earnest, and after he had offered them Carthaginian citizenship once Rome had been defeated, the Taurini pledged allegiance and joined Hannibal's campaign. It is said that during this period of enthusiastic cooperation Hannibal even learned some phrases of Celtic and conversed with tribal kings without an interpreter.

In the event, it was the Celts who finally let Hannibal down and led to his defeat. At a battle fought in a driving blizzard on the Trebia, a tributary of the Po, Celtic mercenaries were supposed to hold the centre while the Carthaginian army advanced in a pincer movement, but the Celts crept away under cover of the blinding snow. This was an unusual event, since the Celts were famed for their zeal and almost insane bravery in battle. Pausanias's account of the Celtic raid on Delphi in thunder and lightning, mentioned earlier, and Livy's account of the dismal scattered retreat in the blizzard on the Trebia both reinforce the classical notion of the Celts as desperately fickle and superstitious in battle, ready to accept defeat at the merest hint that the gods who control the wind and the rain might be against them. Describing an earlier battle, Livy talks of Hannibal's conviction 'that there was more smoke than fire in Gallic resistance'. The Carthaginian army survived, but the decisive impetus was lost. Rumours spread among the Celtic tribes that Hannibal had deliberately put the mercenaries in the most dangerous positions since they were considered to be more expendable. A general disaffection with Hannibal became widespread. The war degenerated into a series of guerrilla campaigns. Hannibal was finally defeated at the Battle of Zama in 202 BC.

The Boii and the Insubres were subdued within the next decade, and those who were not physically annihilated were culturally absorbed. Gradually, Gallia Cisalpina became Gallia only in name: all that was Gallic and Celtic was subsumed into the rapidly expanding territory of Rome.

Hannibal's erstwhile and half-hearted Iberian allies did continue to resist Rome for many more years, and there remains to this day a small enclave of Celtic culture in Galicia in northwestern Spain (compare the name with Galatia), with its own Celtic dialect *gallego* (Gallic), and a distinctively Celtic style of music and dancing.

THE ROMAN CONQUEST OF GAUL

Gallia Transalpina, Gaul beyond the Alps, was also Romanized in its turn, although this was clearly and emphatically the work of one man – Julius Caesar. Suetonius tells us of Caesar's vanity (he combed his thin hair forward over his bald spot, and rejoiced when the senate awarded him the honour of wearing a laurel wreath on all occasions; he added fringed sleeves to his tunic; he plucked his body hair with tweezers), but for most classical commentators, and even some modern ones, Caesar was the epitome of all the virtues, especially of courage and military skill. As a general and military tactician, his abilities were not, in fact, exceptional, but his gift for self-promotion was extraordinary. His ambition was vaulting, and the fulfilment of his ambitions had a greater impact on Celtic society than that of any other individual in history.

A portrait of Julius Caesar, from a contemporary coin.

The Celtic tribes of Gaul and principal Roman settlements.

The four great rivers of modern France, namely the Loire, the Seine, the Garonne and the Rhône, are associated with the ancient Celtic tribal lands which Caesar successively subdued. In the south and east, which was Gallia Transalpina, the tribes who lived close to the Loire were the Saluvii, close to the Mediterranean, and, further north, the Allobroges and the Ambarri. In the south and west, closer to the Garonne, lived the Tolosates (who gave their name to modern Toulouse), the Ruteni, the Cadurci and the Arverni (who gave their name to modern Auvergne). To the north and east lived the Helvetii, who gave their name eventually to Helvetia (i.e. Switzerland), and the Sequani, after whom the River Seine takes its name. Finally, to the north and west, along the lower waters of the mighty Loire River, lived the Aedui and the Bituriges, who were so distinctively alien to Rome that this area was actually called Gallia Celtica (Celtic Gaul) or Gallia Comata (literally, long-haired Gaul).

Rome had always been interested in the narrow strip of Gallia Transalpina which secured land access to the Iberian peninsula, on account of its obvious strategic importance. The Greek settlement of Massalia (the Romans called it Massilia, we call it Marseilles) and the importance of the Rhône for trade, as well as the richness of the lands of the Piedmont and Entremont, led to Roman wars against the Saluvii, and the early establishment of a Roman stronghold at Aquae Sextae (Aix, France). The Allobroges were brought into these wars in 122 BC, when they refused to surrender the king of the defeated Saluvii, who had taken refuge among them. At the same time, the Aedui, the long-haired barbarians further to the north in Gallia Comata, unexpectedly established a treaty with Rome to help them against their tribal enemies, the Arverni. Great tribal blocs began forming: the Aedui took the powerful Bituriges and Senones, the Ambivareti, the Bellovaci and some of the Boii into clientship or submissive alliance; the Sequani to the east began developing a similar hegemony with smaller, client tribes. It was the personal ambition of Julius Caesar which made the rest of Gaul attractive, and it was the divided and often mutually hostile nature of Gallic tribal society which made the conquest of Gaul possible.

Not only did the Celtic tribal alliances in Gaul change rapidly during this period, but the internal political structures changed also. Some of the more powerful tribes, notably the Aedui and the Helvetii, abandoned traditional kingship altogether. Instead, they elected magistrates, from whom was chosen a *vergobret* or chief magistrate. This is a very interesting development, because it seems almost impossible for it to have taken place without the consent of the druidic priesthood. Indeed, the fact that some classical authors tell us that it was the priesthood which elected the *vergobret* in times of war suggests strongly some kind of intertribal conference between druids to establish a more consistent form of government, removed from the petty machinations of sometimes weak and foolish tribal kings. The laws of election to the magistracy decreed that no person could hold the office of magistrate during the lifetime of an incumbent from the same family, which suggests that this was a deliberate attempt to break the strongholds of the established royal and noble families.

The Nervii went further. They established a 300-strong senate of senior nobles, with crude but nevertheless recognisably parliamentary procedures: Strabo tells us that if a speaker was heckled or interrupted, a sergeant-at-arms would come and cut a piece off the heckler's cloak as a fine for speaking out of order.

Caesar hacked through the Gallic hinterland like the proverbial knife through butter. His incursion was technically illegal: he was elected consul in 59 BC and set out on his conquest of Gaul in 58 BC, but the Roman senate had given him no command or even permission to do so. His pretext was the supposed intent of the Helvetii to expand westwards, thus threatening the alliances with the central Gallic tribes under the Aedui, and perhaps even threatening the land crossing to Spain through Gallia Narbonensis. It was a thin pretext, yet, according to Caesar's own figures, over a quarter of a million Helvetii died for it. Caesar even defied senate policy, when his personal sense of occasion demanded. A case in point is that of the German mercenary leader, Ariovistus, whom the Sequani had brought in to support their attacks against the Aedui, but who was technically an ally of Rome, and recognized in the senate as such. Caesar ignored the alliance, and destroyed Ariovistus and his German mercenaries. Such was the subsequent glory and cultural achievement of the expanded Roman empire, we tend to forget that Caesar's original ambition was not much different to Hitler's, although in a very different context.

By 55 BC, Caesar had subjugated most of Gaul, and millions of Celtic tribesmen had died. The Nervii were almost obliterated, and the Eburones ceased to exist as a people. Caesar's own account of the annihilation of the Nervii includes handsome praises of their courage, and ends with a self-righteous account of how decently he behaved by the defeated enemy:

> So ended this battle by which the tribe of the Nervii, and even their name, were virtually wiped out. Their old men had, as I have already said, been sent away with the women and children into the tidal creeks and marshes, and when news of the battle reached them they realized that nothing could stop the victorious Romans or save the defeated Nervii. With the consent of all the survivors they sent envoys to me and surrendered. In describing the disaster their tribe had suffered, they said that from the council of 600, only three men had survived, and barely 500 from their fighting force of 60 000. Wishing it to be seen that I treated unfortunate supplicants mercifully, I took the greatest care to keep them safe. I told them to keep their lands and *oppida* (fortifications), and I gave orders to the neighbouring tribes to refrain from doing them any damage or injury and to see that their people did the same.[11]

In similar fashion, Caesar tells us that he sent the remnant of the defeated Helvetii back to their homelands, and even ordered the Allobroges to supply the defeated warriors with grain, although in this account he is honest enough to admit the real political motive behind his apparent philanthropy: if the fertile Helvetian lands were to remain unoccupied and unfarmed, they would provide an irresistible temptation for German tribes to cross the Rhine and occupy them.

The Aedui, the Arverni and the Remi, who had allied themselves to Caesar's cause, prospered and expanded their territories, while most other tribes were made the poorer, at the very least, by the annual tribute of 400 000 gold pieces which they now had to pay to Rome. The famous Asterix cartoons, amusing as they are, are set in a period which was actually filled with desperation and bitter anger for most of the Celtic tribes. The imposed *pax Romana* made cattle raids and internecine warfare illegal, so that the traditional Celtic methods by which a tribal king might restore his people's welfare and sense of pride in themselves were no longer available. The incentive was very great for

Celtic kings and nobles to throw off their plaids and adopt the Roman toga, Roman entertainments, Roman statuary and even Roman religion, and archaeological evidence confirms that this is exactly what happened. Long after the conspirators murdered Julius Caesar in 44 BC, his legacy remained. In 27 BC Gallia Comata was divided into three provinces. Aquitania expanded to take in all the tribes living south of the Loire. Lugdunum (modern Lyons) became the capital of the new province of Lugdunensis. The old Gallia Transalpina, the corridor of land between the Alps and the Pyrénées, was renamed Gallia Narbonensis, after its capital, Narbo. The eastern territories of Gaul were now called Germania Superior (between the Rhône and the Rhine), Belgica (around the capital Durocortorum, modern Rheims) and Germania Inferior (the northern Rhine valley).

There were sporadic Celtic revolts, most notably that of Vercingetorix in 52 BC, which is discussed in Chapter Six. The revolt of AD 21 was led by Julius Florus and Julius Sacrovir (both Gauls, the former from the Treveri, the latter from the Aedui), and their very names tell us how much Gaul had changed in the seventy years since Caesar's conquest: the Romanization of Gaul was extremely rapid. The revolt of AD 68 was led by Julius Vindex, who claimed descent from the Aquitanian kings, but his purpose was not to re-establish Gaul as a Celtic state – it was to protest against the excesses of the emperor, Nero; the revolt received little support from other Celtic provinces, and it was quickly put down by legions brought in from the Rhine stations.

There had been a time when the Celtic tribal influence stretched undiluted from Gaul in the west to Galatia in the east. Now the only place where the Celtic tradition remained untrammelled by outside influence was that mysterious group of islands beyond Boreas where the Hyperboreans lived among the swirling fogs and damp mists – Britain and Ireland.

Notes

1 Tacitus, *Germania*, 43.
2 Livy, *The Early History of Rome*, I.43.
3 Livy, I.45.
4 Livy, I.57.
5 Livy, I.23.
6 Livy, I.16.
7 Graham Webster, *The Roman Imperial Army*, New York, 1969, pp. 134–137.
8 Livy, V.36–39.
9 Livy, XXI.4.
10 Livy, XXI.28.
11 Julius Caesar, *The Gallic War*, II.26–28.

FOUR

✳

CELTIC BRITAIN

THE EARLIEST TRIBES

HE first inhabitants of Britain were not Celts. Apart from that, we can say very little about them. Archaeological evidence, usually from grave sites, reveals the same patterns of hunting and farming, and of the developments in metalworking, which we find in continental Europe, but there is no clear cultural identity as there is with, say, the ancient Egyptians, even though it could be argued that, in their own way, some of the henges and barrows of the first Britons are as impressive as the Pyramids. In Greek mythology, there was a legend of a land to the north, shrouded in a permanent fog, where the Hyperboreans, the beyond-the-north-wind people, lived. There is some evidence that tin may have been worked from streams and small open-cast workings in Cornwall as early as 2500 BC. There are barrows and burial chambers, quoits and menhirs, stone rows and stone circles; there is the extraordinary alignment of timber posts at Flag Fen in the wetlands of East Anglia, which appears to have been a ritual site from about 1200 BC; and then there are the spectacular sites like Stonehenge (completed about 1500 BC), Avebury and Silbury Hill (although we have convincing evidence that ritual sites like Stonehenge, Flag Fen and Avebury were subsequently used by Celts, it was not Celts who built them). Each tells us something about the pre-Celtic peoples who inhabited Britain, but collectively we still know very little about them.

Nor are we certain when the first Celtic tribes came to Britain. Some time after 250 BC, there is evidence of La Tène culture, which has generally been interpreted as being evidence of either invasion or intense cultural interaction with the tribes of Belgica in Gaul. It is possible that the same Celtic tribal movements around 450 BC which led Celtic tribes south into Italy also led Celtic tribes north into Britain. It is possible that Celtic incursions into Britain began some hundreds of years earlier, although any date earlier than 900 BC appears highly unlikely. Indeed, any specific date before 250 BC, when we have definite evidence of La Tène culture, seems speculative. The generally accepted timetable, vague as it is, is that Goidelic Celts may have settled in Britain and Ireland as early as 900 BC, Brythonic Celts perhaps from about 600 BC, and a wave of Belgae from Gaul from the end of the second century BC.

Britain has an abundance of ancient hillforts, and while it is certain that many of them predate the arrival of the Celts (some show evidence of inhabitation from as early as 1000 BC), it is equally certain that many of them were later occupied by Celtic tribes, with considerable extensions and additions. Some, like that which sits 460 metres (1 500 ft) above sea level on Mam Tor in Derbyshire's Peak District, were probably used in summer only, at times of maximum danger. Some, mostly from later periods, are so small that they are really fortified farms or permanent homesteads, rather than hillforts in the traditional sense. At some stage in the development of hillforts, the Celts introduced a very effective system of double walling; Caesar calls it *murus gallicus*, 'the Gallic wall', and gives a detailed description of how the inner and outer ramparts were separated by an infill of rubble which made the whole construction extremely resistant to penetration – the later wall built by Emperor Hadrian followed the same design principle. Among the best examples of developed hillforts in England are the promontory hillfort at Crickley Hill in Gloucestershire, probably first occupied in about 600 BC; Cissbury and Torberry on the Downs in Sussex; Hembury in Devon, occupied from about 600 to 400 BC; Ingleborough in Yorkshire, and Carrick Fell in Cumbria, both accessible only after a steep climb, but well worth it for the magnificent views; and Hambledon Hill in Dorset, where the ramparts, ditches and walkways have been exceptionally well maintained. Perhaps the most spectacular hillfort in Britain is Tre'r Ceiri, Gwynedd, Wales, which offers commanding vistas across the Menai Strait to Anglesey, down the Lleyn peninsula, and across the mountains towards Harlech.

Llyn Fawr (Great Lake), a sacred lake in Wales, was dredged in 1911 and 1912, and yielded a horde of bronze and iron objects which had been cast into the lake about 650–600 BC, including finely worked harnesses and vehicle fittings in the Hallstatt style, and two bronze cauldrons of local manufacture. Llyn Cerrig Bach (Lake of the Little Rock) in Anglesey produced similar artefacts, clearly votive offerings, but dating from the second century BC through to the first century AD.

Miranda Green describes a more recent find from the fourth century BC which has aroused considerable interest:

In August 1984, a mechanical digger turned up part of a human body in a peat bog at Lindow Moss in Cheshire. The body was that of a young man who had been placed, crouched and face-down, in a shallow pool within the marsh. The man was not a peasant: his

fingernails were manicured and his moustache carefully clipped with
a razor. . . . His body had been painted in different colours. . . . The
young man had been pole-axed, garotted and his throat cut, before
being kneed in the back and thrust into the pool. He wore nothing
but an armlet of fox fur when he met his death. Just prior to being
sacrificed, Lindow Man had consumed a kind of wholemeal bread
consisting of many different kinds of grains, perhaps a ritual meal.
The most striking feature of the stomach contents was the presence of
mistletoe pollen, which has led to speculation that the man may have
been the victim of a druidic sacrifice. . . . Certain Irish mythological
stories allude to a ritual threefold killing of the sacral king – by
wounding, drowning and burning. It is tempting to link this with the
triple injuries to Lindow Man; he was hit on the head, strangled and
his throat cut.[1]

If Lindow Man was a British Celtic king, he is the earliest for whom we have
any evidence. We do have limited but convincing evidence of trade between
Britain and the Mediterranean from the Iron Age onward. Pythias of
Marseilles supposedly visited Britain before 300 BC and recorded many
details of his visit, only to be branded a liar by later classical authors. There
is evidence to suggest that Pythagoreans – perhaps even Pythagoras himself,
who had certainly visited India and Africa – might have visited Britain even
before 500 BC, but no classical author substantiates that story. Modern
archaeology has identified connections between burial practices in the Marne
area of eastern Gaul in the early fourth century BC and burial practices in
East Yorkshire and Humberside, in both of which obviously wealthy persons
were buried alongside two-wheeled chariots; this Arras culture, as it is called,
may represent an early migration of a particular tribe or group from Gaul to
Britain.

Diodorus Siculus identifies a promontory which he calls Belerion, and
within that region a particular island called Ictis, as the centre of the tin trade.
From the description of the island and its causeway which is revealed at low
tide, we have every reason to believe that the promontory is Cornwall, and
that the island is St. Michael's Mount. However, the ancient and original
Cornish name for St. Michael's Mount is *Karrek Loes y'n Koes* (Grey Rock
in the Wood), which tends to confirm the tradition of a much lower sea level
in pre-Roman times, when St. Michael's Mount would have been not an
island, but rather a prominent granite hill on a sloping coastal plain.

Diodorus tells us specifically that the ancient trade route came south
'across the strait to Gaul', and that the merchants then made their way
through Gaul on foot for some thirty days, bringing their wares on horseback
eventually to the mouth of the Rhône. Hengistbury Head, near Christchurch
in Dorset, appears from archaeological evidence to have been an important
centre for trade with the Mediterranean during the Iron Age and into early
Celtic times. Caesar tells us that the trade routes across the English Channel

and through Brittany were controlled by the Veneti, a Gallic tribe whose territories were centred around modern Quiberon. Assuming that the wisdom that carrying heavy goods by water is much easier and cheaper than carrying them by land is as much ancient as it is modern, there is an obvious trade route from southern Britain around Ushant and Brittany into the Bay of Biscay and from there directly into the mouth of the Loire and into central Gaul, connecting overland to the upper reaches of the Rhône, or from Biscay further south into the Garonne to Tolosa in the western reaches of Gallia Transalpina, and from there briefly overland to Narbo and Massalia (Marseilles) and the whole of the Mediterranean. For many years, the assumption was that Britain became Celticized by a succession of invasions (and Irish mythology specifically names the tribal successions), but modern archaeology suggests that there was sporadic but significant trade between Britain and the continental mainland, and that Celtic settlement may have come about in a rather more complex way than simply by a series of discrete territorial invasions.

THE BRITISH CELTIC TRIBES

Tacitus's view was that the climate of Britain was 'wretched', and that even its seas were 'sluggish and heavy to the oar', so it was hardly an attractive place to visit, let alone to conquer and inhabit. Julius Caesar's explanation (or excuse) for his expedition to Britain in 55 BC was that he was punishing the British tribes for having given their support to the tribes of northern Gaul. A more likely explanation is that the potential glory of subjugating this remotest and least known region of the world, a territory beyond which the Earth simply fell away and ended, was too tempting to resist. Tacitus, dramatizing a supposed speech by his father-in-law Agricola, later governor of Britain, gives him the following dialogue, which might just as well describe Caesar's motives: 'And there would be glory, too, in dying – if die we must – here where the world and all created things come to an end.'[2] Whatever his real motives were, it is to Caesar that we are indebted for the first political geography of Britain and its tribes, a geography which was greatly clarified and expanded following the second invasion a hundred years later.

The invasion of 55 BC actually achieved very little other than almost destroying the Roman fleet in a storm, so it was the second attempt, in 54 BC, which achieved the first real contact with the insular tribal Celts. Caesar was vigorously opposed by Cassivellaunus (the Celtic original was probably Cassibel, Cassibelin or Catubelin – Shakespeare's version, Cassibelan, is very credible) who, by Caesar's account, was acting as king and leader not only of his own tribe but also of the southern tribes as a whole. Caesar was very impressed by the Celts' skilled use of chariots in warfare:

These are the tactics of chariot warfare. First they drive in all directions hurling spears. Generally they succeed in throwing the ranks of their opponents into confusion just with the terror caused by their galloping horses and the din of the wheels. They make their way through the squadrons of their own cavalry, then jump down from their chariots and fight on foot. Meanwhile the chariot drivers withdraw a little way from the fighting and position the chariots in such a way that if their masters are hard pressed by the enemy's numbers, they have an easy means of retreat to their own lines. Thus when they fight they have the mobility of cavalry and the staying power of infantry; and with daily training and practice they have become so efficient that even on steep slopes they can control their horses at full gallop, check and turn them in a moment, run along the pole, stand on the yoke, and get back into the chariot with incredible speed.[3]

However, Cassivellaunus was quickly defeated, and was required to pay tribute and to submit to an agreement that he would not attack the Trinovantes to the east, who had already submitted to Roman rule.

At this time, mainland Britain south of the Tees was divided into several clearly defined tribal kingdoms. The Canti or Cantiaci occupied what is now Kent and eastern Surrey, although a later administrative division also included the tribal name of Regnenses. North of the Thames, where Essex and Suffolk now stand, lived the Trinovantes, who were later (circa AD 10) defeated and overrun by their western neighbours the Catuvellauni, led by their king Cunobelinus, whom we shall discuss in more detail shortly. To the north of the Trinovantes, where Norfolk now takes the brunt of the cold winter winds from the North Sea, lived the fierce and hardy Iceni, whose most famous leader was Queen Boudica. South of the Catuvellauni, in what is now Berkshire, Hampshire, Surrey and West Sussex, lived the Atrebates, and south of them, the Belgae, almost certainly related to the Belgae of Belgica in Gaul. Their western neighbours, from the edge of the New Forest through Dorset and most of Somerset, were the Durotriges. The far southwest, modern Devon and Cornwall, was the homeland of the Dumnonii. The Midland tribes were the Catuvellauni, already mentioned, and the Dobunni, who ruled the western part of the central Midlands, modern Avon, Gloucestershire, Herefordshire and Worcestershire. Immediately to the west of the Severn, through Gwent and westward to the Brecon Beacons in Powys, lived the Silures, who were so swarthy that Tacitus assumed that they were related to the Celtiberians of Spain. The Demetae occupied the western part of southern Wales, modern Dyfed. The Ordovices ruled central and northern Wales, including the important druidic centre on Anglesey, although the tract of land east of the Conwy (modern Clwyd) and north of Chester to modern Birkenhead and Wallasey was ruled by another tribe, the Deceangli. The Cornovii (the name means 'horned people' and is related to the name Kernow, or Cornwall) occupied a triangle of territory from modern Liverpool in the north to Shrewsbury in the south and almost as far east as Nottingham. The rest of northern Britain was divided into four kingdoms, two small and two very large. The Parisi lived in the small triangle of land north of the Humber defined by Kingston in the south, York to the west and Scarborough in the north. South of the Humber was the great kingdom of the Coritani or Corieltauvi, covering the modern counties of Lincolnshire, South Yorkshire, Nottinghamshire and Derbyshire. The largest kingdom in terms of geographical territory was that of the Brigantes, stretching almost from Stoke in the south to Newcastle in the north. Lastly, in the region where the remains of the western end of Hadrian's Wall still stand, around modern Carlisle, lived the Carvetii, a small but powerful tribe who managed to resist assimilation from their mighty southern neighbours, the Brigantes.

The Celtic tribes of Britain and principal Roman settlements.

Relief statue of Brigantia, eponymous goddess of the Brigantes,
the most powerful tribe of northern Britain.

We have no way of knowing how stable these territorial kingdoms were before the Romans arrived, but they were certainly not very stable after the Roman invasion, as the story of King Cunobelinus indicates. Cunobelinus provides an interesting example of how the pattern of tribal kingship in early Celtic Britain was affected by contact with Rome.

The name Cunobelinus has two elements: the first, *cun*, means 'dog' or 'hound', and was a common epithet symbolizing courage in battle; the second, *beli* or *belin*, is the god's name Bel, the god of warriors, who was celebrated at the spring festival of Beltane, 'Bel's fire'. Some readers will be more familiar with the name in the form Cymbeline, which is how Shakespeare wrote it.

Cunobelinus ruled the Catuvellauni, one of the most powerful tribes in all of Britain. During the second century AD, the Catuvellauni conquered the neighbouring tribe of the Trinovantes. Although Cunobelinus was of the Catuvellaunian royal blood, he established his *lys* or palace at the settlement which the Romans called Camulodunum (modern Colchester), which was a sacred centre of the Trinovantes. There were tactical advantages to the site – it is close to the Thames, and would have been particularly advantageous for sea-borne trade with the Roman garrisons on the Rhine, as well as for continental trade in general – but there was also an important *Celtic* reason for establishing the power base at Camulodunum.

The similarity between Camulodunum and Camelot is not entirely fortuitous. The *dunum* element is Latin: it means 'fortification', and is a Romanization of the Celtic word *dun* or *din* or *dinas*, which has the same meaning – it is found in the Cornish place names Castle Dinas and Pendennis (*penn*, 'head' and *dinas*, 'fortification'). The *Camulo* element is from Camulos, the name of a Celtic war god. There is a River Camel in Cornwall, although the traditional derivation of that name is from *kamm hayl*, 'crooked estuary'. Dedicatory inscriptions to the god Camulos have been found near Rheims in France, the ancestral tribal area of the Remi, as well as much further east in Dalmatia. The place name Camulosessa in lowland Scotland means 'seat of Camulos', and there is a Latin inscription 'to the god Mars Camulos' on the Antonine Wall, which suggests that the legionaries also took up worship of the Celtic god and equated him with Mars, god of war. So, Cunobelinus's motives in establishing his power base at Camulodunum may have been tactical, or political, but there was also a much deeper symbolism in his continuing to use the area as his royal seat: he was invoking the power of the god and of his blessing, the royal prerogative of association with the divinities of place, the marriage of monarch with the land and its ruling gods and spirits. Shakespeare's Cymbeline is a much more urbane and Romanized figure than the historical Cunobelinus probably was in reality – he talks of how he was 'knighted' by Augustus Caesar and 'gather'd honour' from him – but Shakespeare gives Cymbeline's queen a stirring speech in reference to Augustus's uncle, Julius Caesar, which has a stronger sense of the defiant Celtic spirit:

> Remember, sir, my liege,
> The kings your ancestors, together with
> The natural bravery of your isle, which stands
> As Neptune's park, ribbed and paled in
> With rocks unscaleable and roaring waters,
> With sands, that will not bear your enemies' boats,
> But suck them up to the topmast. A kind of conquest
> Caesar made here, but made not here his brag
> Of 'came, and saw, and overcame': with shame –
> The first that ever touch'd him – he was carried
> From off our coast, twice beaten; and his shipping –
> Poor ignorant baubles! – on our terrible seas,
> Like egg-shells mov'd upon their surges, crack'd
> As easily 'gainst our rocks . . .[4]

Despite this spirit of resistance, the Claudian invasion of AD 43 made final the Roman occupation of Britain which had first been attempted a century

The emperor Claudius, from a statue found in the River Alde in Suffolk, England, perhaps left there by Boudica's troops after the destruction of Camulodunum (Colchester).

earlier. Claudius, the lame, half-deaf cripple chosen to be Emperor by the Praetorian guard as a joke after the assassination of his nephew Caligula, desperately needed a *iustus triumphus* – a 'legitimate triumph' – to secure support in Rome. The invasion of Britain was a very reasonable gamble: the place was so remote that it offered no threat of retaliation to Rome if the invasion failed, but its association with the earlier, failed attempt at conquest by the illustrious Julius Caesar offered the hope of real glory if the invasion could somehow be made to succeed – it would be out-Caesaring Caesar.

The invasion did work, and for the next four centuries Celtic culture and the Roman culture of the legions underwent a process of fusion to produce a Romano-British culture. It was a slow process, with a great deal of Celtic resistance to Roman assimilation. While Julius Caesar had claimed that many Britons were treated no better than slaves, Tacitus comes closer to the insular Celtic spirit when he tells us that 'the Britons readily submit to military service, payment of tribute, and other obligations imposed by government, provided that there is no abuse. That they bitterly resent; for they are broken in to obedience, but not as yet to slavery.'[5]

THE ROMANO-BRITISH CELTS

The southern British tribes succumbed to Roman influence earliest. The Romans introduced the word *oppidum* (plural *oppida*), which means 'town', to Britain. An oppidum was smaller than an *urbs*, or city. From Caesar's descriptions, it is clear that sometimes the word signified nothing more sophisticated than a fortified wood or hillside. Gradually these Roman oppida developed into small army garrison towns, by which stage the name *castra* might be added to them. *Castra* means 'camp', and survives in modern English place-names as the element -chester, -cester or -caster, as in Lancaster, Gloucester and Worcester. Indeed, three of the earliest Romanized settlements were Chichester, Winchester and Silchester.

In AD 41, just prior to the Claudian invasion, when the mad Caligula was still emperor, the death of Cunobelinus triggered a power struggle between his three sons, Caratacus, Togodumnus and Adminius. Adminius fled to Rome, where Caligula promptly declared him King of Britain, a meaningless gesture, since Britain was still free of Roman occupation. However, after the Claudian invasion, the tradition of Rome nominating a king for the Celtic tribes, first established with Cunobelinus, continued – so much so, that when the Roman commander of the British fleet, Marcus Aurelius Carausius, took advantage of Emperor Diocletian's partition of the Empire in 285 AD and tried to seize control of the islands, he declared himself King of Britain, since the Celts were so deeply attached to the notion of royalty.

The first legions to occupy Britain were the II Augusta, the IX Hispana, the XIV Gemina and the XX Valeria, with assorted auxiliaries – a rum collection of troops from all over continental Europe. The first governor of consular rank to be appointed to Britain was Aulus Plautius, a fine soldier but a cruel and inefficient governor. He was succeeded by Ostorius Scapula, governor from 47 to 52, who fought against the Silures in Wales, driving Caradoc or Caratacus north for refuge among the Brigantes, and eventually securing his capture.

Within the first decade of Roman occupation, some Celtic kings were already suing for special consideration and status. King Cogidubnus or Cogidumnus was the first in a succession of Celtic puppet monarchs who rapidly switched allegiance to Rome and were therefore accorded kingship – for what it was worth – of the occupied province. Tacitus, whom one might expect to be more pro-Roman, wryly calls this 'the long-established Roman custom of employing even kings to make others slaves'. Cogidubnus is commemorated in an inscription found at Chichester, which names him as 'Ti. (Tiberius) Claudius Cogidubnus, king, legate of Augustus in Britain'. The adoption of Roman names – the Celtic original was probably Coghdubh ('Black Pate') – must have seemed very strange and precious to unromanized Celts, in the same way that Fredus Claudius Smithus or Sallia Esmerelda Jonesiana would sound fairly laughable to us today. Some of these kings – notably Cunobelinus, Commius, Tincommius, Tasciovanus and Verica – had coins minted, after the Roman imperial fashion, depicting their noble features or exploits, and native coins (which were also produced before the Roman invasion) have provided much useful information to archaeologists and historians as a result. For example, a large number of native coins found at a Romano-British temple at Wanborough in Surrey were deposited below the Roman levels, which indicates that the site was a sacred place for the free Celts before the occupation, as well as later.

King Commius, one of those who deemed himself worthy of appearing on coinage, was from Gaul. His tribe, the Atrebates, must have had cousins, or a sub-sept or clan, living in Britain, because that is where Commius fled in 52 BC, having formerly been the pro-Roman envoy to the island. Commius had, in fact, brought about thirty horsemen in support of Caesar's invasion in 54 BC, and they had killed a large number of Britons in the name of Rome, so Commius must have had singular political skills to persuade his fellow-Celts that he was now sufficiently trustworthy to serve as their king. It is thought that it was Commius who built the pre-Roman sanctuary at Hayling Island in Hampshire, a shrine which was greatly expanded after the occupation.

Didius Gallus ('the Gaul') and Veranius were the next two governors of Britain after Ostorius Scapula, both of them undistinguished. Veranius's successor, Suetonius Paulinus, whom Tacitus describes as 'hard-working and sensible', conquered fresh territory and led an attack on the druidic stronghold of Anglesey in AD 61 (see page 94), but his governorship is better remembered for the rebellion led by Queen Boudica of the Iceni, which almost lost the whole of Britain for the Romans. Paulinus defeated Boudica, but Nero replaced him as governor with the more experienced diplomat Petronius Turpilianus, who in turn was succeeded by Trebellius Maximus, followed by Vettius Bolanus. By 71, the southern part of the province was at peace. Petilius Cerealis, appointed by Emperor Vespasian in 71, made further advances against the Brigantes in Yorkshire, and his successor Julius Frontius (74–78) harassed the Silures of south Wales. In AD 78, Julius Agricola was appointed Legatus Praetorius in Britain, and it is his six-year governorship which is described in detail by his son-in-law, the historian Cornelius Tacitus, from whom much of our knowledge of the early British Celts is obtained.

Caratacus (whose name would be better Romanized as Caradocus, since the Celtic original was Caradoc), son of Cunobelinus, led the Celtic resistance against the Claudian occupation, but was betrayed by Queen Cartimandua, captured and sent to Rome, where he made a famous speech pleading for clemency and dignified treatment; we shall return to this story in detail in Chapter Seven. The Romans advanced west and north very quickly, isolating Celtic resistance into three main areas: south and west of the Bristol Channel; Wales; and the north.

The southwest succumbed very quickly and easily, and was so remote that its influence was negligible. To this day, there remains in Devon and Cornwall very little evidence of Roman occupation, other than the traces of one or two isolated villas and the occasional salt mine.

The Celts of Wales (they did not yet call themselves 'Welsh') offered much fiercer resistance, which led in AD 61 to the Roman destruction of the druidic centre on Anglesey, a massacre described in detail by Tacitus. There has never yet been any convincing explanation for Suetonius Paulinus's actions. It was Roman practice to subvert or assimilate religious cults in conquered territories, not to attempt to eradicate them by force, since such attempts almost always served merely to strengthen the resistance and resolve of the conquered peoples. For some reason, Suetonius Paulinus made an exception in the case of the druids of Anglesey. Some authors have suggested that Anglesey, known as Mona to the Romans (and, therefore, occasionally confused with the Isle of Man), was an important centre for grain storage and distribution for the Celts, and therefore a legitimate military target, but the explanation is not very plausible: it suggests a level of supra-tribal cooperation and organization which is not at all in accord with what we know about Celtic society generally.

In the same year, AD 61, there began a bloody revolt to the east, led by Queen Boudica of the Iceni, to which we shall return in Chapter Seven. This was an isolated and unexpected rebellion, which almost lost the Romans control of Britain – the Iceni had seized Camulodunum, Verulamium and Londinium (Colchester, St. Albans and London). However, with this threat averted by Paulinus's decisive victory over Boudica, the main threat continued to come from where it had always come from, the north. The northern campaign was always difficult and, in due course, Hadrian's Wall (AD 120 onwards) and, further north, the Antonine Wall (AD 140–160), were built in an attempt to contain the menace of the barbarian tribes of the Scottish lowlands.

Hadrian's Wall, about which there is a very extensive literature, was a remarkable achievement – probably the only one of Hadrian's achievements which the proverbial man in the street would recognize. Hadrian decided to build the wall after personally visiting Britain in AD 122. It was designed to be over 117 kilometres (73 miles) long, 2.4 metres (8 ft) thick, and at least 4.6 metres (15 ft) high to the rampart walk, with a parapet adding another 1.8 metres (6 ft) of protection. In front (i.e. to the north) was a ditch 8.2 metres (27 ft) wide and 2.7 metres (9 ft) deep, and behind was another ditch (mistakenly called the Vallum for centuries – *vallum* should really refer to the wall itself) which was 6.4 metres (21 ft) wide at the top and 3 metres (10 ft) deep. At every Roman mile stood a milecastle or fortified turret containing one or two barrack blocks for up to fifty men.

The Antonine Wall, built by order of Antoninus Pius in the AD 140s, was much shorter, much less impressive and much less effective than Hadrian's Wall. Built of turf on a stone base, it was sited further north, stretching from the estuary of the River Clyde in the west to the Firth of Forth in the east. By 155, its defences had been breached so often that it was abandoned and its forts were systematically dismantled.

The invading army could not physically control all the territory conquered, so it relied on client kingdoms to protect its boundaries, notably that of Queen Cartimandua and the Brigantes in the north. The Romans used the natural geographical boundaries of middle England to establish the frontier of actual occupation: the River Exe in the south; the Avon valley, the lower Severn and the Bristol Channel in the west; the Humber Estuary in the north. The four legions seem to have been disposed as follows: Legio XX at Camulodunum (Colchester), the most important garrison for communications with the continental mainland; Legio IX in the north, probably divided between Longthorpe and Newton-on-Trent, and occupying Lincoln from about 65 AD; Legio XIV in the Midlands, probably at Mancetter, a little north of Nuneaton in Leicestershire; and Legio II Augusta, initially split up in the southwest, but reassembled at Exeter in about AD 48.

Suetonius tells us that in AD 54 the new emperor, Nero, considered abandoning Britain altogether. How different the subsequent history of the Celts would then have been! The rumours were so strong that Seneca started calling in some loans which he had made to British kings, causing widespread alarm, which in turn became a factor in the rebellions of AD 61. In the event, Nero was reluctant to appear indifferent to the glories of his adoptive father, Claudius, so instead of abandoning Britain he appointed Veranius as the island's new governor and told him, presumably, to get a grip on the place and sort out those painted barbarians.

The Romans took advantage of civil war among the Brigantes to consolidate their northward advances, and Agricola actually carried the Roman forces all the way into Scotland, defeating the Caledonian tribes at the Battle of Mons Graupius in AD 84. (The name Grampian is actually a misspelling of the original name, due to a scribe's error.) By this stage, there were Celtic mercenaries from the subdued northern tribes fighting with the Romans against their Celtic cousins – but it was an advance that could not be sustained in the long term. One of the key factors was the strength of the Roman fleet: Tacitus tells us that captured Britons had told the Romans that 'now that the secret places of their sea were opened up, they felt that their last refuge in defeat was closed against them'. However, the success of the fleet was very difficult to maintain as effectively in winter as in summer, particularly along the dangerous and inhospitable northeast coast. York (the original Roman name was Eboracum) and Chester (Castra) became the base strongholds for a chain of garrisons stretching into the Scottish Lowlands.

The northern campaigns were a bloody business, as one of Tacitus's vivid and dramatic descriptions illustrates:

> The tactics of the Britons now recoiled on themselves. Our squadrons, obedient to orders, rode round from the front of the battle and fell upon the enemy in the rear. The open plain now presented a grim awe-inspiring spectacle. Our horsemen kept pursuing them, wounding some, making prisoners of others, and then killing them as new enemies appeared. On the British side, each man now behaved according to his character. Whole groups, though they had weapons in their

hands, fled before inferior numbers; elsewhere, unarmed men
deliberately charged to face certain death. Equipment, bodies and
mangled limbs lay all around on the bloodstained earth; and even the
vanquished now and then recovered their fury and their courage.
When they reached the woods, they rallied and profited by their
local knowledge to ambush the first rash pursuers. Our men's over-
confidence might even have led to serious disaster. But Agricola was
everywhere at once. He ordered strong cohorts of light infantry to ring
the woods like hunters. Where the thickets were denser, dismounted
troopers went in to scour them; where they thinned out, the cavalry
did the work. At length, when they saw our troops, re-formed and
steady, renewing the pursuit, the Britons turned and ran. They no
longer kept formation or looked to see where their comrades were,
but scattering and deliberately keeping apart from each other they
penetrated far into trackless wilds. The pursuit went on until night fell
and our soldiers were tired of killing. Of the enemy some 10 000 fell;
on our side 360 men . . . [6]

Ireland (known to the Romans as Hibernia) and Scotland (Caledonia) presented too many challenges for Rome, although Tacitus tells us that Agricola
was very sanguine about the prospect of conquering Ireland at least:

> Ireland, lying between Britain and Spain, and easily accessible also
> from the Gallic sea, might serve as a very valuable link between the
> provinces forming the strongest part of the empire. It is small in com-
> parison with Britain, but larger than the islands of the Mediterranean.
> In soil and climate, and in the character and civilization of its
> inhabitants, it is much like Britain; and its approaches and harbours
> have now become better known from merchants who trade there. . . .
> I have often heard Agricola say that Ireland could be reduced and held
> by a single legion with a fair-sized force of auxiliaries; and that it
> would be easier to hold Britain if it were completely surrounded by
> Roman armies, so that liberty was banished from its sight. [7]

Despite Agricola's confidence, Ireland and Scotland never did yield to Roman
occupation, although both were greatly influenced by non-Celtic peoples, the
Vikings in Ireland and the Picts in Scotland.

Tacitus explicitly uses the term 'kings' (reges) to distinguish the former
leaders of the Celtic tribes from the 'chiefs' (principes) who ruled them during the Roman occupation. Rex and princeps have as precise a difference in
meaning as their English cognates, king and chief. He says of the British
tribes, 'Once they owed obedience to kings; now they are distracted between
the warring factions of rival chiefs.' This is an interesting distinction. It suggests that the ancient pattern of divine kingship was already beginning to
change in Britain at the time of the Roman invasion, perhaps in a similar way

to the change in Gallic society from kings to magistrates or *vergebretos*, but not quite so radically.

As we saw in Chapter Two, Celtic gods and Roman gods began to be worshipped together in Roman-style temples, often combining their separate names into one. There was a strong cult of Mithras among the legionaries, and some elements of Mithraism may have spilled over into the worship of Bel, who was also a god of light and fire. The Mithraic ceremonies included a seven-stage symbolic disrobing (the erotic Dance of the Seven Veils is a vulgar pastiche of the ancient ritual), and meetings were often held secretively in caves or underground chambers, especially those with associated springs or pools, which would have made the ceremonies very attractive to the Celts, who venerated such places.

Two well-known chalk figures date from the early Romano-Celtic period. One is the famous white horse of Uffington, in Oxfordshire, which has been variously dated from 50 BC to AD 50. A bronze horse statue found at Silchester, where the Atrebates had their palace, is so similar in style to the chalk horse of Uffington that it is sometimes assumed to be their tribal emblem. Similar stylized horses, with long, sinuous bodies and cat-like faces, are frequently found on Celtic coins. The second figure is the giant of Cerne Abbas in Dorset, an ithyphallic, club-wielding, Hercules type of god,

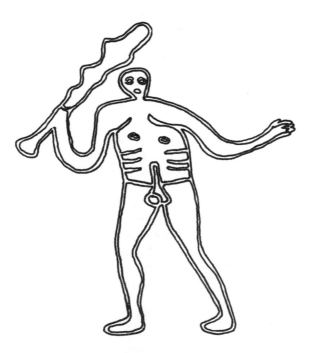

The giant of Cerne Abbas in Dorset, England, dating probably from the second century AD.

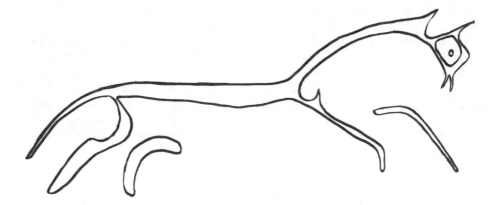

The white horse of Uffington, Oxfordshire, England.

presumably a symbol of potency. Maypole dances, which also have long associations with fertility, were held close to the giant's head in the early 1900s, and local history suggests that days for cleaning the giant were set aside as annual holidays, but he is now well fenced off from intruders, to protect the site, and the dancers no longer twirl.

In the third century AD, a typical Romano-Celtic sanctuary was that built at Lydney, overlooking the River Severn in Gloucestershire. The shrine was dedicated to Nodens, a Brythonic healing god whose name is etymologically related to that of Nuada Argat-Lam ('Nuada of the Silver Hand'), a Goidelic god, one of the Tuatha De Danann, or Children of Dana. The sanctuary included a temple, guest rooms, baths and an *abaton* or sleeping chamber, in which the god would be invited to enter the supplicant's dreams and cure from within. Sometime during the fourth century, a mosaic floor was added to the temple, dedicated by a priest called Titus Flavius Senilis, who was responsible for organizing temple ceremonies. Visitors could choose from a container a number of letters worked in bronze, and nail them to a wooden board, thus creating an individualized inscription or dedication, in the same way that we now have our names put on tee shirts at the fairground. Many of the bronze pieces were in the shape of a dog, which suggests that Nodens may have been worshipped in that form. He also appears in a sunchariot, surrounded by tritons and anchors, and the marine imagery also reappears in the temple mosaic. Miranda Green suggests that the temple may have been sited to obtain commanding views of the famous Severn Bore, the tidal race up the river estuary which is very impressive to this day, and would certainly have been impressive, and probably magical, to the Celts.[8]

The most impressive and famous Romano-British temple complex was at Bath. The natural hot springs would certainly have been a sacred place for the Celts long before the Romans came there. The tutelary goddess of the site was Sulis, a goddess of wisdom and healing, whom the Romans quickly identified with Minerva, their version of the earlier Greek goddess, Athene. The name Sulis also relates the goddess to the sun, and she is a prime example of Celtic attribution of a female deity to the sun, unlike the more familiar Apollo-types of later centuries. The Romans displayed typical religious pragmatism in renaming the goddess Sulis Minerva and building a massive temple to her at the site of the hot spring, possibly as early as AD 70. The site rapidly became a shrine of great renown, attended by the great and good as well as by the humble. Over 16 000 coins were thrown as offerings into the main pool. Subsidiary temples and altars were set up and dedicated to Mars Loucetius, to Nemetona, to the Triple Mother, and to the divine couple, Mercury and Rosmerta. The site, which has been thoroughly excavated and excellently restored and preserved, is probably the most important Romano-Celtic site in Britain. Less well known, but also of interest, is Buxton in Derbyshire, where a similar temple complex called Aquae Arnemetiae ('the waters of Arnemetia') was built around a sacred spa and hot spring in the tribal lands of the Corieltauvi.

Britain's natural resources were of great benefit to the empire. Her grains, particularly barley and oats, were plentiful and easily transported by boat to the army garrisons on the Rhine and on the plains of northern Gaul. Lead was mined in the Mendips, and the tin trade from Cornwall continued to flourish. There were profitable gold and silver mines. Tacitus even mentions trade in British pearls, which he describes as being 'of a dark, bluish-grey colour', and Julius Caesar is supposed to have dedicated a breastplate decorated with British pearls to Venus Genetrix in her temple at Rome. Above all, the famous British wool continued to furnish the best cloaks in the empire.

In return, the Romans brought to Britain not only the obvious wine, but also new livestock, like rabbits, and new fruits and vegetables, such as cherries and peas. The fourth century AD, when Constantius had reintroduced central Roman rule to Londinium after the revolt of Carausius, was so prosperous and peaceful that it is sometimes called the Golden Age of Roman Britain. Commemorative medallions were struck in Constantius's honour portraying him as 'Restorer of the Eternal Light'. His son, Constantine the Great, became semi-mythologized as Costentyn in early mediaeval Celtic literature. Constantine, whose name is commemorated in the town of the same name near Helston, in Cornwall, reunited the empire in 312.

The process of cultural assimilation had begun much earlier, even while the battle blood was still drying on the ground. Tacitus tells us, with typical candour and dry wit, how Agricola had deliberately implemented 'schemes of social betterment':

Agricola had to deal with people living in isolation and ignorance and, therefore, prone to fight; and his object was to accustom them to a life of peace and quiet by the provision of amenities. He, therefore, gave private encouragement and official assistance to the building of temples, public squares and good houses. He praised the energetic and scolded the slack; and competition for honour proved as effective as compulsion. Furthermore, he educated the sons of the chiefs in the liberal arts, and expressed a preference for British ability as compared with the trained skills of the Gauls. The result was that instead of loathing the Latin language they became eager to speak it effectively. In the same way, our national dress came into favour and the toga was everywhere to be seen. And so the population was gradually led into the demoralizing temptations of arcades, baths and sumptuous banquets. The unsuspecting Britons spoke of such novelties as 'civilization', when in fact they were only a feature of their enslavement.[9]

To give Agricola his due, he also introduced a great deal of sensible legislation as governor; for example, ordinances to break up the corrupt cartels which had formed to distribute grain. But in the course of curtailing the activities of crooks, the laws and schemes for social betterment introduced by Agricola and his successors also curbed the activities of kings. The old tribal allegiances, with their fierce loyalties to the clan's royal household, were rapidly eroded by Roman influence.

When Constantine died in 337, he converted to Christianity as he was lying on his deathbed. It was a significant conversion. Christianity was kept alive in Britain by the Celtic Church until the advent of Augustine in 597. Picts and Caledonians crossed Hadrian's Wall in 360; Niall of the Nine Hostages, High King of Ireland, raided Chester and Caerleon in 395, and a series of pirate wars continued until Niall was killed in a sea battle in 405; Saxons made frequent raids on the east coast. Throughout these troubles, Celtic Christianity continued to grow in importance.

POST-ROMAN BRITAIN

In 436, Roman troops left Britain for good. Almost immediately, waves of Angles, Saxons and Jutes attacked and invaded from the east, bringing with them new languages and new gods. Anglish became English. Woden, Thor and Freya supplanted Lugh, Bel and Brigid, at least in mainland Britain. The invading warriors called the western Brythonic Celts, whom they drove across the Bristol Channel, by a Saxon word, *weahlas*, which means 'foreigners': it is the origin of the name Wales. Those who fled south of the Severn were also *weahlas*, and the Celtic southwest, presently Somerset, Devon and Cornwall, was known as West Wales until early mediaeval times.

One of the Celtic kings who resisted these Germanic invaders was Arturus, or Arthur, whose legends were later to grow into the whole Matter of Britain. Taliesin ('Shining Brow'), the legendary Celtic bard and magician on whom Myrddin or Merlin may have been modelled, also comes from this period. Arthur, almost certainly a Romanized Christian, was defeated and killed at the Battle of Camlann around AD 550, at about the same time as St. David was just beginning to convert Wales to Christianity. It was to be another six hundred years before the first Celtic vernacular texts were actually written down, but many of the legends, both pagan and Christian (and some a curious mixture of both), which are so characteristic of Celtic lore and literature have their origins in this extended period of gradual marginalization. The saints' stories are filled with miracles that look like magic, and the pagan tales are filled with magic that looks like miracles. There are gods, but there are also demi-gods, and god-like heroes; gods who die, and mortal kings who visit the underworld without dying. For example, Pwyll, Prince of Dyfed, exchanges his mortal realm and takes the place of Arawn Pen Annwn ('Arawn King of Hell') for a year, even sleeping in Arawn's bed with Arawn's wife. Or Sylvester, supposedly a Cornish saint rather than a warrior or hero, defeats a dragon which has been dining too frequently on the local youth. St. Meryasek, the patron saint of my home town of Camborne in Cornwall, and certainly a real historical figure since he was actually an appointed bishop in Brittany, travels between Wales, Cornwall and Brittany, striking rocks with his staff and producing instant holy wells, or performing other routine miracles. St. Piran, patron saint of Cornwall and of tin miners, sails from Ireland on a millstone and establishes his tiny oratory among the sand dunes of Perranporth.

The heathen Angles, Saxons and Jutes pressed inexorably northwards and westwards. It was the Battle of Deorham in AD 577 which separated the *weahlas* north and west of the Bristol Channel and turned them (eventually) into the Welsh. The Celts of the southwest were later further subdivided when continued Germanic incursions precipitated a Celtic migration across the sea to that northwestern tip of Gaul which the Romans called Armorica, but which subsequently became known as Breizh, Bretagne or Brittany (land of the Britons or Bretons).

When Augustine landed at Thanet in 597, the Angles, Saxons and Jutes themselves began a conversion to Christianity. As the monasteries began to spread, yet another layer was added to the complex of influences leading to Celtic marginalization. The Celtic Church had grown used to its independence, and the gradual process of annexation and realignment with Rome which took place during the seventh and eighth centuries provoked considerable conflict. When St. Aidan began his missionary work in Northumbria in 640, he must have met a bizarre mixture of ancient Celtic paganism, including some remnants of Mithraism, ancient Norse paganism, and Celtic Christianity. In 669, St. Chad founded the Bishopric of Lichfield in the English kingdom of Mercia and, in the same year, Theodore of Tarsus became Archbishop of Canterbury. As the centuries progressed, Canterbury and York (established in 735) came to dominate the British Christian church. In the thirty years between 655 and 685, all the following were founded: the Benedictine monastery at Peterborough; Whitby Monastery; Ripon Monastery; Lichfield

Cathedral; Ely Abbey; Hereford Cathedral; Gloucester Abbey; and the Saxon cathedral at Winchester. Wells Cathedral was founded in 705.

In 825, Egbert, King of Wessex, defeated the Mercians at the Battle of Ellandun and in 828 he was recognized as Overlord of England by other English kingdoms. In 835, he crushed an uprising in Cornwall led by the petty Cornish kings and supported by Danish mercenaries; it was one of the last writhings of the dying Celtic body in what was becoming an increasingly unified England.

The most significant marginalizing event was the Norman Conquest which began in 1066. Now began the period when Old English became Middle English as it absorbed a vast Norman French vocabulary. Modern English still retains traces of the social and historical circumstances which changed the language. For example, we herd cows, sheep and pigs, but we do not eat roast cow, sheep stew or a nice slice of pig: instead we use the descendants of the Norman French words for these meats, *boeuf*, *mouton* and *porc*, because it was the Saxon underlings who looked after the animals but the Norman overlords who ate the meat. While these great changes were taking place, Celtic language and culture retreated to the far west and north and were dispersed into isolated groups on the Atlantic seaboard. Cumbria, with its name related to Cymru, lost its Celtic identity entirely. Cornwall remained Celtic in language and in spirit, but a gradual English encroachment began from the east and continued for centuries, until eventually the Cornish language survived in only the remotest and most inaccessible parts of Penwith, the far west of the peninsula. Welsh survived intact as a language, largely because a Bible was printed in Welsh, and Wales as a political and cultural entity also survived, as we shall examine more closely in Chapter Ten. Ireland and Scotland both had complex interactions with the emerging English, but both retained a clear sense of their Celtic identity and nationhood, a pattern which obtains to this day.

Notes

1 Miranda J. Green, *Dictionary of Celtic Myth and Legend*, p. 132.
2 *Agricola*, 33.
3 *The Gallic War*, IV, 33.
4 *Cymbeline*, Act III Sc. I, ll. 16–29.
5 *Agricola*, 29.
6 *Agricola*, 37.
7 *Agricola*, 24.
8 *Dictionary of Celtic Myth and Legend*, pp. 136–137.
9 *Agricola*, 21.

FIVE

❋

CELTIC IRELAND

THE INVASION MYTHS

IRE, or Ireland, is named after the Celtic goddess, Eriu. Irish mythology describes a series of invasions which led to the establishment of Celtic Ireland, summarized in the mediaeval *Lebor Gabala Erenn* ('Book of Invasions of Ireland'). The invading tribes were, in succession, the Cessair, the Partholon, the Nemed, the Fir Bolg, the Tuatha de Danann and, lastly, the sons of Mil Espane, or Milesians. Eriu was a goddess of the divine race of the Tuatha de Danann, or People of the Goddess Danu. She and two other goddesses, Banbha and Fodla, each extracted a promise from the conquering Milesians that Ireland would henceforth take its name from her and her alone. The *fili* ('poet' or 'visionary') Amhairghin (Amergin) reassured Eriu that Ireland would be named after her; in return, she promised that the sons of Mil Espane would rule Ireland for all time. The Tuatha de Danann retreated to the dark and secret places, caves, forests, burial chambers, under the waves of the sea, beneath the hillsides, under the streams, where they still live to this day as faery folk.

Many of Ireland's provincial towns and capitals also took their names from goddesses. Tara, seat of the High Kings, is named after the goddess Tea; Tailtiu is the eponymous goddess of Tailtiu or Teltown, the site of a famous traditional fair; and Emhain Macha, the capital of Ulster, was named after the war-goddess Macha. We can reasonably suppose that most deities of the land, local, regional or national, were also female.

Eriu, like Sulis in Britain, was a solar deity. Her husband was the Tuatha god Mac Grene ('son of the Sun'). But every mortal king of Ireland was also her husband, at least for the period of his reign. The king was the physical embodiment of a divine concept, and acted as intermediary between the goddess and the land; behind every successful harvest, indeed behind every natural act of procreation within his kingdom, lay a deep, mystical union, a marriage between the mundane and the eternal. One of the reasons that Ireland, which is a tiny country geographically and in terms of population, has such a clear and distinctive identity on the world stage is that this sense of the numinous, the miraculous, the eternal and the perfect lying just behind the drabness of the mundane world has been part of Irish culture for century upon century. Tir n'an Og, the Land of the Ever Young, lies just beyond the western shore, and once in a rare while it may be seen as a summer's eve sunset shimmers on the waves. Even in the grimmer streets of Dublin, and there are several such streets, or in troubled Belfast, this numinous character and sense of timelessness invests and enhances the Irish identity, and its origins are to be found in the intense association between religion and authority. It is not surprising that modern Ireland is staunchly Christian (Catholic or Protestant − in the grand scale of things, the distinction is hardly material), since ancient Ireland was staunchly devout to its gods, goddesses, demi-gods, heroes, ogres, druids, magicians and faery folk. In ancient Ireland, the profound faith was extended also to the king or queen who ruled the land; the mortal monarch, by marriage to the land, became a temporal channel or conduit for the timeless forces which make life happen, which propel the seasons and their harvests. For that reason, the distinction between mythical kings and actual historical kings is extremely blurred in early Irish history. This blurring is not the result of romanticism or deliberate obfuscation; it is rather a reflection of the Celtic world view, which has survived more powerfully in Ireland than anywhere else. In this view, the gateways between this world and the next are many, and it is a simple matter to pass through them.

My wife and I once spent a magical day on the tiny island of Innisfallen, which lies in one of the great lakes near Killarney. The island, so small that one could walk its circumference in less than half an hour, can be reached by a rowing-boat hired from the lake shore. On it are the remains of a monastery. Legend has it that a former abbot of the monastery was awakened early one morning by the most exquisite bird song he had ever heard in his life. He was so enchanted by the beautiful melody that he pursued the bird around the island, never quite catching sight of it, but following it until the sun was setting. When he returned to the monastery, he was astonished to discover that he did not recognize any of the monks, and even their way of speech was strange to him. Little by little, the monks managed to convey to him that once, three centuries previously, a former abbot had mysteriously disappeared, following, so the legend said, a singing bird; he had been presumed drowned. With humility, it dawned on the abbot that his day had, in the mortal world, been over three hundred years, and that he had been granted a foretaste of eternal paradise. With fitting prayers, he yielded his soul to God, and, as he died, a shining bird appeared and hovered over his body, singing its heavenly music for all the monks to hear.

When Mary Jane and I first rowed out to Innisfallen, we knew nothing of that legend. All we knew was that we had this tiny, beautiful island to ourselves for a day, and that its atmosphere was as richly charged as any we had ever known. When we later discovered the legend by reading about it in Killarney's town library, we were not surprised. Celtic Ireland is filled with such legends and such numinous places – thousands upon thousands of them. That is why sites such as Tara, the seat of the High Kings of Ireland, or Navan in County Armagh, where Emhain Macha, the ancient capital of Ulster, once stood, still exert such a powerful influence over the Irish landscape; ancient Ireland and modern Ireland are still very closely linked.

The mediaeval account of successive waves of invasion is not supported by archaeological evidence. The Fir Bolg ('Bolg Men'), for example, may have been Belgae from Gaul – the name seems to suggest it. But the overall pattern seems to have been more complex than a simple series of tribal incursions. Most of the material artefacts are either in the early Hallstatt style, or in the late La Tène style (from about 250 BC). There is virtually no evidence for the expected intermediate stages of late Hallstatt and early La Tene. There seems to have been a more or less continuous development out of the Bronze Age, with La Tène elements arriving rather later than in Britain. A few artefacts, such as the torc found at at Clonmacnoise dating from about 300 BC, appear to have been imported from the continental mainland.

Part of our difficulty stems from the fact that Ireland and the mountains and highlands of Scotland were never occupied by the Romans, so we have no classical sources of information; we have only what archaeology tells us, and what the vernacular literature reveals. The archaeological evidence, as always, raises questions of interpretation, and the vernacular evidence is limited and distorted, because it was written down largely by Christian scribes many centuries after the events which it describes actually took place.

In a little more detail, the waves of invasions story runs as follows:

The Cessair were a tribe of Amazons, or goddess-women, who invaded Ireland before the time of the Great Flood. Their leader was Cessair, supposedly a great-granddaughter of the Biblical Noah. When the Flood came, the only member of the Cessair to survive was a male god, Fintan, who was Cessair's consort. He survived because he had the power of shape-shifting: he became a salmon, an eagle and a hawk; he spent the first year of the Flood living under the waters in a cave called 'Fintan's Grave'. He lived to Christian times, was a witness to all the succeeding invasions, and was therefore the supreme authority for all questions of history or tradition.

After the Cessair came the Partholon, also named after an individual. Ireland had lain unpeopled for untold ages after the Flood, and Partholon led the restoration of the land to fertility. Unfortunately, fertility also brought disease, and the Partholon all perished in a great plague. As with the Cessair, one survivor was left to tell the tale: this was Tuan Mac Starn. In modern Ireland, there is still celebrated a day of Partholon or Parthanan, in which the god is transformed into an agricultural demon who has to be trapped and bound in the last stooks of corn, in similar fashion to the ancient Crying of the Neck ceremony in Cornwall.

Nemed was the leader of the next group of invaders, the Nemed. After internal disputes, they abandoned the country. The name Nemed is clearly the same as the word which appears, in Greek form, as *nemeton* in the classical texts. The nemeton was the sacred grove or shrine after which the goddess Nemetonia took her name. It may be that the Nemed represent an ancestral memory of the arrival of druidism, rather than of a particular conquering tribe, although this is only a speculative interpretation.

The Fir Bolg (men of the Belgae) were descendants of the Nemed. They were still in possession of the land when the next wave, the Tuatha de Danann, arrived. The Fir Bolg were defeated at the First Battle of Mag Tuired and forced to flee to the islands, notably Islay, Arran, Man and Rathlin. During this battle, Nuadu, king of the Tuatha, had his arm severed. The blemish meant that he could no longer be king, and a prolonged contention over rights of sovereignty ensued.

The Tuatha de Danann were wizards and magicians who had learned their arts by living in the remotest northern islands of the world. They had four inestimable treasures: the Great Fal was a prophetic stone, which uttered a cry when, and only when, it was touched by the future king of Ireland (*cf.* the Arthurian legend of the sword in the stone); the spear of Lugh guaranteed victory to whoever held it; the sword of Nuadu could not be escaped, once it had been drawn from its scabbard; and the cauldron of the Dagda ('good god') was inexhaustible, so that no company could ever leave a feast unsatisfied. All the other invasions had been sea-borne, but the Tuatha de Danann, using their magic, flew to Ireland in dark rain clouds and were literally rained on to the mountain of Conmaicne Rein in Connaught, where their falling obscured the sun for three full days. The greatest of the Tuatha de Danann became Ireland's gods and goddesses: Danann herself, mother of the gods, and Lugh, Nuada and the Dagda, already mentioned; the Morrigan ('Great Queen'), goddess of battle and the Dagda's consort; Brigit, goddess of light and fire, daughter of the Dagda; Manannan Mac Lir ('son of the sea'), who gave his name to the Isle of Man; Dian Cecht, the 'sage of leechcraft' and god of healing; and many others.

The Second Battle of Mag Tuired was fought by the Tuatha de Danann against the Fomoire or Fomori, a race of grotesque giants. They were led by Cichol Gricenchos Mac Goll, whose mother, Lot, had lips in her single breast and four eyes in the back of her head. The name Fomori probably means 'under sea'. Nuada was succeeded as king by Eochaid Bres ('Eochaid the handsome'), who was of mixed Danann and Fomorian descent.

Eochaid, almost certainly still a mythological rather than genuinely historical figure, is sometimes described as the first true king of Ireland. It was Eochaid who first divided Ireland into the 'five fifths' of Ulster, Connaught,

Meath, Leinster and Munster. Book Four of the Lebor Gebala says of Eochaid: 'There was no wetting in his time save only dew: there was no year without harvest. Falsehoods were expelled from Ireland in his time. By him was executed the law of justice for the first time.'

In the meantime, Nuadu was fitted with a prosthetic arm crafted by Dian Cecht, and took the name Nuadu Argat Lam, which means Nuadu of the Silver Arm. (Dian Cecht's son, Miach, later miraculously healed Nuadu's real arm, so that he was made whole again.) There now began a series of terrible wars between the Tuatha de Danann and the hideous Fomori, whose champion, the one-eyed giant Balor, was invincible. The tales of these wars form one of the great mythological cycles of the Irish vernacular literature.

While the Tuatha de Danann and the Fomori were still at war, the last invasion came. This was led by Mil Espane (Milesius of Spain), so that the tribe he led is called either Sons of Mil Espane or, more simply, Milesians. The legends give the date of this invasion as a thousand years before Christ. It seems strange to think of most modern Irish people as being descended from Spaniards – we are reminded of Tacitus's geographical error in placing Spain to the west of Ireland. However, the legendary accounts all agree that the Milesians were, indeed, the last race to conquer Ireland. Moreover, they were a mortal race, whereas the Tuatha de Danann and the Fomori, who were never entirely banished from the island, were gods and magicians.

What emerged from these 'three derivatives of one stream', as Seumas MacManus calls it,[1] was a group who called themselves, and still call themselves, Gaels. Their language is Gaelic (pronounced by the Scots as Gallic). Ironically, the name Gael is probably Brythonic in origin. The Welsh word for an Irishman is Gwiddol (the Cornish cognate is Gwydhal), and this seems the most likely source for the term Gael. There is a much more fanciful story which attributes the origin to Gaodhal Glas, an Egyptian (yes, an Egyptian!), who, as a child, was cured of a snake bite by Moses (yes, *that* Moses). Gaodhal's grandson, Nual, left Egypt for Spain. Mil, one of Nual's descendants, married the Pharaoh's daughter, Scota, and left Spain to find Inisfail, the Island of Destiny. He found it, and called it Eire. His Egyptian wife, Scota, gave her name to the Irish tribe of the Scoti or Scotti, who eventually crossed the Irish Sea and gave their name to what is now Scotland. (Such convoluted stories are par for the course in most early histories of Ireland.)

We have to be careful in all these discussions not to confuse culture with race. There is no Celtic race, not even the Irish, who are the most Celtic of nations. Studies of blood groups in Ireland show that about a quarter of the genes of the people in the Republic are derived from Anglo-Norman and English settlers. There is an unusually high incidence of blood group O in the western parts of Ireland, and a common trait of the unusual combination of dark hair and light eyes, both of which may be derived from pre-Celtic stock.[2] The other common Irish attribute of red or fair-red hair is probably Nordic in origin, following the invasions of the Vikings.

CLASSICAL AND HISTORICAL ACCOUNTS

The mythological accounts of the peopling of Ireland were accorded the status of gospel truth, even until quite recently, for the same reasons that partially invented British histories, like those of Nennius and Geoffrey of Monmouth, were also accorded legitimacy: they were neat and tidy, and they were religiously orthodox. They reconciled Biblical stories and early mythologies with contemporary situations, and they provided rattling good entertainment into the bargain. In Ireland, the histories served another, very specific purpose: they legitimized the ancestries, and therefore the right to rule, of the High Kings. The key name in the pedigrees was Aithechda (the name is actually a derivative of *aitheach*, which literally means 'rent payer' or 'churl') son of Magog son of Japheth son of Noah. More recently, the pseudo-histories of the vernacular texts have also served to support the claims of the romantic nationalist movement.

For the Celts of continental Europe and mainland Britain, we have accounts from classical authors, at least some of which were based on genuine first-hand contact. For the Celts of Ireland, we have only hearsay and brief mentions. Ireland was most commonly referred to by classical authors as Hibernia, although the name Scotia was also sometimes used. The sixth century BC poet Orpheus uses the name Ierna, as does Aristotle. Plutarch uses the term Ogygia, after Ogyges, an ancient ruler of Beotia in Greece: the name merely signifies great antiquity. Pomponius Mela used the term Iuvernia in the first century AD, saying this of the country:

> Beyond Britain lies Iuvernia, an island of nearly equal size, but
> oblong, and a coast on each side of equal extent, having a climate
> unfavourable for ripening grain, but so luxuriant in grasses, not mere-
> ly palatable but even sweet, that the cattle in very short time take
> sufficient food for the whole day – and if fed too long, would
> burst. Its inhabitants are wanting in every virtue, totally destitute
> of piety.[3]

Strabo went even further, claiming that the Irish were cannibals, a claim later repeated by St. Jerome. Solinus, who wrote at the beginning of the third century AD, called the Irish 'inhuman beings who drink the blood of their enemies, and besmear their faces with it'. There is no other historical evidence of any kind to support any of these claims. In the third century AD, a very obscure historian called Marcianus Heracleota reported that he had met sixteen different Irish clans and visited eleven of their palaces or 'cities of note', but gave no further details.

Remains of wattled huts found near Lough Neagh have been dated to the period 7000 to 4000 BC. It is probable, from the location of these settlements near the Lough and along the banks of the River Bann, that the pre-Celtic people who lived in them survived mainly by fishing, presumably for eels and salmon, which remain plentiful to this day. They appear to have followed the coastal routes and inland waterways, westwards through Fermanagh and along the Shannon, and down the east coast to Dublin and Wexford. By 1800 BC, there is extensive evidence of their pottery, known as Sandhills ware. The mesolithic salmon fishers of the Boyne appear to have been the first to devise the small skin-covered boat called the *curragh*, which has the distinction of being one of the very few Stone Age artefacts to have survived in regular use until the present day.

As in Britain, there are many megalithic sites about whose origins and purposes we remain uncertain. The most impressive of these is the circular passage grave complex at New Grange, which lies close to the River Boyne, east of Knowth and south of Monknewtown. Although the cairns and court-graves are fewer in number than their contemporary counterparts in mainland Europe (particularly Brittany), they have generally been exceptionally well preserved. It was long assumed that these megalithic chambers and mounds were built by new settlers, either from Brittany or from the Iberian peninsula, but of the 1 250 surviving megalithic sites the vast majority are to be found north of the River Boyne, which suggests that they were the work of indigenous peoples.

As was suggested earlier, finding a precise date for the arrival of the Celts in Britain and Ireland is no easy task. The Lebor Gabala mythical accounts date the arrival of the Cessair to 1000 BC. Certainly there was in the Late Bronze Age, from about 900 BC, a sudden appearance of new tools and weapons in Ireland; new metal-working techniques included the hammering and riveting of bronze sheets to make huge cauldrons, of the kind which figure so prominently in Celtic lore and literature. However, real evidence of distinctively Celtic metalwork (by now mostly in iron) is not found until about 200 BC. As in Britain, the Celts' culture was not imposed in one fell swoop on the pre-Celtic natives; rather, a gradual process of cultural and linguistic assimilation took place. For example, it has been suggested that typical Irish syntax such as that found in the sentence, 'I'll be after having my dinner,' is pre-Celtic in origin, and that while the vocabulary of Gaelic is Celtic, much of the structure of the language represents the skeletal remains of the language spoken by the natives whom the Celts eventually subjugated.

It was probably the Celts who brought oats to Ireland. While the older cereals, wheat and barley, continued to play an important part in the lives of the British Celts, oats were found to be particularly well suited to the even damper Irish climate; oats flourished in poorer soils, and with less careful cultivation. To this day, oatcakes and oatmeal porridge are identified more particularly with the Celts of Ireland and Scotland than with the Brythonic Celts.

The Irish Celts also built hillforts and other defences, known by the Irish words *crannog*, *rath* and *cashel* or *caher*. The crannog was a lake-dwelling, usually a small artificial island connected to the shore by a walkway. The word means 'piece of wood' or 'pole' (*crann* is the Gaelic for 'tree'), but it is used to refer to any wooden frame or structure, like a hut, a pulpit or rostrum, or the crow's nest on board a ship. The narrow timber walkways made the crannog easy to defend from the land. The rath was a circular ringwork or succession of earthworks in concentric ramparts; the word *rath* indicates piling up or gathering – it is used to describe a layer of thatch, and the phrase *rath sneachta* means 'snow drift'. The word *dun*, occasionally found in Ireland to describe more heavily fortified sites, is imported from the Latin *dunum*, which in turn came from Brythonic *din* or *dinas*, as mentioned in the previous chapter.

While we are describing Irish vocabulary for fortifications and defensive earthworks, it is worth mentioning one other important word: *sid* or *sidh* (pronounced 'sheedh', plural *sidhe*). The *sidh* was a mound or hill in which lived the faery folk or spirits. These were not little winged creatures of the Tinkerbell type. The gods, demi-gods and mythical heroes of the Irish tales have the *sidhe* as their strongholds, and they are places of great power. It is supposedly to the underground fortresses of the *sidhe* that the Tuatha de Danann fled, and where they reside to this day. Even in modern, Christian Ireland, there remain strong traces of the druidic belief in the special potency and magic of lakes, caves, wells and springs, those places of transition between this world and the Otherworld, and of the *sidhe*, the underground fortresses where Ireland's former gods and goddesses still dwell.

If the rath was built in stony ground, especially in the hills, so that the ramparts were rather dry stone walls than earthen embankments, the fortification was then usually called a *cashel* or *caher*. Some of these are indeed castle-like. The cashel known as the Grianan of Ailech in Donegal was a royal palace, and was extensively restored at the end of the nineteenth century; Staigue Fort in Kerry has stone stairways leading to wallwalks, and cells and galleries inside the wall, almost like an early Norman castle; and on the Aran Islands, where there are many cashels, stands Dun Aengus, a particularly impressive promontory fort protected on one side by a 90 metre (300 ft) cliff which rises sheer from the sea.

There are some souterrains in Ireland (and several more in Cornwall, where they are called fogos or fogous). These underground passageways, sometimes single-ended like a cave but usually double-ended, and roofed with granite slabs, have caused much acrimonious debate, because nobody really understands how they were used. The most common explanation is that they were places of cold storage for grain and meat, but their permanent dampness presents difficulties for that explanation. They may have been places of refuge from marauding tribesmen, they may have been places of emotional or religious sanctuary, or they may have served some combination of these purposes. We shall never know for certain. The Irish souterrains are found only in Ulster, which suggests that the practice of building them may have been imported from northern Britain or Scotland. Tree-ring dating has led to suggestions that the crannog may also have been imported from Scotland, perhaps as late as the sixth century AD.

SOCIAL STRUCTURE

We have to suppose that the invasion myths contain at least some elements of truth about the character of early Irish Celtic society, and we can be encouraged by the many similarities we find with the better-documented Celtic tribes of Britain and Gaul. In Ireland, as elsewhere in the Celtic world, the social units were the tribe, sept and clan, with the king or queen playing an essential unifying role. There seem to have been many small kingdoms with petty kings, but there was also a very special king, the *Ard Righ* or High King. In some of the vernacular tales, the Ard Righ performs so many miraculous feats that he is indistinguishable from the other gods and demi-gods of pure mythology; yet there is also historical evidence for genuine Ard Rithe, High Kings of All Ireland. As with much early Irish history, we have to uncoil some of the mist of legend in order to reach historical truth, and the mist can be very persistent. We shall investigate the High Kings in more detail in Chapter Nine.

The word used to describe an individual tribe or kingdom, or its people, was *tuath* (pronounced too-uh), which we have already met in its plural form *tuatha* (too-uh-huh) in the Tuatha de Danann, the Tribes of Danu (or, sometimes, the Children or People of Danu). Each *tuath* had a chief, usually the *ri tuatihe*, or territorial king. In modern Irish, *tuath* can also refer to the laity (*cleir agus tuath* means 'clergy and laity') or even to rural territory itself: *amuigh faoin tuath* means 'out in the countryside'. The *tuath* was divided into smaller units, usually thirty in number, each known as a *baile biataigh* (*baile* means 'home' or 'town', and is easily seen in the many Irish place names which begin with Bally-). The *baile biataigh* was approximately equal to 194 hectares (480 acres) of arable land, or, as the ancient Irish laws described it, sufficient land to supply grazing for four herds of seventy-five cows each, 'without one cow touching another'. The *baile biataigh* was again subdivided into smaller units, each known as a *seasrach*, literally a 'standing', each being a single ploughland or farm ranging anywhere from 16 to 48 hectares (40 to 120 acres) in size, perhaps even larger in sparsely grazed upland country.

The social structure within the *tuath* was very complex. Highest ranking were the king, the royal entourage and other nobles, the druid and his entourage of poets, seers and herbalists, and a few leading professional men, notably metalsmiths, jewellers, weapon makers and ostlers. Below the highest ranks, there obtained a complicated system of clientship, known as *ceilsine*. The base word, *ceile*, is usually translated as 'tenant' in this context, but actually means 'companion' or 'spouse'; it is related to the word *ceili* or *ceilidh*, which can describe a friendly call or visit, a social evening, or a dancing session. Under *ceilsine*, the *ceile* who possessed cattle of his own, or whose debts to his superiors were light, had a much higher social standing than the *ceile* who had to borrow or rent all his stock; the former was sometimes referred to as a 'free' tenant, while the latter was 'unfree'. Between the true noble and the *ceile* was an intermediate rank, the *bo aire* ('cattle lord'), who was rich enough to lend stock, although he was not himself of the royal family, or even distantly related (unless he chose by judicious marriage to bring himself closer). Next below the free and unfree *ceile* came the *bothach* and the *sencleithe*, the shanty-dwellers and labourers, horse-boys and herds-men, who were usually retained by individual families, although they were not related to them; they were considered members of the tribe, but they had no property or voting rights. Lowest of the low were the *fuidir* (the modern Irish is *fuad*, meaning 'thief', 'vagrant' or 'wretch'), who were strangers, war prisoners, hopeless debtors or criminals. The *fuidir* were treated like serfs, but this was not a rigid caste system: even a *fuad*, if he could show sufficient determination and effort, could improve his social status by working hard and acquiring wealth, and could eventually become a member of the *feine* or freeholders. Furthermore, the law offered protection to the *fuidir* as much as to the nobility, and the law (which was based on druidic teaching) was pro-foundly respected, so that even a *fuad* could obtain a judgment against a king.

These laws, almost certainly druidic in origin, were variously codified and explicated in succeeding centuries. They have received particular atten-tion because they were supposedly codified by St. Patrick, and they are referred to as either *An Seanchas Mor* ('The Great Law') or as *Cain Padraig* ('The Statutes of Patrick'). In the tenth century, the historian Cormac explained many of the ancient and sometimes obscure early terms, in a work which is subsequently known as Cormac's Glossary. Collectively, the ori-ginal laws and their various glosses have become known as *The Brehon Laws*, after the title *Brehon*, which was given to the chief justice or arbitra-tor in the early Irish royal courts. Some of the obscurity in the laws was deliberate: judgments and prophecies were given in cryptic, poetic language, so that only the initiated could interpret the meanings, which is why Cormac felt the need to supply a glossary. The *Seanchas Mor* is, strictly speaking, only the civil part of the legal code. Unfortunately, not only is the original language obscure (so much so that even a modern native Irish speaker would not be able to read it), but the codification was undertaken, if not by Patrick himself, by Christian scholars who excised many of the pagan references and probably bowdlerized many others. The introduction to *An Seanchas Mor* explains:

> It was then that all the professors of the sciences in Erin were assem-bled, and each of them exhibited his art before Patrick, in the presence of every chief in Erin. . . . Now the judgments of true nature which the Holy Ghost had spoken through the mouths of the Brehons and just poets of the men of Erin, from their occupation of this island, to the reception of the faith, were all exhibited by Dubthach to Patrick. What did not clash with the Word of God in the written law and in the New Testament, and with the consciences of the believers, was confirmed in

the laws of the Brehons by Patrick and by the ecclesiastics and the chieftains of Erin; for the law of nature had been quite right, except the faith, and its obligations . . .[4]

The king was elected from the leading family, and the election did not always go to the eldest son. Inheritance generally was also not decided by primogeniture; on the father's death, land and stock were equally divided among all the sons. In Britain, and to some extent in Gaul, there is clear evidence of matrilinear inheritance, and we know that there were British and Gallic queens of considerable status and importance. There are queens among the early Irish gods and goddesses, and there are mythological queens of great power and significance, notably Queen Medb, in the Irish literature, but the later social pattern, certainly as it had developed by Christian times, was clearly patriarchal.

It is highly likely that the druids played a very important role in the selection of the king. The candidates would be the sons of the deceased king, but also his brothers, uncles, nephews and grandsons. Physical perfection, without a blemish of any kind, was an absolute requirement. Proven prowess in battle was usually also required. The druidic concept of the 'fitness of things' also played an important part: there would be some particular feature or characteristic of the ideal candidate which would emerge or be revealed, sometimes by invocatory magic (*cf.* the practice of *tarbhfhess* at Tara, described on page 114), and that feature would be distinctive and unmistakable, like (in the British mythology) Arthur's drawing of the sword from the stone. On occasion, the title would be determined by combat, either between candidates themselves, or with the candidate represented by his *airechta* or champion, although that was always a dangerous method, since intrafamilial feuds and vendettas would almost certainly follow in due course. There were so many feuds springing from disputed succession that, in later centuries, there developed a system in which the king's successor was chosen while the king was still alive; the king-elect was called *tanaiste*, a word used in the modern Irish Dail or Parliament to refer to the deputy of the Taoiseach, or Prime Minister.

The king of the *tuath* owed allegiance directly to the king of the *cuig*, or province, who in turn owed allegiance to the Ard Ri or High King. These allegiances were cemented by a ritual exchange of tribute known as *tuarastal*: each overlord paid an annual stipend to his retainers, usually in the form of cattle, jewellery, cloaks or weapons. The king would also host many assemblies, usually on feast days, at which the entertainments would be generous to a fault. Among the nobility, bathing was highly valued, and offering a valued guest a bath with scented oils and fragrant herbs after the day's hunting was an important courtesy. Dinners would be accompanied by a variety of amusements, including musicians, dancers, jugglers and *seanchaithe*. The *seanchai* (sometimes written *seanachy*, pronounced shon-a-hee) was a historian and story-teller, who would recite ancient lore and tales of the gods and heroes around the fireside. *Ficheall* (sometimes written *fidchell*), a chess-like board game, was also very popular among the royal families, and there are many tales, including some Brythonic ones, in which matters of great import are decided by success at the chessboard.

Tara in County Meath, the holy seat of the High King, was supposedly the ancestral seat of the god-kings Bres and Nuadu Argat Lam. The goddess-queen Medb pronounced that no king could rule at Tara unless he first mated with her. A special kingship ritual, called the *tarbhfhess* or 'bull sleep', was associated with Tara in particular. A druid would eat the flesh of a sacrificed bull, and drink of the broth in which it had been cooked, and then sleep. During his sleep, while four other druids chanted over him, a vision of the next king would come to him. There is a 2 metre (6 ft) standing stone inside the Rath na Rithe (Fort of the Kings) at Tara which may well be the Stone of Fal, the legendary stone of destiny which shrieks when, and only when, it is touched by the rightful king of all Ireland.

The other great royal capital, Emhain Macha, is situated at Navan Fort near Armagh. It is the traditional royal seat of the kingdom of Ulaid (Ulster). The word *emhain* means 'twins', and the name refers to the twin sons of the goddess Macha, who died in a horse race after giving birth to them. Emhain Macha is the central site of the Ulster mythological cycle, which features King Conchobar Mac Nessa, and the successive feats of the god-hero Cu Chulainn, in particular those recorded in the *Tain Bo Cuailnge* ('Cattle Raid of Cooley').

THE DIVISIONS OF IRELAND

The division between north and south in Ireland is by no means a recent phenomenon, nor is it based solely on the distinction between Protestant and Catholic. It begins right back in the mythological era of the Milesians. Of the Sons of Mil who led the invasion, the most prominent were Donn the king, and his brother Ir; Amhairghain the druidic poet and judge; Eremon the military leader and his brother Eber. After Donn and Ir had both died, a dispute arose about the kingship, which Amhairghain settled by giving the judgment that Eremon should rule first, followed by Eber after his death. Eber, however, was dissatisfied with the judgment, and proclaimed his own kingship of the south, while Eremon remained king of the north.

These kingships were mythological and symbolic, rather than actual. For example, the northern kingdom was supposedly the home of all skill in speech and intellectual endeavour, while the southern kingdom was the place where music, fine art and spiritual sensitivity resided; the poets lived in the north, the harpists lived in the south. The northern half of Ireland acquired the name *Leth Cuinn*, 'The Half of Conn' or 'The Half of the Head', while the southern half became known as *Leth Mogha*, 'Mogh's Half' or 'The Half

The five fifths of Ireland.

of the Servant'. In modern Irish, the word *mugadan* means 'a pretentious youth, someone who puts on airs and graces'. The traditional boundary between these northern and southern halves was Eiscir Riada, a broken line of low hills which runs from Galway Bay in the west to Dublin in the east.

I mentioned earlier King Eochaid, who divided Ireland into the 'five fifths' of Ulster, Connaught, Meath, Leinster and Munster. Only four of those names are commonly used for today's regions; Meath, which historically occupied the centre, is not now used as a regional name, although there is a County Meath. The modern division between north and south, or more precisely between Northern Ireland and the Republic of Ireland, does not follow the ancient Eiscir Riada but is more or less consistent with the ancient division between the kingdom of Ulster and all the other kingdoms. Yet, although there are only four 'fifths', an Irish speaker understands the historical origins: the modern Irish word for 'five' is *cuig*, and the modern Irish word for 'province' is *cuige*, literally 'a fifth'. So, the four provinces are Cuige Chonnacht (Connaught), Cuige Laighean (Leinster), Cuige Mumhan (Munster) and Cuige Uladh (Ulster), and the whole of Ireland is Cuig Cuigi na hEireann, 'the five fifths of Ireland'.

The early Irish literary tradition includes a group of writings called *dinnseanchas*, which might be translated as 'poems of place' or 'geographical poems'. (The modern translation is 'topography', and *dinnseanchai* means 'a topographer or geographer'.) These ancient *dinnseanchas* did more than just record basic geographical features, like the famously ridiculed lines of Wordsworth:

> Not five yards from the mountain-path,
> The thorn you on your right espy;
> And to the left, three yards beyond,
> You see a little muddy pond
> Of water, never dry;
> I've measured it from side to side;
> 'Tis three feet long, and two feet wide. [5]

The Irish *dinnseanchas* not only describe the place, they also describe its spiritual and historical significance. They were written in a very strict pattern of metre and rhyme, with each stanza consisting of 4 lines, all rhyming, with exactly 7 syllables, a variant form allowing for 3 syllables in the first line only. Here, for example, is the opening of the description of Ard Ruide (Ruide Headland):

Tri tuili	(Three flood-tides
bit i ndun Ardda Ruidi:	there are in the dun of Ard Ruide:
tuile ocan, tuile ech,	a tide of young men, a tide of horses,
tuile milchon meic Luigdech.	the tide of the greyhounds of Lugaid's son.)

The *dinnseanchas* collectively ascribe a series of characteristics to each of the five fifths or provincial kingdoms. Connaught in the west is the kingdom of learning, the seat of the greatest and wisest druids and magicians; the men of Connaught are famed for their eloquence, their comeliness, their ability to pronounce true judgment. Ulster in the north is the seat of battle valour, of haughtiness, strife, boasting and vainglory; the men of Ulster are the fiercest warriors of all Ireland, and the queens and goddesses of Ulster are associated with battle and death. Leinster in the east is the seat of prosperity, hospitality, the importing of rich foreign wares, like silk, or wine; the men of Leinster are noble in speech, and their women exceptionally beautiful. Munster in the south is the kingdom of music and the arts, of harpers, of skilled *ficheall* players, and of skilled horsemen; the fairs of Munster were the greatest in all Ireland. The last kingdom, Meath, is the kingdom of kingship, of stewardship, of bounty in government; in Meath lies Tara, the traditional seat of the High King of all Ireland. The ancient earthwork at Tara is called Rath na Rithe (Rath na Righi or Rath na Riogh are dialectal variants), meaning 'Rath of the Kings'.

The literary cycles of the Irish heroes and demi-gods are closely associated with these ancient geographical divisions. The tales of the hero Cu Chulainn are often referred to as *The Ulster Cycle*, although they actually chronicle a series of battles between Ulster and Connaught. The stories of the *Tuatha de Danann* are set mostly in Connaught; Danann's Children are said to have first appeared descending from the clouds on a mountain of Conmaicne Rein in that kingdom. *The Fenian Cycle*, the stories of Finn or Fionn, is set mostly in Munster. Fionn (whose name means 'white' or 'fair'), has a Brythonic counterpart in Gwynn, whose name means exactly the same. Gwynn is still commemorated in the many British place names which have Win- as an element, like Winchester or Wincanton.

Apart from Tara, which may have acquired its status as capital of all Ireland only when Ui Neill ('the descendants of Niall') became kings in the fifth century, there were other traditional royal capitals. I have already mentioned the capital of Ulster, Emhain Macha. The royal seat of Leinster was Dun Ailinne, now called Knockaulin, in County Kildare. A large complex of earthworks at Rathcroghan is presumed to have been the seat of the kings of Connaught; it was also believed to be an entrance to the otherworld, and was for many years the site of fairs and druidic gatherings.

The ancient regions (apart from Meath, which survives only as a county within Leinster) are now divided into counties: in Ulster are Antrim, Armagh, Down, Fermanagh, Londonderry or Derry, and Tyrone; Leinster comprises Carlow, Cavan, Monaghan, Leix or Laois, Offaly, Dublin, Kildare, Kilkenny, Longford, Louth, Meath, Westmeath, Wexford and Wicklow; in Munster are Clare, Cork, Kerry, Limerick, Tipperary and Waterford; lastly, Connaught comprises Donegal, Galway, Leitrim, Mayo, Roscommon and Sligo.

Classical authors used the term *Scotti* to describe the Irish tribes which began launching series after series of raids on Britain from the end of the third century AD. The term, which eventually became embodied in the name of Scotland, was not a tribal name: it was a generic term meaning 'raiders', from an Irish Gaelic verb meaning 'to plunder'. In modern Irish, *scot* means 'reckoning' (this is the origin of the phrase to go 'scot free', i.e. without punishment or reckoning), and *airgead scoit* means either 'compensation for trespass' or, more mundanely, 'a picnic feast on raided or stolen food'. The most renowned of the Scotti, and one of the earliest Irish kings who was undeniably a real historical figure and not just a mythological hero or demi-god, was Niall Noigiallach, whose name means 'Niall of the Nine Hostages'. His descendants, mentioned earlier, were known as Ui Neill. Niall's seat of power was Tara, but the Ui Neill came to dominate Ireland in two kingdoms, one in Ulster and one in the south, as well as to continue incursions into the British mainland. We have precise dates for Niall's raids on Chester and Caerleon, which took place in AD 395, and for his death, which occurred during a sea battle of 405.

The original Celtic name for Scotland was Alba. The name Albion was later understood to mean England, so a whole series of name confusions began with the first incursions of the Scotti into Scotland and northern England, and those confusions have continued to this day. Several classical authors use the term Scotia to refer to Ireland. Adamnan, an Irish historian who moved his residence to Scotland, used the name Scotia to refer to his original homeland, not to his adopted one. Even as late as the eleventh century, the Irish exile Marianus was called Marianus Scotus, and he referred to his own Irish compatriots as Scots. However, by the time we reach the thirteenth century, the name Scot appears to have changed its reference. John Duns Scotus (c.1265–1308), the most famous British mediaeval philosopher, was born in Scotland.

The first Irish kingdoms in Scotland are collectively known as the Dal Riada, supposedly after Carbri Riada, son of King Conaire the Great of Munster, who led a great expedition from Kerry, via Antrim, across Sruth na Moill to the coast of Scotland, establishing the first colonies in what is now Argyle. The Dal Riada existed on both sides of the water, in Alba and in Antrim. Three of the largest Scottish clans are supposedly descended directly from the kings of the Dal Riada, namely the Campbells, the MacAllens and the MacCullums. In 576, King Aedh was declared king of the independent Scottish Dal Riada at the Convention of Drimceatt, and for the next century and a half there was an uneasy coexistence between the Pictish tribes of northern and eastern Scotland and the Irish Scots kingdom of Dal Riada. The first Celtic king of all Scotland (or at least the greatest part of it) was Cinnead (Kenneth) MacAlpin, who conquered the Picts, and the few Danish and northern British settlers in the southeastern regions, in AD 850. From this date onward, the country as a whole came to be known as Scotia Minor, to distinguish it from Scotia Major (i.e. Ireland), and the name Scotia, and finally Scotland, came eventually to apply to it alone, although, as we saw earlier, name confusions continued to exist for another three or four centuries at least.

One of the British citizens captured and brought as a slave to Ireland by the Ui Neill was Magon or Magonus, the son of a wealthy Romano-British family in Carlisle. His father was a tax collector for the Romans. He was captured by Irish pirates at the age of 16 and sold into slavery in Ireland. Six years later, he escaped on a merchant ship bound for Gaul. Some years later, he returned to Britain, was ordained, and later became a bishop, abandoning his real name of Magonus and taking on the Roman name Patricius, 'the fatherly one or patrician'. He decided in about AD 455 to return to Ireland, where he became a missionary, establishing his bishopric at Armagh, only a walking distance from Navan or Emhain Macha. He is now revered as Saint Patrick, or Padraig in the Irish spelling. The diminutive form of Padraig, Paidin, is the origin of the nickname 'Paddy'.

Within two hundred years, Ireland became, and remains to this day, one of the most important centres of Christianity in the world. The development of the Irish Celtic church was, in the best Celtic tradition, erratic and idiosyncratic; it depended far more on monastic authority, and on the growth of individual monasteries, than on bishoprics. Clonmacnoise and Glendalough, to name two of the most important monasteries, became international centres of learning in Ages which have been called Dark. The English historian, Bede, wrote in the eighth century a description of how British travellers had been received in Ireland a century earlier:

> About this time there were in Ireland many nobles and people of the lower classes who had left their country. . . . Some immediately devoted themselves to the monastic life, others preferred to travel and study under different teachers. The Irish welcomed them all with hospitality, and asked for no payment, but gave them food, books and teaching.[6]

Visitors came to the great Irish monasteries not only from Britain but also from all over Europe, and scholars and missionaries from the monasteries

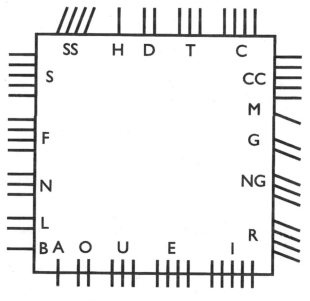

The Ogham alphabet.

visited the rest of the known world, including Asia and Africa. Great voyages of discovery were undertaken, notably that of St. Brendan, which will be described more fully in Chapter Twelve.

The piratical raids on Britain were replaced by missionary exchanges. St. Piran, patron saint of Cornwall, was originally Kieran of Ireland. Many of the parishes of Cornwall, Wales and southern and western Britain have names derived from Irish missionary saints, like St. Crewenna, who gave her name to Crowan near Camborne, or Ia, after whom St. Ives is named. A new kind of art work appeared, which achieved its full flowering in later treasures like the *Book of Kells*, the *Lindisfarne Gospels* and the *Book of Durrow*. This new art combined Anglo-Saxon, Celtic and Pictish elements.[7]

Ogham inscriptions began to appear frequently during this period, mostly on memorial stones. This lettering system later spread to Britain, almost certainly via Irish settlements in Wales. We saw in Chapter Two (see page 51) that Ogham was deified as the god Ogmios, a bald old man with a golden chain from his tongue linked to the ears of his followers. The deification represents a deep-seated Celtic belief in the power of correct utterance, what the Welsh and Cornish call *an gwir erbyn an bys*, 'truth against the world'.

The Viking incursions into Britain's east coast began at the end of the eighth century – Lindisfarne was sacked in 793. Two years later, Vikings landed near Dublin. Within a decade there were Viking settlements along the Shannon River, and the Celtic Irish way of life was transformed for ever. After the Vikings came the Anglo-Normans, then the Elizabethan English, and the long succession of foreign political and military interventions which, at least in part, have led to today's tragic sectarian strife.

Notes

1   Seumas MacManus, *The Story of the Irish Race*, New York, 1944, p. 1.
2   Brian de Breffny (ed.), *The Irish World*, New York, 1978, p. 7.
3   Quoted in *The Story of the Irish Race*, p. 20.
4   *The Story of the Irish Race*, p. 133.
5   William Wordsworth, *The Thorn*, in the enlarged edition of *Lyrical Ballads*, published in 1800.
6   Bede, *Ecclesiastical History*, III.27.
7   See *Treasures of Early Irish Art*, the catalogue of the exhibition which toured New York, Boston, Philadelphia, Pittsburgh and San Francisco in 1977, published by The Metropolitan Museum of New York, 1977 and 1978, ISBN 0-87099-164-7; or Carl Nordenfalk, *Celtic and Anglo-Saxon Painting*, pub. George Braziller, New York, 1977, ISBN 0-8076-0825-4.

SIX

TWO WARRIOR KINGS: VERCINGETORIX AND VORTIGERN

VERCINGETORIX and Vortigern were both Celtic kings who took calculated political risks, provoked warfare and distinguished themselves in battle, but who ultimately died wretched deaths. They came from different eras, however, with different enemies. Vercingetorix's enemy was Julius Caesar, and the critical siege of Alesia, at which Vercingetorix was finally forced to surrender, took place in 52 BC. Vortigern's enemies, the Saxons under their leaders Hengist and Horsa, were originally his allies (or so he thought), and his battles date from the fifth century AD. What the men had in common was their distinctively Celtic style of

Vercingetorix as a young man, from a Gallic coin.

Vercingetorix depicted on a Roman coin. Note the beard (to indicate 'barbarian') and the spiky, lime-washed hair.

leadership. Long before the historical Arthur, let alone the mythologized Arthurian legends and the chivalric code which emerges from the Matter of Britain, the lives of leaders like Vercingetorix and Vortigern exemplified a typically Celtic pattern of personal courage, battle skill, political intrigue, high honour and a certain vanity combined with vaulting ambition. These were warrior kings whose exploits were inspirational to their peoples. To this day, Vercingetorix remains a potent symbol of Gallic nationhood to the French, and his name, and by implication the fierce spirit of independence which he represents, are still invoked in modern French political rhetoric. Vortigern, whose political machinations were more sophisticated, has also become semi-mythologized. These two men were very different in character and ambition, but their deeds and exploits tell us a great deal about the Celtic style of kingship which they had in common.

VERCINGETORIX

Vercingetorix was a prince of the Arverni, a powerful tribe of central Gaul at the time of Caesar's occupation. His father was Celtillus. The *-rix* element is a title, meaning 'king'; *ver* means 'over' or 'higher', and *cinget* means 'warrior'. Celtillus, whose relationship to the royal Arvernian household is unknown, had been killed by the tribal elders because he had tried to seize personal power in 80 BC and declare himself king. The Arverni had suffered few casualties during Caesar's earlier campaigns, and had shown few signs of intending further resistance, so Caesar assumed, incorrectly, that they were pacified. Vercingetorix must have had some very impressive personal qualities to have persuaded the tribal elders that he deserved the kingship. One of these must have been eloquence: Caesar tells us of Vercingetorix assembling his retainers and having 'no difficulty in exciting their passions'. We can assume that he had inherited at least some of his father's ambition, and a measure of Celtic pride in restoring the family honour may have been a contributory factor to his character. According to Caesar's account, another of his qualities was a ruthlessness bordering on savagery:

> Himself a man of boundless energy, he terrorized waverers with the
> rigours of an iron discipline. Serious cases of disaffection were
> punished by torture and death at the stake, and even for a minor fault
> he would cut off a man's ears or gouge out one of his eyes, and send
> him home to serve as a warning to others of the severe chastisement
> meted out to offenders.[1]

By 52 BC, Caesar had secured a tenuous grip over most of Gaul. To the far north were the tribes collectively known as Belgae, and to the far northwest the Armorican tribes. The most secure part of Gaul was the narrow strip in the southeast known as Provincia ('The Province'), which protected the overland crossing from northern Italy to the Pyrénées and down into the Iberian peninsula. The least secure part of Gaul was the Massif Central, where large and powerful tribes were kept in check by a complex series of political deals involving tribute and protection. Early in 52 BC, a senior official, Publius Clodius, was assassinated in Rome, and the senate ordered all men of military age to be sworn in. When the Celts of Gaul received news of these events, it sounded as though Rome was about to enter a period of civil turmoil. Caesar was forced to return to the Province, and so was separated from his Gallic army. Caesar tells us that the Celts thought they might be able to prevent him from rejoining his troops:

> The prospect of such a chance spurred them into action. They were
> already smarting under their subjection to Rome, and now began
> to plan war with greater confidence and boldness. The leading men
> arranged meetings at secluded spots in the woods. . . . They
> complained of the miserable condition of the whole country, and
> offered tempting rewards to induce some of their hearers to open
> hostilities and risk their lives for the liberty of Gaul.

Vercingetorix must have been a key player in these meetings. The 'secluded spots in the woods' to which Caesar refers may well have been sacred groves, which raises the possibility that there was a strong druidic influence in the political decisions which ensued. Druids were not only priests and leaders of civic ceremonies; they also acted as judges and as political advisors. In the event, Vercingetorix received a previously unknown level of confidence and support: he was elected King of Gaul, and very quickly secured the allegiance not only of his own powerful tribe, the Arverni, but also of the Senones, Parisii, Cadurci, Turoni, Aulerci, Lemovices, Andes, Pictones, Santoni and Aquitani. To the best of our knowledge, no Gaulish king had ever been afforded that title or honour.

There now began a series of internal campaigns, involving rapid political realignments. The intention was to organize before Caesar could rejoin his army. Vercingetorix marched against the Celtic tribes which had pledged allegiance to Rome, beginning with the Bituriges. The Bituriges sent for help from their overlords, the powerful Aedui. The Aedui sent cavalry and infantry, but when they reached the River Loire (which marked the boundary between Biturigan and Aeduan territory), the Aeduan forces halted and then turned back, saying that they feared treachery from the Bituriges. The Bituriges promptly ceased their resistance and joined forces with Vercingetorix. In similar campaigns and counter-campaigns, the Gallic tribes tried to decide where their best interests lay. Some, like the Aedui, had received very generous terms from Caesar and prospered as a result, while others had suffered far more severely under the Roman occupation and bitterly resented the hostages and tribute which they had been forced to send to Caesar. It was not a time for indecision: it became plain within a short while that the campaigns of this one year would probably result either in the complete Roman subjugation of Gaul or in the exact opposite, the liberation of all Gaul.

The Celts had taken their initial impetus from two circumstances: there was political turmoil in Rome, and they believed Caesar was holed up in Provincia with no opportunity to rejoin his Gallic army, because it was winter and the Cevennes mountains were impassable. They were wrong, however, as Caesar himself explains:

> The Cevennes mountains, which form a barrier between the Helvii
> and the Arverni, were at this season – the severest part of the winter –
> covered with very deep snow, and the passes blocked. But the soldiers
> cleared stretches of the path by shovelling away drifts up to 6 feet
> deep, and by prodigious exertions enabled Caesar to get across into
> the land of the Arverni, taking them completely by surprise, for they
> thought that the Cevennes gave them as secure protection as a solid
> wall, since the passes had never been considered practicable even for
> single travellers at that time of year.

Once Caesar had rejoined the Gallic army, he began a series of cavalry raids to announce his presence and sow as much fear and confusion among the Gauls as possible. Vercingetorix retaliated by attacking Gorgobina, the stronghold of the Boii. The Boii were a weak tribe, clients to the more powerful Aedui, who in turn were loyal to Rome. When Vercingetorix defeated the Boii, it was the equivalent of the mediaeval throwing of the gauntlet:

This move greatly embarrassed Caesar. If he kept the legions all together until the end of the winter, and allowed a people subject to the Aedui to be overpowered without interference, it was only too likely that the whole of Gaul would desert his cause, since it would be evident that his friends could not look to him for protection. On the other hand, if he withdrew the troops from their quarters so early in the year, he might be hard put to it to supply them with food, owing to the difficulties of transport.

In the event, Caesar had no choice but to act, and he accordingly set out for the country of the Bituriges. The war which followed was not conducted in a series of pitched battles; it became instead a series of sieges and counter-sieges, with control of supply lines and materials a constantly recurring factor. Vercingetorix deliberately destroyed towns, bridges and fortified *oppida* in an attempt to deny supplies to the legions. While the control of materials and supply routes is basic to all military strategy and is not in itself remarkable, what is immediately striking about Vercingetorix's strategic command is its unprecedented scale in the Celtic world, and its extraordinary sophistication. Just securing simple military cohesion among so many different tribes, each with its own petty king and fierce tribal allegiances, was an extraordinary feat, but to conduct the kind of cat-and-mouse, supply-line based warfare which Vercingetorix achieved must have required extraordinary cooperation among the tribes, extremely swift and diligent information gathering from spies and scouts, and very effective intertribal communication.

The Celts also demonstrated considerable adaptability and ingenuity in siege warfare. Remember that most classical descriptions of Celts in battle portray them as frenzied, uncontrollable savages, screaming their battle shouts and scarcely answerable to their own leaders, let alone to some super-king not even of their own tribe. Caesar gives a more generous account of their skills:

To baffle the extraordinary bravery of our troops the Gauls resorted to all kinds of devices; for they are a most ingenious people, and very clever at borrowing and applying ideas suggested to them. They pulled aside our wall-hooks with lassoes, for example, and when they had made them fast hauled them inside with windlasses. They made our terraces fall in by undermining, at which they were expert because they have extensive iron mines in their country and are thoroughly familiar with every kind of underground working. . . . They counter-mined the subterranean galleries that we were digging towards the walls, and prevented their continuation by throwing into them stakes sharpened and hardened in a fire, boiling pitch, and very heavy stones.

At the siege of Avaricum, from which the description above is taken, the faith of the tribal kings in Vercingetorix began to waver. Caesar, in siege formation about the city, had advanced on the Celtic camp by night, only to discover by daylight that his legions were in marshland with the Celts on high ground above them. To the frustration of his commanders, he withdrew his forces back to the safety of the Roman camp. Vercingetorix had established his first headquarters twenty-six kilometres (sixteen miles) from Avaricum, where marshes and forests presented better defences. He then advanced his cavalry to the higher ground closer to Avaricum where Caesar had found them. Then, after Caesar had declined battle there, Vercingetorix returned to the original Celtic camp, where the remaining kings and tribal elders had, by now, become decidedly unsettled. Caesar continues the story:

> On returning to his main body Vercingetorix was accused of treachery for having moved his camp nearer the Romans, for going off with all the cavalry, and for leaving such a large army without anyone in supreme command. . . . All this could not have happened by accident, they said, but must have been deliberately planned; evidently he would rather become King of Gaul by Caesar's favour than by the gift of his fellow-countrymen.

This chessboard approach, with each move and counter-move deliberately considered, must have been very frustrating for the Celtic tribal kings, who were accustomed to much more direct approaches. Nevertheless, Vercingetorix's command was not challenged. Caesar's account puts in Vercingetorix's mouth a cunning piece of political oratory which persuaded the other Celts to continue trusting him, but the speech has a very contrived Roman flavour.

Nor, astonishingly, did the Celtic kings abandon Vercingetorix when the Roman siege finally prevailed against Avaricum and its inhabitants were slaughtered. Caesar left the ruins of Avaricum smouldering behind him and advanced directly into Arvernian territory, Vercingetorix's own power base. He attacked the oppidum of Gergovia.

Vercingetorix had originally proposed to the other Celtic kings that Avaricum be destroyed ahead of the advancing Romans, as were the other potential sources of supply and materials cleared in the slash-and-burn plan. It was only because the Bituriges had pleaded for Avaricum's survival that the siege and subsequent defeat had come about at all, so to some extent Vercingetorix was vindicated. He had been right after all. More significantly, he had begun to acquire that special status which is unique to inspirational military leaders: he appeared prescient and invincible. In the Celtic context, this powerful emotional appeal would have enormously strengthened his position; whatever names each tribe used for its gods, they could see the god working in the man. Here was a king who had not only the usual divine charge and energy, but a king apparently for all Gaul. He had Celtic tribesmen building siege fortifications, which even Caesar acknowledged as being 'an unheard-of thing in Gaul'. He had different tribes moving in single formations; he had battalions commanded by kings and elders of other tribes, to whom they had never before shown allegiance, and some of whom had even been formerly in the pay of Rome. It was an astonishing political feat, and speaks greatly of Vercingetorix's dominant character.

Shortly after Caesar had begun the siege of Gergovia, fate again appeared to step in on Vercingetorix's side. Among the Aedui, staunch and powerful allies of Rome, there arose a petty internal dispute which refused to go away. Two candidates for the post of chief magistrate were at each other's throats. One was Convictolitavis, a wealthy young noble. The other was Cotus, a widely connected politico whose brother had held the post the previous year. Caesar, fearful that the dispute would weaken the Aedui when he most need- ed their support, journeyed in person to the Aeduan capital of Decetia and resolved the dispute by announcing Cotus ineligible for the office under Aeduan (i.e. Celtic) law. Convictolitavis and his supporters were no doubt delighted. However, Caesar's choice was proved disastrously wrong. Within a month, Convictolitavis had accepted cash bribes from the Arverni and was openly preaching abandonment of the treaty with Rome. Within another month, the Aedui defected and Caesar was left abandoned by his most pow- erful Celtic ally, isolated in a hostile land with no immediate sources of sup- ply or support, cut off from his lieutenant Labienus in the north.[2]

When Vercingetorix next engaged the Romans, his apparent intention was to destroy the Roman cavalry, presumably because doing so would make both scouting and foraging more difficult for them; it was a continuation of the strategy of containment of supplies and materials. Vercingetorix's forces captured the small Aeduan garrison town of Noviodunum on the Loire, to which Caesar had sent Celtic hostages captured in previous battles, stores of grain and coin, and even some of his personal baggage. The Celts stripped the town:

> Accordingly they massacred the garrison of Noviodunum and the
> merchants who lived there, shared the money and horses, had all the
> hostages taken to the magistrates at Bibracte, and carried away as
> much grain as they had time to stow into boats, the rest being thrown
> into the river or burnt. The town itself they thought they could not
> possibly hold; so they burnt it to prevent it being of use to the
> Romans.

This was a humiliating reverse for Caesar, and his calm account of the events, written with hindsight, belies the exasperation he must have felt. The Loire was swollen with snow melt and apparently unfordable, and he was desper- ately short of supplies. It looked as though his only option now was to retreat to the Province and let Vercingetorix become King of Gaul in fact as well as in title. However, Caesar took the bolder course. He unexpectedly struck north to rejoin forces with Labienus. His men forded the freezing river, carrying their arms and equipment over their heads, the cavalry crossing upstream to try to break up the flow of the current. After some difficult trials and tribulations of his own, Labienus managed to rejoin Caesar and the Roman army was reassembled. To reinforce his depleted cavalry, Caesar sent for German auxiliaries from across the Rhine.

Vercingetorix, smelling victory, pressed the attack on what he thought was a thoroughly depleted and demoralized Roman army. It was a disastrous mistake. Not only did the Roman columns hold, they also inflicted heavy casualties on the Celts, with the imported German horsemen playing a particularly effective part. Vercingetorix retreated to a hilltop oppidum called Alesia, where Caesar immediately laid siege. Around Vercingetorix's position he built an outer rampart 22 kilometres (13 miles) long, fortified at regular intervals, and an inner wall fortified with wooden towers, ditches, stakes and pits.

It was a classic siege. The defenders soon began to starve, despite the fact that Vercingetorix had organized the distribution of corn and cattle with excellent military sense, imposing the death penalty on any tribesman who tried to violate the rationing arrangement – a further example of his ability to transcend the traditional tribal patterns of rank and entitlement. Vercingetorix also managed to send envoys out through the Roman lines to all the other Celtic tribes of Gaul. The whole Gallic cause was now in the balance, as Caesar himself recognized. If the Gauls survived this siege, the Romans would have no option but to retreat to Provincia.

Caesar gives us precise numbers for the Celtic tribes which responded to Vercingetorix's call for help, but the numbers are difficult to believe. By Caesar's account, his army of 50 000 Romans prevailed over a Celtic host of over a quarter of a million men. He gives details:

Aedui, with their dependent tribes (Segusiavi, Ambivareti, Aulerci Brannovices and Blannovii):	35 000
Arverni, with their dependent tribes (Eleuteti, Cadurci, Gabali, Vellavii):	35 000
Armorican tribes (Coriosolites, Redones, Ambibarii, Caleti, Osismi, Veneti, Lexovii, Venelli):	20 000
Sequani, Senones, Bituriges, Santoni, Rutini, Carnutes:	12 000 each
Bellovaci, Lemovices:	10 000 each
Pictones, Turoni, Parisii, Helvetii:	8 000 each
Suessiones, Ambiani, Mediomatrici, Petrocorii, Nervii, Morini, Nitiobroges, Aulerci Cenomani:	5 000 each
Atrebates:	4 000
Veliocasses, Aulerci Eburovices:	3 000 each
Rauraci, Boii:	1 000 each
Total:	265 000

Even if Caesar's total is an exaggeration, and it almost certainly is, this nevertheless was, and remains, the largest Celtic army ever assembled in one battle. The Celtic relief force attacked the Roman positions, confident that they could penetrate to the central hillfort and their besieged fellow-Gauls.

Unfortunately, the one leader who could command authority among so many diverse tribes, namely Vercingetorix, was trapped in the hillfort, and unable to lead the vast Celtic army. Instead, the relieving army was led by a quartet of commanders: Commius, a king of the Atrebates who had formerly been an ally of Rome; Viridomarus and Eporedorix, Aeduan kings; and Vercassivellaunus, who was Vercingetorix's cousin. Caesar tells us that they were accompanied by 'associated representatives of the various tribes, to act as an advisory committee for the conduct of the campaign'. If there is anything which could be said to be definitively untypical of early Celtic society, it is an 'advisory committee' for warfare. No, these tribal representatives were not a committee, or anything like it: they were an assemblage of individuals, including kings and senior nobles from the tribal royal families, possibly with some druids and their retinues, each representing his own tribe first and foremost, and protecting its interest and good name, with the general Gallic cause as a secondary objective. What Vercingetorix had been able to do was to somehow present himself as a king for all the Gauls. Without his active command, the petty squabbling over disputes of honour returned.

There were several impressive assaults on the Roman positions, conducted with typical Celtic courage and impetuosity, but with little overall coordination. At one point, it looked as though a night attack might allow the relieving force to get through to Vercingetorix, but the attack failed. The details of Caesar's account are illuminating:

> Meanwhile, hearing the distant shouting, Vercingetorix sounded the trumpet and led his men out of the town. The Roman troops moved up to the posts previously allotted to them at the entrenchments, and kept the Gauls at a distance with slingstones, bullets, large stones and stakes which were placed ready at intervals along the rampart, while the artillery pelted them with missiles. It was too dark to see, and casualties were heavy on both sides. The generals Mark Antony and Gaius Trebonius, who had been detailed for the defence of this particular sector, reinforced the points where they knew the troops were hard pressed with men brought up from redoubts well behind the fighting line. As long as the Gauls were at a distance from the entrenchments, the rain of javelins which they discharged gave them some advantage. But when they came nearer they suddenly found themselves pierced by the goads or tumbled into the pits and impaled themselves, while others were killed by heavy siege-spears discharged from the rampart and towers. Their losses were everywhere heavy, and when dawn came they had failed to penetrate the defences at any point. . . . The besieged lost much time in bringing out the implements

that Vercingetorix had prepared for the sortie and in filling up the first stretches of trench, and before they reached the main fortifications heard of the retreat of the relief force. So they returned into the town without effecting anything.

Every detail about the Roman strategy speaks of preparedness: strategically placed towers and ramparts; pre-dug pit traps; fresh reinforcements kept well behind the battle lines. Everything about the Celtic strategy speaks of impetuosity and confusion: abandoning strong positions; rushing into unfamiliar ground; failing to bring men and materials into position in an orderly, timely fashion; lack of communication and coordination.

The relieving army made a few more sorties, but when Sedullus, king of the Lemovices, was killed, and Vercassivellaunus, Vercingetorix's cousin, was captured, the Celts lost heart. They scattered, and those few who managed to escape the Roman pursuits returned to their tribal homelands. Vercingetorix surrendered to Caesar the following day.

Plutarch tells us that over a million men died during the Gallic wars, and a further million were made slaves. After Vercingetorix's rebellion had failed, the Romans subdued and pacified the remaining tribes with purposeful severity. After defeating a small Celtic army at Uxellodunum, Caesar had every captured Gaul brought forward to have his hands cut off, to serve as an example to others of what happened to those who dared to take up arms against Rome. Even more severe were the general privations inflicted on the defeated tribes; famine was widespread, yet Caesar insisted on punitive levels of tribute. By contrast, Caesar himself made vast capital out of his conquest of the Gauls; literally, in the gold and other wealth which he took back to Rome to finance his political campaigns, and metaphorically in the public acclaim which his victories brought him – a thanksgiving festival of twenty days was proclaimed in his honour, an unprecedented statement of popular approval.

Vercingetorix was taken prisoner and brought to Rome, where Caesar left him languishing in prison for six years, an imprisonment which must have been a severe torment to the Celtic leader's soul, knowing how deeply his people were suffering. We have to presume that Caesar saw some advantage in keeping Vercingetorix alive as a prisoner – perhaps he was more effective alive as a symbol of the hopelessness of the pan-Gallic cause than dead as a potential martyr to it. Finally, however, in 46 BC, Caesar held a public triumph at which Vercingetorix was paraded in chains before the people, then brought back to the city centre for ritual disembowelling and execution.

Since Alesia was Vercingetorix's last stronghold, and Vercingetorix has exercised the French imagination for many centuries, there were prolonged debates about where exactly Alesia was. Two small towns vied for the honour: Alaise, in Franche-Comté, and the slightly larger Alise-Sainte-Reine in Burgundy, on the lower Seine, where shrines to the Celtic horse-goddess Epona have been found, along with images of the Matrones and other deities.

Napoleon III had excavations conducted at Alise-Sainte-Reine, and an archaeological expedition of 1861–1865 produced bones of humans and horses, equipment, weapons and all the signs of a major battle, plus the most convincing evidence, signs of a defensive ditch 5.5 metres (18 ft) wide, and other entrenchments and fortifications. Alise-Sainte-Reine is still a relatively small and uncommercialized town, but it is proud of its apparent Vercingetorix connection.

VORTIGERN

The name Vortigern has caused some confusion, because it has been applied both to a real historical figure and to a mythological figure. In British mythology, Vortigern is a king who appears in the following dynastic sequence:

Constans, a monk, is the eldest of three sons of the Emperor Constantine of Rome. His two brothers are Aurelius Ambrosius (Emrys, in the Welsh traditions) and Uther Pendragon. When Constantine dies, Constans renounces the monastic life and assumes the crown. The usurper Vortigern, however, has Constans assassinated and takes the throne. Aurelius Ambrosius invades Britain, and Vortigern flees to a wooden tower, in which he is burned to death. Aurelius Ambrosius succeeds Vortigern and, in turn, is succeeded by Uther Pendragon, who is the father of King Arthur. In some versions of the legend, Vortigern is originally a monk, while elsewhere he is portrayed as a druid or magician. The Welsh historian Nynniaw, better known as Nennius, whose *Historia Britonum* was published in AD 810, gives us an account of Vortigern's life which is clearly more myth than history, which we shall examine in more detail shortly.

The name Vortigern may not even be a name. In the original British, it would have been Gwrtheyrn, or something like it. The first part, *gwrth-*, or *gwr* (*gor*), survives in modern Brythonic, with the meaning 'super'. For example, the Cornish for 'market' is *marghas* and for 'supermarket' it is *gorvarghas*. Dr. Chadwick has suggested that the name Gwrtheyrn or Vortigern is actually a title meaning 'High King', exactly like the Irish *Ard-Ri*.[3] The name of his son Gwerthefyr (Vortimer), is also taken to be a title, signifying 'supreme king'. In early mediaeval texts, Vortigern's name has many variant spellings, including Guorthigirnus and Wyrtgeorn. There is a ninth-century inscription to Vortigern on a pillar at Valle Crucis Abbey near Llangollen which describes him as the son-in-law of the Romano-British leader Magnus Maximus (Macsen Wledig in Welsh legend), although the dedication was made to support the genealogical claims of a prince of Powys and probably has no basis in historical fact.

The historical Vortigern was a British king at the time of the arrival of the Saxons under Hengist and Horsa in the sixth century AD. Rather like Arthur (although to nothing like the same extent), the myth of the king grew to such proportions that discovering the historical reality of the man has been very difficult, although there is no serious dispute that Vortigern may be safely regarded as a genuine historical figure. The historian Gildas tells us that he was the grandson of a Welsh border prince, Gloiu Gwalltiu ('Gloiu of the Long Hair'), who may have given his name to the city of Gloucester. We know that Vortigern established supra-tribal rule over southern Britain, that he was harried by Picts and Scots from the north, and that, in order to protect his own territories, he entered a pact with Hengist and Horsa, offering them land in return for political and military support, a deal which they accepted with eagerness. Nennius's account tells us that the pact was cemented by Vortigern marrying Hengist's daughter, although Nennius, the sole source for that part of the story, is unreliable.

The Saxons arrived in Kent, at Ebbsfleet according to some accounts. The Welsh chronicles give the landing date as AD 428, while the later English authorities date the Saxon arrival to somewhere between 450 and 455. The historian Bede describes the inhabitants of Kent as being of Jutish descent, rather than Saxon (he uses the term *Iuti*), and it is certain that the Jutes, as distinct from the Angles and Saxons, maintained a separate identity in Kent, the Isle of Wight and Hampshire, especially the New Forest, up to Bede's own time (the first half of the eighth century). However, we know that Hengist and Horsa made their first settlement on the island of Thanet, that northeastern corner of Kent insulated by two branches of the River Stour, where Margate, Broadstairs and Ramsgate are now the chief towns.

It did not take long for quarrels to spring up between the Britons and the Saxons. Kent began to develop as a separate Jutish kingdom, although it kept a name from the original Celtic inhabitants, the tribal name of the Cantiaci. The *Anglo-Saxon Chronicle* (a compilation probably made under the direction of Alfred the Great) records a battle between Vortigern and Hengist and Horsa at a place called Aegaels threp (*threp*, which survives in many English place names as -thorp or -thorpe, means 'homestead'). In this battle, dated AD 455 by the chronicles, Horsa was killed. Hengist continued to reign in Kent, together with his son Aesc (the name means 'ash tree' or 'spear'). Both the *Anglo-Saxon Chronicle* and Nennius's *Historia Britonum* record three subsequent battles, although they differ about the outcomes. What is certain is that the Celts were driven out of Kent, which marked the beginning of the long drive westwards and northwards of the Celtic kingdoms as they retreated before the advancing Angles, Saxons and Jutes. Hengist is supposed to have died in 488, his son Aesc in 512. The dates of the Anglo-Saxon invasions are unreliable, but the following sequence is widely accepted: 477, Ella and his three sons; 495, Cerdic and Cynric; 501, Port, who founded the town of Portsmouth; 514, Stuf and Wihtgar; 547, Ida, founder of the kingdom of Northumbria.

(Parenthetically, it is worth noting how peculiar it is that England should have acquired that name. The early kingdoms of Mercia and Northumbria were certainly of Anglish origin, but there was never an Angle-land as such.

After the Saxons, England was ruled predominantly by Danes, up to and including the Danish King Harold who was shot with an arrow by William the Conqueror's men in 1066. By the logic of probability, England should have ended up being called Saxonland, Daneland, or even New Normandy.)[4]

As Winston Churchill pointed out,[5] the place names of Sussex suggest that the westward expansions of the Saxons either exterminated or eliminated the Celts entirely in the southern parts of England, while in other areas there may have been a more gradual change in hegemony, and even some assimilation. A West Saxon legal code of AD 694 makes provision for various degrees of *weahlas* ('Welshmen', foreigners) who perform particular tasks. Churchill points out that hill, wood and stream names are often Celtic (the word *avon* means 'river', for example, so the River Avon is the River 'River'), even in areas where the town and village names are Anglo-Saxon.

There is no certain historical record of what happened to Vortigern after his battles with Hengist and Horsa. The Saxons and Britons are supposed to have met to discuss the terms of a truce, but the treacherous Saxons brought long daggers hidden in their boots with which they intended killing Vortigern and his retinue. The king escaped, but the event came to be known as the Night of the Long Knives, a phrase still commonly used to refer to an act of treachery by supposed allies.

From this part of the story onwards, mythology predominates. The main accounts are those given by Gildas (*Book of Complaint on the Ruin of Britain*, AD 547); Nynniaw or Nennius, in 810; and Geoffrey of Monmouth (*Historia Regum Britanniae*, a supposed translation of an earlier Welsh history of Britain, 1147). All three accounts are fantastic to varying degree, and the myth has been embellished with many exotic details in other versions.[6] The rest of Vortigern's story, therefore, is told on that basis, with occasional reference to possible actual historical connections.

After the Night of the Long Knives, Vortigern fled to north Wales to take refuge in the bleak fastnesses of Snowdonia. He ordered his people to build a tower (castle in some versions) directly under the shoulder of Mount Snowdon. However, some deep and powerful magic prevented his men from completing their king's order: whatever they managed to build by day disappeared during the following night, without apparent cause or explanation. Vortigern consulted his druids, who told him that he must find a boy without a father and have him brought to the spot (to be sacrificed, according to some versions). Circumstances of unusual birth are very common in Celtic tales of gods and heroes, so it is clear that the boy, whoever it would turn out to be, would be no ordinary mortal. Such a boy was found in south Wales, and brought northwards to Snowdon to be presented to the king. The boy gave his name as Ambros (which became Celticized as Emrys) and boldly declared that from henceforth the spot where they were standing would be known as Dinas Emrys ('Ambros's Palace'). This Emrys is clearly Aurelius Ambrosius, a highly respected Romano-British leader of the early post-Roman period, and a genuine historical figure, although by the time he had earned his military reputation he was clearly a man, not a boy. In Geoffrey of Monmouth's version of the story, the boy is not Ambros, but Myrddin, better known now as Merlin.

The druids came to challenge the boy, but instead he posed them a question: what was it that was hidden under the paving slab on the summit of the hill? They did not know. Ambros/Myrddin told them that there was a pool there, and in the pool two containers. If they drained the pool and opened the two containers, two winged serpents (i.e. dragons), one white and one red, would emerge and begin to fight. The white dragon would win the first few skirmishes, but would eventually be defeated by the red dragon. Then a bear would come sweeping up from Cornwall and confirm the red dragon's conquest for all time. As for Vortigern himself, his day was done, and his palace would never be built on that spot. Vortigern's druids opened the chamber, drained it as instructed, and everything which had been prophesied subsequently took place.

The symbolism of the prophecy is not difficult to interpret. The white dragon represents the Saxon invaders, the red dragon the British defenders. We are familiar now with the red dragon as the emblem of Wales, principally because it was adopted by the Tudors, originally from Anglesey, who, after the Battle of Bosworth in 1485 at which Richard III was defeated, came to rule Britain. Henry Tudor had picked up the emblem from the seventh-century Welsh king Cadwaladr. The bear sweeping up from Cornwall is Artos (the Latin for 'bear') or Artorius; in other words, King Arthur. The story of the fighting dragons also appears in the legends of Nudd, or Lludd, who is the Brythonic counterpart of Nuada Arghat Lam, Nuada of the Silver Arm, the Irish god. It has been suggested that Lludd gave his name to London (Lludd plus *din*, 'fort', later Romanized as Londinium); Ludgate is named after him, in the same way that Billingsgate is named after the Celtic god Belinus.

According to the legend, Vortigern fled to the remotest isolation he could find, the Lleyn peninsula. There he lived in a valley which, to this day, is called Nant Gwrtheyrn, 'Vortigern's Valley'. A burial chamber in the valley, known by local people as Castell Gwrtheyrn ('Vortigern's Castle'), was supposedly excavated in the eighteenth century to reveal the bones of a tall man buried in a stone coffin. In other versions of the story, he was burned alive in the wooden tower which he had managed only partially to build.

The historical truth is probably that Aurelius Ambrosius (Ambros, or Emrys) succeeded Vortigern (Gwrtheyrn) as king, either by defeating him in battle or by being elected king after Vortigern had been deposed. The Romans had introduced the notion of a single leader of Britain in the form of the Governor, and, as was noted earlier, it may be that the very name Vortigern indicates a 'High King' rank over all the tribes of Britain, including the lesser kings. Certainly, by the time we come to Ambros's successors, his brother Uther Pendragon and his nephew Arthur, the title 'King' clearly implies King of Britain, although the earliest historical reference to Arthur uses the Latin term *dux*, which means 'commander' rather than 'king' (the word 'duke' derives from it).

The historian Bede conveys us from the privations of the Britons under the marauding Anglo-Saxons to the emergence of Ambros as the new British champion without any reference to Vortigern's demise:

> Public as well as private structures were overturned; the priests were
> everywhere slain before the altars; the prelates and the people, without
> any respect of persons, were destroyed with fire and sword; nor was
> there any to bury those who had been thus cruelly slaughtered. Some
> of the miserable remainder, being taken in the mountains, were
> butchered in heaps. Others, spent with hunger, came forth and
> submitted themselves to the enemy for food, being destined to undergo
> perpetual servitude, if they were not killed even upon the spot. Some,
> with sorrowful hearts, fled beyond the seas. Others, continuing in
> their own country, led a miserable life among the woods, rocks and
> mountains, with scarcely enough food to support life, and expecting
> every moment to be their last. When the victorious army, having
> destroyed and dispersed the natives, had returned home to their own
> settlements, the Britons began by degrees to take heart, and gather
> strength, sallying out of the lurking places where they had concealed
> themselves, and unanimously imploring the Divine assistance, that they
> might not utterly be destroyed. They had at that time for their leader
> Ambrosius Aurelius, a modest man, who alone, by chance, of the
> Roman nation had survived the storm, in which his parents, who
> were of the royal race, had perished. Under him the Britons revived,
> and offering battle to the victors, by the help of God, came off
> victorious. From that day, sometimes the natives, and sometimes
> their enemies, prevailed . . . [7]

CELTIC WARRIOR KINGS

At first glance, Vercingetorix appears the greater hero of these two kings, and Vortigern the greater fool. After all, it was Vercingetorix who almost achieved the establishment of the first Celtic supra-tribal nation state, whereas it was Vortigern who committed the unforgivable error of inviting the cruel Saxons into his country, with devastating consequences for all the Celtic peoples. Ironically, Vortigern later became a saint. He emerges as St. Gwrthiern in the kingdom of Bro Waroch in southern Brittany. Many Celts fled from the Saxons across the Channel, and there are countless Breton saints who came originally from mainland Britain. However, it does seem ironic that the supposedly foolish tyrant Vortigern should end up being canonized.

In reality, Vortigern was in many ways closer to the archetype of the Celtic king than Vercingetorix, who has become a virtual symbol of Celtic leadership. Both kings attempted to achieve a Celtic kingdom larger than the tribe, a pattern which obtained in Ireland in the form of the Ard Ri, but which was never achieved in Gaul and only uncertainly achieved in Britain. In that sense, both kings were atypical. Vortigern, however, was as much a Roman as he was a Celt. In his predominantly Christian Romano-Britain, it could be argued that his invitation to Hengist and Horsa was an error of judgment, but not of principle.

Although Vortigern is historically more modern than Vercingetorix by a few hundred years, in cultural terms he seems infinitely more modern. Statecraft, diplomacy, doing deals with foreigners in the national interest: these were all Roman tricks which would have had no appeal, or even much meaning, to a Celtic king of Vercingetorix's age. Yet Vercingetorix, too, had learned much from the Romans, and not just in terms of how to use sappers and engineers in warfare. For Vercingetorix to have achieved what he did, his diplomatic and oratorical skills must certainly have matched those of Caesar, and probably exceeded them, bearing in mind the intractable nature of the petty Celtic kings with whom he was dealing. So both Vercingetorix and Vortigern have characteristics which set them apart from other Celtic kings, the common feature linking them being their preoccupation with nation rather than tribe. Yet both also have distinctly Celtic characteristics, including inordinate pride and enormous ambition, physical courage and battle skill, a sense of destiny, a firmness which seems tyrannical to modern sensibilities, and the apparently inescapable Celtic fate of ultimately failing. Vercingetorix remains a Celtic hero, and Vortigern a Celtic villain, but in reality their different historical and political contexts explain a great deal about the way they conducted themselves, and their differences in essential character appear to be not so great after all.

Notes

1   Unless otherwise noted, all quotations from Caesar in this chapter are from *The Conquest of Gaul* (also known in other editions as *The Commentaries*, or, more usually, *The Gallic War*), Book VII, trans. S.A. Handford, Penguin Classics edition, 1951 and several reprints, Harmondsworth, Middlesex, England.

2   One of Labienus's campaigns included the burning of a Celtic settlement called Lutetia in the territory of the Parisii. The settlement, on an island in the Seine, later became Paris.

3   Dr. Nora K. Chadwick, *Studies in Early British History*, Cambridge University Press, 1954, p. 37.

4   See Michael Senior's *Gods and Heroes in North Wales*, pub. Gwasg Carreg Gwalch, Llanrwst, 1993, p. 48.

5   Winston S. Churchill, *A History of the English Speaking Peoples*, Vol. 1, Donn, Mead & Co., New York, 1956, pp. 62–63.

6   There are some lively fictional versions of the Vortigern story. Mary Stewart's popular Arthurian trilogy (*The Crystal Cave, The Hollow Hills* and *The Last Enchantment*, Hodder and Stoughton, London, 1970) features the Dinas Emrys prophecy in the first volume.

7   Bede's *Ecclesiastical History of the English Nation*, trans. John Stevenson, Dent Everyman Library, London, 1910 and many reprints, Chapters XV and XVI, pp. 23–24, 1954 edition.

SEVEN

✳

TWO WARRIOR QUEENS: CARTIMANDUA AND BOUDICA

UNLIKE Vercingetorix and Vortigern, Cartimandua and Boudica were contemporaries, which makes comparison between them easier and more direct. Again, the same themes emerge: loyalty and betrayal, heroic representation of the Celtic cause and base abandonment of principle for political expediency. It is tempting to think of Boudica as the counterpart of Vercingetorix, the indomitable warrior, and Cartimandua as the counterpart of Vortigern, the diplomat and deal-maker, but, as with Vercingetorix and Vortigern, the temptation to qualify the actions of one as heroic and of the other as villainous may not be entirely justified. However, the most obvious and significant difference to be discussed first is the simple fact that these two great tribal war leaders were women, not men, a difference of great significance in the ancient world.

WOMEN IN ANCIENT CELTIC SOCIETY

The only other early societies which uniformly afforded high social status to women were the small colonies of Pythagoreans which established themselves under Pythagoras and after his death in various settlements of the ancient world. But these were very tiny groups, and the status was established on a single premise, namely that women could teach mathematics, which, for Pythagoreans, meant the same as saying that women could be priests. In no other early societies (nor indeed in many later ones) were women afforded the same level of status as in early Celtic society. Plutarch, writing in the second century AD, tells us that there was a long-standing Celtic tradition of women acting as mediators or judges in political or military disputes. Caesar tells us that Celtic women were free to choose their own husbands, that property was equally shared between them, and that full inheritance went to either partner after the death of the other. We know from the background to Boudica's story that a king could bequeath his rights and property directly to his daughters, as Prasutagus (Boudica's husband) did. Both Caesar and Dio Cassius describe types of communal marriage or polyandry, with kinsmen sharing wives and the descent becoming in effect matrilinear; Dio Cassius no doubt intended his account to be shocking to the Roman sensibility, and the accounts of polyandry have subsequently been attacked as no more than propaganda to discredit the Celts as barbarians, but it is perfectly possible that multiple marriage was common among the Celts, at least in Gaul. Votive tablets found at many Celtic shrines provide hard evidence that women owned property and businesses in their own names.

Polybius tells us that Celtic women followed their menfolk into battle, driving the supply waggons, and Ammianus Marcellinus tells us that they also took part in the actual combat, and that 'a whole troop would not be able to withstand one Gaul in battle if he summoned his wife to his assistance'. Plutarch's account of the life of Marius includes a description of Celtic women of the Ambrones tribe taking up arms when their menfolk retreated before the Romans, and attacking not only the Romans as the identified enemy but also their own menfolk as traitors. Both Caesar and Tacitus give us descriptions of Celtic women present at battles, usually standing on or near the supply waggons and yelling encouragement to their tribesmen, sometimes being wounded or killed in the action. We have in Cartimandua and Boudica evidence that Celtic queens could be and were supreme commanders in battle and sovereigns over the whole tribe. We know that there were women druids, women poets, women physicians and women sages.

There were at least as many goddesses as there were gods, and they were by no means subservient to their male counterparts, as they often are in the Greek and Roman pantheons; indeed, the Celtic war deities are predominantly female rather than male. Badbh, the war-goddess whose name means 'fury', and the Morrigan or Great Queen both appear as crows or ravens in the Irish mythological tales, and there was obviously a widespread conception of the spirit of battle as a female deity throughout the ancient Celtic world. Badbh Catha (Badbh the shape-shifter) is undoubtedly the same goddess as Cathubodua, the raven-goddess worshipped in Gaul. In Welsh folklore appears Cyhiraeth ('hound of longing'), a goddess of streams, marshes and lonely places whose blood-freezing wails predict death, particularly death in battle. In the tales of Blathnat (Irish, 'little flower') and her Brythonic counterpart Blodeuwedd (Welsh, 'flower'), we find a goddess just as capable of intrigue and murder as her male lover.

Modern Ireland is often viewed as male-dominated because of the influence of the Catholic Church, but the ancient and traditional Celtic pattern in

Ireland certainly afforded women very high status. Even the early mediaeval Brehon laws, which are generally very androcentric, explicitly state that for every nobleman 'to his wife belongs the right to be consulted on every subject'. Under the same laws, a man could not own his wife, and her rights were safeguarded: 'It is only contract that is between them.' A married woman was fully entitled to pursue a case at law, with or without her husband's permission, even if his property or joint property was at risk. Legal separation and divorce were not only possible in pagan Celtic Ireland, they were also accompanied by detailed legal rights for the woman, including the right to keep all marriage portions and gifts, as well as additional amounts for damages. Although inheritance was to the eldest son, a daughter could inherit if there was no son, but she was then obliged to provide and pay for a warrior under military levies unless she herself was prepared to fight in battle, which became increasingly difficult to do after the advent of Christianity.

The Christian influence certainly altered the status of women in Ireland very rapidly. In the earliest Christian period, immediately after Padraig's arrival, we see evidence of continuation of the older pattern: at the sixth-century school of St. Finian at Clonard there were female students, and when St. Mugint went from Ireland to found a school in Scotland in the seventh century, girls were encouraged to attend and study as well as boys. As late as AD 932, the Irish annals record the death of Uallach, chief poet of Ireland and a woman of the greatest learning. However, the law known as Cain Adomnain or Cain Adamnan ('Adamnan's law') passed at the Synod of Tara in 697 exempted (or excluded) women from taking part in battle, and the Catholic Church, as it grew, came more and more to dominate the legal and social mores of the country, so that by the early Middle Ages the ancient Celtic pattern of high legal and social status for women in Ireland had been considerably eroded, and the more common mediaeval pattern of male dominance obtained.

In Gaul and Britain, the same erosion of female social status also took place, first under Roman influence, then later under Christian influence. Boudica and Cartimandua, however, were warrior queens in an age when the unusually high social status of women was an indisputable reality in the Celtic world.

BOUDICA

Boudica was queen of the Iceni, in the area now called East Anglia after the Anglish tribes who later settled there. The name Boudica was spelled Boadicea (and, therefore, pronounced Bo-di-see-uh) in British school history books for many years, but Boudica or Boudicca (pronounced Boo-dee-kuh) are the spellings commonly used more recently, since they more accurately represent the probable original name, which is derived from the Celtic *bouda*, meaning 'victory'.

A marble statue of Boudica and her daughters, carved by J. Howard Thomas in 1913–15 and now housed in Cardiff.

Boudica's husband was Prasutagus, a Roman client-king. We have to assume that Prasutagus was the regent and Boudica the consort, since it was Prasutagus who had negotiated the treaty with Rome. The Roman emperor at the time (AD 61) was Nero, and the military governor of Britain was Caius Suetonius Paulinus. Prasutagus was a weak king, although the Iceni were a powerful people and held sway over all of what is now Norfolk, most of Suffolk, and parts of Cambridgeshire, Northamptonshire and Leicestershire. Prasutagus had made a will bequeathing his property half to his daughters and half to Nero, in what was obviously intended to be a gesture of reconciliation and submission to Rome. It was a very generous gesture, too – the Iceni had prospered in the few years of Roman rule since the Claudian invasion, and the estates of the royal and noble households were heavily stocked with grain and fat cattle.

When Prasutagus died, the temptations offered by such riches were too great for the Roman troops stationed in Iceni territory to resist. The officers began the breach of the treaty by raiding and occupying a few choice farmsteads; they killed the occupying families, or let them escape to fend for themselves, then looted the grain stores, gave themselves feasts on the slaughtered livestock, and took whatever coinage, jewellery or other treasure they could find. As the king's relatives attempted to retaliate, or to reclaim the estates, they in turn were either killed or taken prisoner as slaves. Such lawlessness was unusual in the Roman army; it was Suetonius Paulinus's preoccupation with the druids of Anglesey in the west which kept him distant from his officers, and perhaps made them more reckless.

There were Roman procuring agents, merchants and slaves who lived and worked among the Iceni, some of them even in the royal palace. When news broke of the officers' raids on the royal and noble households, these lesser Romans decided that they, too, wanted a piece of the action. They began looting the palace. Boudica, outraged at the open breach of the treaty, attempted to stop them. She was viciously subdued and taken prisoner in her own palace. First she was publicly flogged. Next, she was made to submit to a far greater torture, being forced to watch helplessly while her two young daughters were repeatedly raped in front of her. To modern sensibilities, it is hard to imagine a more vicious or cruel crime; to the ancient Celts, for whom pride and personal honour were immeasurably important, the humiliation as well as the viciousness of the crime itself would have been unbearable.

This blatant insult to the royal family brought the Iceni immediately to open rebellion, and Queen Boudica immediately became their champion and commander. She was, according to Dio Cassius, an imposing figure:

> In stature she was very tall, in appearance most terrifying, in the glance of her eye most fierce, and her voice was harsh. A great mass of red hair fell to her hips. Around her neck was a large necklace of gold and she wore a multicoloured tunic over which a thick cloak was fastened with a brooch. . . . She grasped a spear to help her terrify all beholders.[1]

It was not difficult to rouse the Iceni. There had been many pent-up resentments of Prasutagus's weak conciliations with Rome, and the tribal families responded vigorously to Be⌣dica's call for support.

Other tribes joined the rebellion, notably the Trinobantes. The expansion of the Roman settlement at Camulodunum (Colchester) by retiring Roman legionaries had driven many of the Trinobantes into exile or slavery in their own territory. The greatest wound of all had been the erection of a temple to the former emperor and now god Claudius on one of the most sacred sites in Trinobantian territory.

So the Iceni and Troniobantes together began the rebellion by attacking Camulodunum. Tacitus tells us how the Britons took heart from an unusual omen as the attack began:

> At this juncture, for no visible reason, the statue of Victory at
> Camulodunum fell down – with its back turned as though it were flee-
> ing the enemy. Delirious women chanted of destruction at hand. They
> cried that in the local senate-house outlandish yells had been heard; the
> theatre had echoed with shrieks; at the mouth of the Thames a
> phantom settlement had been seen in ruins. A blood-red colour in the
> sea, too, and shapes like human corpses left by the ebb tide, were
> interpreted hopefully by the Britons – and with terror by the settlers.[2]

The Roman settlers could not appeal to Suetonius Paulinus – he was still engaged in northern Wales – so they called for help instead from the imperial procurator's agent, Catus Decianus. He sent them fewer than two hundred men, poorly armed. The settlers, scantily supported by Decianus's troops, neglected to build a rampart or even trenches – they had become so accustomed to soft living in the conquered province. Nor did they send away their old people, women and children. As Tacitus observes, 'their precautions were appropriate to a time of unbroken peace'.

Queen Boudica's army rapidly surrounded the settlement, and the Romans were forced to retreat to the temple. The ninth Roman division, commanded by Quintus Petilius Cerialis Caesius Rufus, came to relieve the town, but the infantry was massacred and its commander escaped with his few remaining cavalry. The temple garrison fell, and Boudica's rebels seized Camulodunum.

With scarcely a pause, they advanced southwards towards Londinium. At the time, London was no larger or more important a town than Colchester, although its control of the Thames gave it obvious strategic importance. It did not even rank as a Roman settlement, although it was a busy trading centre. Suetonius Paulinus, alerted by reports of the fall of Camulodunum, marched swiftly from north Wales and reached Londinium before the rebels. We can presume that his original intent was to stand and resist the Celtic forces there, but he appears to have changed his mind. Despite what Tacitus calls the 'lamentations and appeals' of the Roman merchants, he decided to withdraw and let the rebels have Londinium. Under Boudica's command, the Celtic force swept through the city, slaughtering indiscriminately as they went.

(In parenthesis, it is worth noting that this is the only occasion in history when a Celtic army successfully invaded and occupied the city of London as an identifiable territory. The Cornish rebel army of 1497, led by Myghal Josef an Gov and Tomas Flamank, reached London and gave battle against the king, but was defeated at Blackheath. The Celts may be said to have the distinction of having initiated both the first and the last invasions of London.)

Fired by their success at Londinium, Boudica's forces moved on to Verulamium (modern St. Albans), which they also rapidly subdued. As so often happened in Celtic warfare, however, indiscipline, greed and excessive cruelty dissipated the Celtic strength:

> The natives enjoyed plundering and thought of nothing else. Bypassing forts and garrisons, they made for where loot was richest and protection weakest. Roman and provincial deaths at the places mentioned are estimated at seventy thousand. For the British did not take or sell prisoners, or practise other war-time exchanges. They could not wait to cut throats, hang, burn and crucify – as though avenging, in advance, the retribution that was on its way.[3]

In light of the tragic indignities forced upon Boudica, it is perhaps not surprising that the Celts took no prisoners, or that they were thirsty for vengeance in recompense for the gross insult given to their queen. Incidentally, there is no other mention of Celts ever using crucifixion as a method of execution – that was a Roman invention – so Tacitus's account may not be wholly reliable in this particular regard.

Suetonius Paulinus gathered his forces – the fourteenth brigade, detachments of the twentieth, plus auxiliaries, amounting to about ten thousand men – and moved to battle with Boudica without further delay. We do not know where this battle took place, other than that it was somewhere in the Midlands, within open country, and that Suetonius Paulinus ranged his troops in a defile with a wood behind him so that he could not be attacked from the rear. Mancetter in Warwickshire has been suggested as a possible site. Tacitus's account of the battle begins with a rousing speech from Boudica:

> Boudica drove round all the tribes in a chariot with her daughters in front of her. 'We British are used to woman commanders in war,' she cried. 'I am descended from mighty men! But now I am not fighting for my kingdom and my wealth. I am fighting as an ordinary person for my lost freedom, my bruised body, and my outraged daughters. Nowadays Roman rapacity does not even spare our bodies. Old people are killed, virgins raped. But the gods will grant us the vengeance we

deserve! The Roman division which dared to fight us is annihilated. The others cower in their camps, or watch for a chance to escape. They will never face even the din and roar of all our thousands, much less the shock of our onslaught. Consider how many of you are fighting – and why. Then you will win this battle, or perish. That is what I, a woman, plan to do! Let the men live in slavery if they will.[4]

That image of Boudica in her chariot with her daughters beside her is very familiar to Londoners, although they may not know it. A statue depicting the rebel Celtic queen was erected in 1902 on the Embankment opposite the Houses of Parliament, where it is passed by thousands upon thousands of Londoners and visitors every day, a romantic but nevertheless fitting representation of the spirit of British nationhood. It is worth noting that the image of the queen and her two daughters is reminiscent of the image of the Triple Goddess, feared and revered by the Celts over many centuries.

However inspiring Boudica may have been as a commander, her military generalship seems to have been less impressive. By meeting Suetonius Paulinus on flat, open ground, she lost any opportunity she might have had for ambush or for surprise manoeuvres: the collision was head-on, and very straightforward, which was of greater advantage to the more disciplined Roman soldiers. Worse, she had stationed all her supply waggons immediately behind the Celtic positions. When the Romans advanced in wedge formation, the Celts retreated, but were blocked by their own waggons, which could not be moved out of the way quickly enough. The Celtic warriors stumbled backwards into a confused melee of women, children, pack animals and belongings. The Romans pressed their advance with uncharacteristic ruthlessness – giving no quarter in exactly the same way as the Celts had done in earlier battles – and slaughtered warriors, women, children and pack animals alike. Tacitus gives the casualty numbers as four hundred dead and some wounded for the Romans, and eighty thousand dead for the Celts. This is almost certainly an exaggeration. The Roman force actually consisted of XIV Gemina, part of XX Valeria and auxiliaries, perhaps as many as 20 000 in total, with the Celtic forces probably about 50 000 in total.[5]

When the battle was lost, Boudica poisoned herself, according to Tacitus. He does not tell us what became of her body. Suetonius Paulinus had ordered the second division up from Exeter to assist in the battle, but its commander, Poenius Postumus – presumably because he little regarded Suetonius Paulinus's chances against the might of Boudica – refused the order. When he heard of the Roman victory, he stabbed himself to death.

Suetonius Paulinus solidified the victory by bringing in another two thousand regulars from Germany. The procurator Catus Decianus was dismissed, and a new imperial agent, Caius Julius Alpinus Classicianus, was appointed in his place. The rebellious tribes suffered intense famine, and their anger grew even greater, but so also did their sense of helplessness. Nero became concerned about the restlessness in the distant province, and sent a ridiculous envoy in the person of his foppish former slave, Polyclitus, at whom the still rebellious Celts merely roared with laughter. At one point, Nero even considered abandoning Britain altogether, as too remote and rebellious to be worth all the effort. If he could have been persuaded that Gaul would remain uninfluenced by the British tribes, he might have risked it. Eventually, however, Nero replaced the inept Suetonius Paulinus by Petronius Turpilianus, and the period of open rebellion came to an end.

Miranda Green comments on the association recorded by the classical historian Dio Cassius between Boudica and the Celtic war-goddess, Andraste:

> Andraste and the unspeakable rites carried out in her honour are
> described by Dio in connection with the massacre of Roman women
> by Boudica at London. . . . Boudica's female prisoners were sacrificed
> in Andraste's grove, their breasts cut off and stuffed in their mouths,
> before being impaled vertically on great skewers. . . . The propitiation
> of the goddess appears to have demanded blood-sacrifices of especial
> ferocity, while the slaughter of the women seems to have been part of
> a specific rite associated with a goddess of battle.[6]

As with all the classical authors, there is, of course, no guarantee of truth, and Dio's account of Boudica's ferocity may be yet another colourful fiction created to emphasize how barbarous those barbarians really were. However, Miranda Green's main point, namely that there appears to have been some real ritual connection between Boudica as warrior-queen and Andraste, one of the many Celtic goddesses of war, is well made.

It is clear that Boudica, like Vercingetorix, was able to command the respect and allegiance of Celts other than those of her own tribe, and that in itself gives evidence of an extraordinary strength of character. We can deduce that she was physically without blemish, and that Dio Cassius's description of her as large of stature and imposing in aspect may be historically accurate. As with Vercingetorix, we can also easily imagine that Boudica did indeed establish authority by acts of unusual cruelty and savagery. She must certainly have had real battle skills, and real physical courage. We see in coins struck by the Redones and Turones, tribes of northwestern Gaul, images of naked female riders and charioteers waving weapons and shields; although they may be representations of goddesses rather than queens, the image of the woman warrior is quite unmistakable. There have been many attempts to 'soften' the image of Boudica, concentrating on the grievous wrongs done to her and her nobility of spirit, but my personal view is that the most obvious interpretation of her character is also the most likely one: she was probably a physically imposing figure, battle-hardened, ferociously proud and sensible of her royal status and rights, capable of acts of great cruelty herself, a ruthless and determined military leader.

She has certainly made her mark on history; her brief campaign lasted only a few months and ended in failure, yet Boudica has become a symbol of the British fighting spirit and passion for freedom and independence. John Fletcher wrote a play about her in 1619; William Cowper and Alfred Lord Tennyson both wrote long ballads in her honour; John Milton, a noted misogynist, dismissed claims of Boudica's greatness, saying in his *History of Britain* that her story showed only that 'in Britain women were men, and men women'. In the popular imagination, Boudica has acquired some of the attributes of Britannia: she represents all that is noble, determined and independent in the British character.

CARTIMANDUA

Cartimandua, on the other hand, whose political skills and influence were probably considerably greater than Boudica's in her own time, and whose generalship in battle was probably also superior to Boudica's, is now a far more obscure figure. While Boudica has become a symbol of heroic resistance, like Vercingetorix, Cartimandua is remembered, if at all, as a traitor, like Vortigern. In part, ironically, it was Roman historians who helped to perpetuate these simple images. The Roman mother or matron held a place of high honour in Roman culture. Boudica, Rome's implacable enemy, came to represent matronly honour because she was fighting on behalf of her defiled daughters, while Cartimandua, Rome's political and military ally, was a shameless adulteress. For many years, Cartimandua's story was told to Roman girls by their mothers as an example of where unbridled lust would lead them.

Unlike Boudica, Cartimandua was the regent of her tribe, and her husband, Venutius, was merely her consort. The tribe was the Brigantes, whose territory was very extensive: in fact, it was the single largest Celtic kingdom in Britain, covering most of modern Cheshire, South and North Yorkshire, Lancashire, North Humberside, Cumbria, County Durham and Tyne and Wear.

Britain had been subdued as far north as the area of modern Lincoln (Roman Lindum) by the commander Aulus Plautius, who had returned to a triumphal retirement in Rome in AD 47. By AD 51, his successor, Ostorius Scapula, was still wrestling with the problem of subduing the rebellious tribes of the far north, including the powerful Brigantes, but he was presented with a more immediate problem in the shape of King Caradoc or Caratacus, son of Cymbeline. Caradoc summoned to war the Silures, a fiercely independent tribe, probably originally of Celto-Iberian stock, whose territory was in what is now south Wales. The Silures were joined by the Ordovices from the northwest. Caradoc's intention was to mobilize the Silures, Ordovices and Brigantes as one supra-tribal unit against the Romans. It was an ambitious plan, but not unworkable, given the huge numbers of warriors who could be assembled if all three tribes worked in concert. In the meantime, Queen Cartimandua had grown tired of her husband, Venutius. She fell in love with a younger man, Vellocatus, the king's arms-bearer. She was in an awkward position. She could not conduct an open love affair with her husband's servant: the insult would have been unforgivable. So Cartimandua had to devise some method to get rid of her husband. The method she chose was extreme, to put it mildly. She sent envoys to Ostorius Scapula, offering him the whole of the Brigantian tribal area as a Roman protectorate. Ostorius Scapula, who must have been scarcely able to believe his good fortune, accepted immediately.

The divorce was so acrimonious that it triggered intratribal warfare. Cartimandua, obviously an astute tactician, captured Venutius's brother and other relatives and held them hostage. Venutius, infuriated, responded by raising a force against his former queen. Within weeks, a full-scale Brigantian civil war was in progress. Inevitably, the Romans took advantage of the situation. Since Cartimandua had offered the Brigantian territory as a protectorate, they naturally sided with her and against Venutius.

In the meantime, King Caradoc engaged in battle with Ostorius Scapula, as Tacitus describes:

> After a reconnaissance to detect vulnerable and invulnerable points, Ostorius led his enthusiastic soldiers forward. They crossed the river without difficulty, and reached the [Celtic] rampart. But then, in an exchange of missiles, they came off worse in wounds and casualties. However, under a roof of locked shields, the Romans demolished the crude and clumsy stone embankment, and in the subsequent fight at close quarters the natives were driven to the hill-tops. Our troops pursued them closely. While light-armed auxiliaries attacked with javelins, the heavy regular infantry advanced in close formation. The British, unprotected by breastplates or helmets, were thrown into disorder. If they stood up to the auxiliaries they were cut down by the swords and spears of the regulars, and if they faced the latter they succumbed to the auxiliaries' broadswords and pikes. It was a great victory. Caratacus's wife and daughter were captured. His brother surrendered.[7]

Caradoc fled for his life, and he naturally fled to the place he thought safest: Cartimandua's palace. He obviously had received no news of her divorce from Venutius, nor of her offer to Ostorius Scapula. Instead of receiving Caradoc as a fellow Celtic monarch, Cartimandua had him put in chains and thrown into a prison to await collection by the Romans. While in prison, Caradoc learned that Cartimandua had colluded with Ostorius Scapula in planning the battle at which his wife and daughter had been captured and his brother had been forced to surrender. We can imagine how deep his grief and sense of betrayal must have been.

Ostorius Scapula sent Caradoc to Rome, as Tacitus explains:

> The reputation of Caratacus had spread beyond the islands and
> through the neighbouring provinces to Italy itself. These people were
> curious to see the man who had defied our power for so many years.
> Even at Rome his name meant something. . . . There was a march past,
> with Caratacus' petty vassals, and the decorations and neck-chains and
> spoils of his foreign wars. Next were displayed his brothers, wife, and
> daughter. Last came the king himself. The others, frightened, degraded
> themselves by entreaties. But there were no downcast looks or appeals
> for mercy from Caratacus.[8]

Tacitus then proceeds to give us a speech for Caradoc which clearly was an
appeal for mercy, and a very eloquent one. Although the defiant, heady
speech is almost certainly pure invention by Tacitus, it has captured the imagination of Celtic scholars over the centuries, and there are many versions of
it, most of them in Welsh, and most of them much more windbaggish. Here
is Tacitus's original:

> 'Had my lineage and rank been accompanied by only moderate suc-
> cess, I should have come to this city as friend rather than as prisoner,
> and you would not have disdained to ally yourself peacefully with one
> so nobly born, the ruler of so many nations. As it is, humiliation is my
> lot, glory yours. I had horses, men, arms, wealth. Are you surprised I
> am sorry to lose them? If you want to rule the world, does it follow
> that everyone else welcomes enslavement? If I had surrendered without
> a blow before being brought before you, neither my downfall nor your
> triumph would have become famous. If you execute me, they will be
> forgotten. Spare me, and I shall be an everlasting token of your
> mercy!'[9]

Unless Caradoc had learned Latin with remarkable ease, we must assume that
this speech was given in Celtic and translated for the emperor. Claudius
spared Caradoc and his family, who lived on in Rome as famous prisoner-
guests, presumably for some years.

Meanwhile, back in Britain, the Silures were proving to be, as Tacitus
says, 'exceptionally stubborn'. Ostorius Scapula had repeatedly and publicly
promised not just to defeat them in battle, but to exterminate them as a tribe
and people. For Celts, there could be no greater insult or affront to their dignity. At this point, 'exhausted by his anxious responsibilities', Ostorius
Scapula died. He was replaced by Aulus Didius Gallus ('Didius the Gaul'),
who, despite his name, was neither a Celt nor a friend of the Celts. Didius
immediately confirmed his predecessor's deal with Queen Cartimandua, and
sent her Roman reinforcements when rebel tribes tried to invade Brigantian
territory.

In the end, however, it was her own people who defeated Cartimandua. Her abrupt divorce of Venutius and hasty marriage to the much younger Vellocatus was certainly a scandal to Roman eyes, and it appears that even for her own people it was a challenge to the prestige of the royal family. Venutius, campaigning with all the fury of a cuckolded husband as well as the natural anger of a deposed king, persuaded the druids, and through them the rest of the huge tribe, that the ageing Cartimandua was no longer fit to govern. Eventually, she was forced to flee the kingdom, taking Vellocatus with her. They escaped to Camulodunum, where they lived, and finally languished, under Roman protection. We can picture the couple, she now having lost her looks, and he having lost all his ambition to be king, declining into bitterness and regret, virtually confined to the Colchester barracks and its immediate surroundings, perhaps bickering through the long nights over glasses of cheap army wine, a burden and embarrassment to their Roman hosts.

(Just to tidy up the story, Venutius did not have long to glory in his revenge. When Vespasian became emperor, he appointed Petillus Cerealis governor of Britain. Cerealis was dispatched from Rome with an extra legion, II Adiutrix, which joined IX Hispana and XX Valeria Victrix, already stationed in the island. The legions marched northwards to defeat and kill Venutius at a battle site near modern Stanwick in Leicestershire.)

WARRIOR QUEENS

We know from Tacitus that Cartimandua was not the only Brigantian military leader – he describes raids in AD 71 and 83 led by female commanders. Tacitus puts in the mouth of Suetonius Paulinus a speech which includes his incredulity at how among the Celts 'in their ranks there are more women than fighting men'. Even allowing for dramatic licence, the evidence is convincing that Celtic women did, indeed, fight in battle, and that the tribe could be commanded by a queen as well as by a king. It hardly needs saying that this is a very unusual pattern of behaviour in the general historical scheme (certainly before the twentieth century), where the conduct of warfare was almost exclusively a male activity.

On the face of it, Boudica appears a nobler figure than Cartimandua. Her cause was justified by the cruel indignities forced upon her and by the rape of her daughters. She was an inspiring leader, whose appeal went beyond her own tribe. She led her forces to significant victories, including the conquest and sack of the port of London. When she was finally defeated, her sense of honour would not allow her to be taken captive by the enemy; rather than be paraded as a prisoner, she took poison and ended her own life. By comparison, Cartimandua's story of love intrigues, political jockeying, and above all her cold-blooded betrayal of her fellow Celt, King Caradoc, looks tawdry, and her undignified end in a Colchester army barracks seems suitably pathetic.

In many ways, however, Cartimandua may actually have been the more impressive of the two in her own time. She had a much larger and more complex kingdom to deal with, and to have survived for any length of time at all as Queen of the Brigantes must have required considerable political skill. However undignified her motives for casting aside Venutius for Vellocatus (and it may be that political and tactical considerations were actually more important than physical desire), once she had made that decision she reinforced her position with some very impressive military campaigns, outmanoeuvring her former husband on several occasions. It could even be argued that her imprisonment of Caradoc was decisive and bold, since she must have been well aware of the fury that it would engender in the powerful Ordovices and Silures, but was prepared to take the consequences. As with Vercingetorix and Vortigern, we can only interpret Boudica's and Cartimandua's characters through the accounts of their actions, and those accounts were almost invariably hostile to the Celts, and deferential to classical ideas of what constitutes virtue.

Notes

1   Dio Cassius, *Roman History*, LXII.2.
2   Tacitus, *The Annals of Imperial Rome*, XIV.30.
3   *The Annals*, XIV.33.
4   *The Annals*, XIV.34.
5   Graham Webster, *The Roman Imperial Army*, A. & C. Black, London, 1969, p. 229.
6   Miranda J. Green, *Celtic Goddesses*, George Braziller, New York, 1996, pp. 32–33.
7   *The Annals*, XII.33.
8   *The Annals*, XII.35.
9   *The Annals*, XII.35.

✲

EIGHT

'KING' ARTHUR – CHIVALRY'S CELTIC HERITAGE

THE HEROIC SAGAS

N THE figure of Arthur we see epitomized many of the characteristics which define Celtic kingship, yet, paradoxically, there is no convincing evidence that the historical Arthur was a king at all, which explains the inverted commas in this chapter's title. The mythological Arthur is a composite of many heroic and kingly attributes. There are three great sagas, or groups of heroic tales, in Celtic literature. The first two are Irish: the *Ulster Cycle*, featuring King Conchobar and the hero Cu Chulainn; and the *Fenian* or *Ossianic Cycle*, featuring the hero Fionn mac Cumhail (Finn mac Cool) and his poet-warrior son, Oisin or Ossian. The third cycle is the *Arthurian Cycle*, which is Brythonic in origin. The historical Arthur may have been Cornish by birth – Tintagel is reputed to have been his birthplace – but the early legends were mostly Welsh and carried to Brittany by British refugees, so all three Brythonic Celtic nations can lay claims to at least some part of the Arthurian saga. The Breton legends were carried in time to the Norman court, and from there to the world.

There have been literally hundreds of authors and poets who have taken Arthurian material for their theme, but four writers in particular played a major role in establishing the story of Arthur on the world stage. We met two of them in Chapter Four: these were Nynniaw or Nennius, the ninth-century Welsh historian, and Geoffrey of Monmouth, the twelfth-century historian and fabulist whose *History of the Kings of Britain* attained enormous popularity in the early mediaeval period. The third is the mediaeval French poet Chrétien de Troyes, a native of Champagne, who wrote *Le Conte du Graal* ('The Story of the Grail') in 1180. Several other writers took up the stories which Chrétien left unfinished, notably Thomas (no other name is recorded) and his translator Gottfried von Strassburg, who developed the story of Tristan and Isolde. Chrétien's poems were translated into German, Old Norse and even back into Welsh. The fourth great promulgator of the Arthurian theme was Sir Thomas Malory, whose *Le Morte d'Arthur* ('The Death of Arthur') was written in Newgate prison between 1468 and 1471 and published by William Caxton (without acknowledging Malory's authorship) in 1485.

By the time we reach Sir Thomas Malory's version, the legend has already become huge in proportion to the original material, with a long list of main characters and dozens of extremely complex, interwoven stories and themes. These stories, which have become well known by frequent retelling, are sometimes collectively called The Matter of Britain, and they have become a commonly recognized feature of British culture. Although most people have not read any of the original legends, many are familiar with the names Lancelot and Guinevere, or with the legends of the Lady of the Lake or the Sword in the Stone.

We need to look at two Arthurs: the Arthur of history, and the King Arthur of legend. Unfortunately, the legendary saga is so long and complex that there is not space here to examine in detail more than a few selected themes, so before we begin a closer examination I need to set out as background reference the main elements and characters of the story. (This is essentially the Malory version, apart from the Fisher King episode, which comes from Chrétien de Troyes. There are many other variants, and many different spellings for the names of principal characters. In the outline below, name spellings in parentheses are usually the older Welsh or Cornish spellings.)

OUTLINE OF THE LEGEND

Arthur's father was Uther Pendragon ('Chief Dragon'), King of all Britain. Uther was at odds with Gorlois, the rebellious Duke of Cornwall, and killed him in battle near Tintagel, on the north Cornish coast. Uther ordered his prophet and magician, Merlin (Myrddin), to make him look like Gorlois for one night, so that he could sleep with Gorlois's widow, Ygraine (Ygern). Uther appeared in Ygraine's bedchamber in the guise of her husband, whom she believed to be still alive, and slept with her, siring Arthur. Gorlois and Ygraine already had one child, a girl called Morgan, now Arthur's half-sister, who, because of her skill as a sorceress, later became known as Morgan Le Fay.

When the child Arthur was born, Merlin took him and gave him secretly into the care of Sir Ector, a knight, who raised him alongside his own son, Kay (Cei). In childhood, there was great jealousy between the two foster brothers, but in later years Kay became the Royal Seneschal and one of Arthur's most loyal knights.

Uther Pendragon died while Arthur was still a young child, and the kingdom fell into chaos and disarray. The Archbishop of Canterbury, on the advice of Merlin, summoned all the nobles and petty kings of the land to

London on Christmas morning, where they discovered a beautiful sword stuck firmly in an anvil on a marble stone. On the anvil was inscribed in letters of gold: *Whoso pulleth oute this swerd of this stone and anvyld is rightwys kynge borne of all Brytaygne.* Kay had forgotten his sword for a tournament, and sent Arthur to fetch it. Arthur, not understanding what he

THE LADY OF THE LAKE TELLETH ARTHVR OF THE SWORD EXCALIBVR

A young Arthur, accompanied by Merlin, is met by the Lady of the Lake, who, according to some versions of the legend, gives Arthur his magical sword Excalibur. Print by Aubrey Beardsley.

was doing, removed the Sword in the Stone, a feat which no other was able to repeat. (This sword is named as Caledfwlch or Excalibur in some versions of the legend; in others, it is the Lady of the Lake who gives Excalibur to Arthur.) Merlin declared Arthur rightful King of Britain, to which the other nobles and kings assented.

In early manhood, Arthur committed incest and adultery with his aunt, Queen Margawse (Morgeuse), begetting his bastard son Modred (Mordred, Medraut). He later married the daughter of King Lodegreaunce, Guinevere (Gwenhwyfar, meaning 'White Goddess'), but the marriage was childless. Guinevere brought with her, as a wedding gift, a Round Table, which came to symbolize the equality of the knights who served Arthur and the British cause. Arthur established his court at Camelot. After Arthur's marriage to Guinevere, Merlin fell in love with a sorceress, Nyneve (Nimue, Vyvyan), who imprisoned him for ever in an enchanted sea cave below the headland of Tintagel in Cornwall.

Queen Margawse married King Lot of Orkney, leader of the rebel kings of the north and west. Four of their children became Knights of the Round Table: Gawain (Gawan, Gwalchmei Gwyn), Aggravayne, Gaheris and Gareth. King Lot was killed in battle by King Pellinore, Arthur's ally and hunter of the Questing Beast, a creature with the head of a serpent, the body of a leopard, the buttocks of a lion, and the feet of a hart. Gawain avenged his father's death by killing King Pellinore. The pursuit of the Questing Beast was then taken up by Palomides the Saracen. Eventually, Gawain became Arthur's favourite nephew, while his younger brother Gareth became a favourite of Sir Lancelot du Lac.

Lancelot was the son of King Ban of Benwick in France. He was appointed Guinevere's champion by Arthur, but became her lover. Under an enchantment, he slept with Elaine, daughter of King Pelles, and sired Galahad. Guinevere's jealousy drove him to madness for two years.

Arthur set his knights many tasks to perform and feats to achieve. One was the pursuit and capture of Twrch Trwyth, a legendary boar of great courage and ferocity, which kept a magical comb and pair of scissors in its bristling mane. Twrch Trwyth had once been a king, but he had been turned into a boar by sorcery.

After many such battles and challenges, Arthur established a greater cause for the Knights of the Round Table to pursue: it was to seek and find the Sangraal, or Holy Grail, the chalice in which Joseph of Arimathea had collected drops of blood from Jesus Christ at the Crucifixion. A vision of the Grail appeared before all the knights. The quest was pursued by Galahad and Bors, but principally by Perceval (Percival, Parsifal), who was protected by his virginity from temptations by the Devil.

Perceval had been raised by his mother, Acheflour, who was Arthur's sister, in a deep forest near Snowdon, in Wales. She deliberately kept him innocent of all knowledge of the world, including even his own name. He was merely called Fair Son. His father, Bliocadrans, had been crippled by a wound in the thighs during a tournament, and died while Perceval was a child. Acheflour deliberately raised Perceval in the forest so that he would avoid the same fate, but one day he met some of Arthur's knights. Their splendour was so great that he thought they must be angels. When they explained who they were, Perceval determined to leave the forest and join Arthur at his court. During his quest for knowledge about the world, Perceval was granted a vision of the lance which had pierced Christ's side at the Crucifixion, and of the Grail, but he was too innocent to ask what the visions signified. Later, he met a girl (his cousin, although he did not know it) cradling the headless corpse of a knight, her lover. She had spent the night at the castle of the rich Fisher King, who had been wounded in battle by a javelin thrust through both thighs, and who was so crippled and in such constant pain that fishing was his only recreation and occupation. (In some versions of the legend, the first Fisher King was Alains le Gros, who performed a miracle like Christ's feeding of the five thousand, and was thereafter called the Rich Fisher. All keepers of the Grail were thereafter given the title Fisher King. The most famous of the Fisher Kings, and the one whom Perceval meets, is called Amfortas.)

In the end, the only knight to see the full vision of the Grail was Galahad, who took the Siege Perelous (Seat of Danger) at the Round Table, the only knight able to do so and still live. Bors, son of King Bors of Gaul, survived both Perceval and Galahad, and ordered their burial in the Spiritual Palace at Sarras.

Arthur defeated many enemies of the realm in a series of battles. One defeated enemy was King Angwyshaunce of Ireland, who had taken King Mark of Cornwall into bondage. Mark was released by Tristram of Lyonnesse (Tristan, Drustanus). To cement the treaty, a marriage was arranged between King Mark and King Angwyshaunce's daughter, Iseult the Fair (Ysolt Wynn, Ysolde, Isolde), but Tristram and Iseult accidentally drank a love potion together and became inseparably devoted to each other. After their deaths while being pursued by Mark, they were buried in adjoining graves, from which two rose trees grew and entwined themselves into a single tree.

Lancelot's passion for Guinevere also intensified, until the insult to Arthur could no longer be borne. Modred, Arthur's bastard son by Queen Margawse, took advantage of the strife between Arthur and Lancelot and tried to seize the throne. He exposed Guinevere's adultery and publicly denounced her and Lancelot. During the open fighting which broke up the Round Table, Lancelot killed forty knights, including Gaheris and Gareth. Arthur exiled him to France, where, breaking out of the siege imposed by the knights loyal to Arthur, he also mortally wounded Gawain.

While Arthur was in France, Modred attempted to marry Guinevere, who fled to seek refuge in a nunnery. Arthur returned to Britain, and engaged in battle with Modred. Arthur killed Modred, but simultaneously received from his son a single, mortal blow. Arthur ordered his faithful knight Bedivere (Bedwyr) to cast his sword Excalibur (Caledfwlch, 'Hard Handle') back into the lake from which the mysterious Lady of the Lake had appeared to give it to him. Bedivere finally threw the sword into the lake, where it was caught by a hand which appeared from beneath the waters.

Lancelot returned from France to find Arthur dead and Guinevere in a nunnery. He became a monk, and died of a broken heart shortly after Guinevere. He was buried at his own castle, Joyous Garde.

Bedivere casts away Excalibur, which is caught by the Lady of the Lake. Print by Aubrey Beardsley.

As Arthur lay dying, four queens appeared in a mysterious boat. They carried him aboard, and sailed westwards to Avalon (Avallen, Avallon, 'Apple Orchard') in the Isles of the Blessed which lay beyond the western horizon. Arthur was commemorated as *Arturius quondam rex futurusque* ('Arthur, once and future king'). Now, in folklore, Arthur and his knights lie sleeping beneath Britain's hills and mountains, and will rise at a trumpet call in the hour of Britain's greatest need.

THE HISTORICAL ARTHUR

Even told in crudest bare-bones outline, as above, the Arthurian legend is magnificently rich in themes, and tells us a great deal about how early Celtic philosophical ideals were transmogrified, first by Roman influence, later by the Christian Church, and finally by the traditions of the mediaeval French troubadours, into the complex and deeply influential chivalric code which has had such an important impact on moral thinking in the western world, and which still affects us to this day. Before we discuss these themes, however, we should review the evidence for the existence of a real, historical Arthur.

In Chapters Four and Six, we established much of the historical background against which the life events of the real Arthur took place; Britain by the beginning of the fifth century AD was a Christian, Romano-Celtic province, into which hordes of heathen Germanic tribesmen advanced following Vortigern's invitation to Hengist and Horsa to come over and assist him in his fight against the Picts and Scots. We know that for a brief period, approximately AD 515 to 540, the Anglo-Saxon invasion was held in check by British forces.

This check to the invading tribes was supposedly initially led by a single commander, Arthur. The 'supposedly' is justified because there is no definite proof that a historical Arthur even existed, let alone what role he played. However, the general consensus is now that the legend must have had some basis in fact. Pioneering studies by Geoffrey Ashe and others, beginning in the 1950s and 1960s, have all given further credence to Arthur as a real person. His exact role and title remain disputed. He is often described in recent histories as a 'petty chieftain', probably to counteract the image of the legendary Arthur as King of all Britain. He is also often described as Welsh or Cornish, a distinction which would have had no meaning at all in his own time, but which further contributes to his marginalization in our own.

Nennius, the first historian to mention him by name, uses two titles to describe Arthur: *dux bellorum*, which means 'commander of battles', and *comes Brittanorum*, which means 'guardian of the Britons'. Both words, *dux* and *comes*, deserve a little further explanation. *Dux* is the root of the English word 'duke'. In classical Latin, it could mean 'guide' or 'conductor'. It was used, for example, to describe the person at the head of a train or caravan of pack animals. While Caesar, Cicero and Livy use it as a general term for a military leader, Caesar and Cicero also use it to refer to a specific army rank, namely lieutenant-general, as opposed to *imperator*, which originally signified a general or commander-in-chief, and only later came to mean 'emperor'. (The Welsh *amherawdyr*, which we find in the early vernacular texts as a title for Arthur, is simply *imperator* pronounced and spelled in early Welsh fashion.) *Comes* similarly has more than one meaning. Its original sense was 'one who goes with another', 'journey companion' or 'fellow traveller'. It could also mean, more generally, 'sharer' or 'associate'. It was used by Cicero, Horace and Suetonius to refer specifically to the members of the retinue which accompanied magistrates and other officials. Finally, it could mean 'guardian' or even 'tutor', in the sense of a companion who has responsibility for another. So, when we look at these two terms, *dux* and *comes*, which Nennius uses to describe Arthur, we have to bear in mind two things: first, that he is writing in the monkish Latin of the ninth century, not classical Latin; and second, that both words have a range of possible meanings and translations. If we choose 'leader of battles and companion of the Britons', we create a very different effect to that created if we choose 'commander in war and guardian of the Britons'.

One of the main factors contributing to the 'belittling' of the historical Arthur is the fact that no mention is made of his tribe. If he were a king of any standing, the argument runs, his tribe would have been great and prosperous, with extensive territories, and we would have had a real, historical genealogy to study, instead of the endless confusions with Aurelius Ambrosius and the dubious existence of Uther Pendragon, Ygraine, and so on. Not only that, there would have been some discernible geographical pattern to all the battles in which he is supposed to have engaged, a recognizable expansion of territory and influence, instead of the list of engagements all across the country, in no apparent order. Yet, in the historical context, the role of military leader without a specific tribal base is not so far-fetched, as Sir Winston Churchill astutely pointed out many years before Geoffrey Ashe brought the historical Arthur into the public spotlight:

> What could be more natural or more necessary than that a commander-in-chief should be accepted – a new Count of Britain, such as the Britons had appealed to Aetius to give them fifty years before? Once Arthur is recognised as the commander of a mobile field army, moving from one part of the country to another and uniting with local forces in each district, the disputes about the scenes of his actions explain themselves. Moreover, the fourth century witnessed the rise of cavalry to the dominant position in the battlefield. The day of infantry had passed for a time, and the day of the legion had passed for ever. The Saxon invaders were infantry, fighting with sword and spear, and having little armour. Against such an enemy a small force of ordinary Roman cavalry might well prove invincible. If a chief like Arthur had

gathered a band of mail-clad cavalry he could have moved freely about
Britain, everywhere heading the local resistance to the invader and
gaining repeated victories.[1]

A specifically Celtic factor, not mentioned by Churchill, is the long tradition
of druidic leadership, which was always intertribal. I am not seriously suggesting that Arthur was a druid (although it is a very interesting idea to play
with), but the Celts had long had a system which very effectively limited
intertribal conflict and promoted cooperation, namely the Celtic law as
administered by the druids, who were judges and ambassadors as much as
they were priests. Someone with a burning sense of mission, and a clear sense
that what he was doing represented natural and universal law, would have
appealed very strongly to the Celtic tribal leaders not just, as Churchill suggests, because he represented a Roman sense of rightness and fair play, but
also, and more significantly, because he would have reminded them very
forcefully of the ancient Celtic druidic traditions.

Churchill's point about the military significance of the Celtic cavalry's
superiority over the Anglo-Saxon infantry is well made. One of the reasons
that the Norman knights took such a fancy to the Arthurian tales in the
eleventh and twelfth centuries was because they, also, were horse-riders,
while King Harold's Saxons at Hastings were footmen. The words 'cavalry'
and 'chivalry' are both derived from Latin *caballus* ('pack-horse') and mediaeval French *cheval* ('horse'). Tales of chivalry originally meant tales about
warriors on horses.

Nennius lists twelve great battles fought by Arthur, as follows:

> The first battle was at the mouth of the river called Glein. The second,
> third, fourth and fifth upon another river called Dubglas and is in the
> district Linnius. The sixth battle upon the river which is called Bassas.
> The seventh battle was in the Caledonian wood, that is Cat Coit
> Celidon. The eighth battle was in Fort Guinnon. . . . The ninth battle
> was waged in the City of the Legion. The tenth battle he waged on the
> shore of the river which is called Tribruit. The eleventh battle took
> place on the mountain which is called Agned. The twelfth battle was
> on Mount Badon (*Mons Badonicus*), in which nine hundred and sixty
> men fell in one day from one charge, and no-one overthrew them
> except himself alone. And in all the battles he stood forth as victor.[2]

There have been many attempts to find modern counterparts for these place
names. Glein may be the River Glen in Lincolnshire, in which case Linnuis
might be Lindsey in the same county. However, the name Dubglas certainly
appears Goidelic rather than Brythonic, and Caledonia is explicit enough, so
some of these battles at least appear to have taken place in Scotland. (The
legendary Arthur is supposed also to have fought battles in Ireland.) Cat Coit
Celidon is not as helpful as it might appear: it is simply Welsh for 'the battle

of the wood of Celidon'. We can identify the City of the Legion: that was Caerleon on the bank of the Usk in Monmouthshire, the site of the former Roman garrison of Isca, where Legio II Augusta was stationed during the earlier suppressions of the Silures. The site was excavated in 1908, and by the National Museum of Wales in 1926 and 1928, yielding extensive evidence of the Roman barracks, but none of Arthur. There is a steep headland at St. Agnes in Cornwall, which may or may not be related to Agned. Mount Badon and Bath have frequently been linked, partly because of the many legends surrounding Arthur which are set either at nearby South Cadbury (see below), or at nearby Glastonbury, where Arthur and Guinevere were supposed to have been buried. Other candidates are Badbury, near Swindon, which has the ancient British hillfort of Liddington Castle close by, and another hillfort in Dorset called Badbury Rings.

The monk Gildas (the source of some of Nennius's material) tells us that the Battle of Badon took place in the year of his birth, which we can deduce to have been about AD 517 or 518. The Battle of Camlann, at which Modred reputedly slew Arthur, is usually dated at about 538. We assume, then, a period of about twenty years (518 to 538) of peaceful rule by Arthur, with the Anglo-Saxon advances temporarily but significantly checked. That would certainly have been long enough to have registered itself in the Celtic memory as a Golden Age.

One of the early confusions between the historical Arthur and the legendary Arthur arose because of his name. Arthur was originally Artus, Arturius or Artorius, a Latin name derived from Greek αρκτοσ (*arktos*) meaning 'bear' (the Latin is *ursus*). However, the god Bran, a prominent warrior-god in the Brythonic pantheon, was commonly known by the epithet Arddu (pronounced Ar-thyew), meaning 'the Dark One'. (This name also appears in the Welsh Bible as an epithet for Satan.) This close similarity in names could easily have led to some of the god's heroic attributes (and legends) being transferred to the real, historical military leader. There is one other significant historical fact concerning the name itself. Before the sixth century, there is no record of any native Briton using it. By the end of the century, however, it had become a very popular Celtic name, in widespread use across the whole of Britain – there was even a prince of Argyll who used it. The logical inference is that there must have been one individual Artus or Arturius whose exploits were so impressive that others wanted to adopt the name of the national hero.

South Cadbury, a British hillfort of great antiquity which stands just south of Sparkford, has long been considered the chief contender for the site of Camelot, Arthur's legendary palace; or, rather, for one of the genuine fortresses used by the historical Arthur on which the later legends of Camelot were founded. John Leland, the sixteenth-century antiquary, wrote without any hesitation or qualification: 'At South Cadbyri standith Camallate, sumtyme a famose toun or castelle.' The hill stands about 152 metres (500 ft), but looks higher because it is set in the great level of the Glastonbury marsh plain.

The hill-top, which is reached by ascending through four immense earthen ramparts, covers about 7.3 hectares (18 acres) and commands a very impressive view across the plain towards Glastonbury Tor, which is clearly visible at a distance of about 19 kilometres (12 miles) to the northwest as the crow flies. The site was briefly excavated in 1913, then more thoroughly in 1966 by a Camelot Research Committee which included Ralegh Radford, Sir Mortimer Wheeler and Leslie Alcock. The excavation uncovered pre-Roman material, evidence of Roman occupation, including a fourth-century temple, evidence of continued occupation through the fifth and sixth centuries, and of a stone wall built about 1020 during the reign of Ethelred the Unready. A more extensive dig in 1967, which was televised, revealed evidence of significant additions to the ramparts during the sixth century. In 1968, traces of a hall in a commanding central position were also discovered. As Leslie Alcock said at the time, if these fortifications were not built by Arthur himself, they were built by someone who, at the very least, was an Arthur-type figure.[3]

The first book to give us any detail about Arthur's life was Geoffrey of Monmouth's *History of the Kings of Britain*, completed in about 1136. The most obvious difficulty with the book is that much of it is clearly invented. More importantly, the inventions are of the most pernicious kind: we are given precise troop numbers and battle alignments for battles which never actually took place, for example, or detailed lineages which include completely fictional names, so that untangling the genuine from the fabulous is extraordinarily difficult. A more precise example will help to illustrate the point: Geoffrey gives us a very detailed picture, with lots of topographical and architectural information, of a plenary court held by Arthur at the City of the Legions, Caerleon-on-Usk; what we are unable to disentangle is whether this detailed information came a) from Geoffrey's original sources, b) from his personal knowledge of the city or c) purely from his imagination.

Geoffrey himself gave his primary source as 'a certain very ancient book written in the British language' (which must mean early Welsh), which he claimed was given to him by Walter, Archdeacon of Oxford. This book has never been found. Yet, despite the difficulty with Geoffrey's book which all historians have acknowledged, some elements of the genuine historical background do appear somehow to 'break through' the fictions, as Lewis Thorpe describes:

> Much of this background material is twisted almost beyond recognition; but in earliest essence it has some element of truth. Geoffrey did not invent it. . . . In addition to the debt which he acknowledged to Walter's 'very ancient book' and to the book of the 'Prophecies of Merlin' which he said he translated, also from British, to please Alexander, Bishop of Lincoln, Geoffrey made many cross-references in the Vulgate text to such writers as Cicero, Juvenal, Lucan, Apuleius, Bede, King Alfred, etc. He can also be shown to have drawn upon Livy, Orosius and Virgil. . . . Finally, there is the archaeological

evidence, the fact that strange light has been thrown upon certain
of the alleged fancies of Geoffrey of Monmouth by subsequent
archaeological discoveries.[4]

The classic example of the last point is Geoffrey's account of how Merlin
magically brought the stones of Stonehenge piecemeal from Mount Killaraus
in Ireland to Salisbury Plain. The story was so fantastical that it was obviously one of Geoffrey's pure fictions. That was the prevailing historical view,
at least, until twentieth-century archaeology revealed that the Stonehenge
bluestones had, indeed, come overland and by sea from the Prescelly mountains in Wales, so that the essential idea of a colossal act of transportation
over a huge distance was shown to be historically accurate.

So what do we learn, if anything, about the historical Arthur from
Geoffrey's book? It is Geoffrey who first introduces the story of Merlin's
magic assisting Uther Pendragon to seduce Ygraine, wife of the Duke of
Cornwall. Does that mean that the real Arthur was born in Cornwall? The
answer is: possibly. Excavations at Tintagel headland have revealed extensive
fortifications dating from the Norman period, and monastic cells dating from
much earlier. There is a sea cave beneath the rocky isthmus which local
legend identifies as the cave in which Merlin was sealed for ever by the
enchantress Nimue or Vyvyan. Tintagel is an isolated headland, almost an
island, providing a virtually unassailable natural fortification; it is certainly
within the realms of possibility that it could have been one of the principal
fortifications of a Cornish king or chieftain of the sixth century. More persuasive are the references in some of the early Welsh vernacular texts to the
childhood home of Arthur as *Kelliwyk*. The name is Cornish, meaning 'wood
grove', and it is verifiably recorded as an earlier name for Callington, which
lies between Liskeard and Launceston at the junction of the A388 and A390.
Interestingly, the early Norman-French texts speak of Arthur's home as
Logres, which is derived from early Welsh *Lloegr*, the name for England,
which seems to suggest that the Welsh themselves, despite subsequent claims
to the contrary, knew that Arthur was not a Welshman by birth.

By the standards of modern fiction (let alone factual history), Geoffrey's
book is strangely uneven. Over a fifth of the book is devoted to Arthur, yet
this principal character leaves the main stage almost unnoticed. Geoffrey tells
us 'Arthur continued to advance, inflicting terrible slaughter as he went,' then
adds a few lines later, 'Arthur himself, our renowned King, was mortally
wounded and was carried off to the Isle of Avalon, so that his wounds might
be attended to.' Geoffrey tells us that Arthur 'handed the crown of Britain
over to his cousin Constantine, the son of Cador Duke of Cornwall: this in
the year 542 after our Lord's Incarnation'.[5] That is the last we hear of Arthur
in Geoffrey's book.

Constantius or Constantine was a very common ruler's name; it was
given to several of Rome's emperors. In its Celtic form, Costentyn, it was also
a common name in Brythonic legend, particularly in Cornwall. There is a

small parish between Falmouth and Helston which is still called Constantine. The first Constantine (clearly not the Constantine to whom Geoffrey refers) was converted to Christianity by a vision of a flaming cross, and took for his monogram the chrismon or chi-rho, which remains a potent symbol of Christian faith to this day. The name Constantine therefore became closely associated with the notion of constancy (that is the name's meaning) to the Christian faith. Therefore, even if the historical event of a dying Arthur giving his crown to a new King Constantine is one of Geoffrey's fictions, there is good reason to infer a historical fact from the fiction, namely that Arthur was, in all probability, a practising Christian. Gildas (as cited by Nennius), in the entry for the year AD 518, tells us that Arthur 'carried the cross of Our Lord Jesus Christ for three days and three nights on his shoulders and the Britons were the victors' at the Battle of Badon. Does this mean that Arthur literally carried a wooden cross for three days in some kind of ritual display, or is it a figurative expression meaning that Arthur represented the Christian cause ('carried the cross') during a battle which took three days to win? We shall never know the answer, but we can reasonably suggest that the evidence for Arthur's religious affiliation is sufficient.

Ironically, Arthur is recorded in various early accounts of saints' lives as an enemy of the church. In the *Life of St. Cadoc*, he demands cattle from Cadoc's abbey at Llancarfan (the cattle turn into ferns – one of the saint's miracles). In the *Life of St. Padarn*, Arthur is buried up to his neck as punishment for trying to steal from the saint. In the *Life of St. Carannog*, Arthur actually steals the saint's altar, and returns it only after the saint has helped him destroy a dragon which has been troubling the neighbourhood. There is a very plausible historical explanation for these apparently bizarre tales, as Geoffrey Ashe points out:

> The truth behind these queer stories may be that the real Arthur
> seized church property to supply his army, so the monks remembered
> him chiefly as an unwelcome visitor making demands on them. He
> sounds like a local ruler who sometimes leads forces outside his home
> territory. Although he is powerful, both churchmen and laymen can
> and do stand up to him.[6]

The title 'King' (*rex*) is first given to Arthur in these tales of saints' lives, not by Geoffrey of Monmouth. However, the implication is that this is a local or territorial king, not *the* King of all Britain.

Arthur's death was a matter of hot political debate in the twelfth century. Henry II came to the throne in 1154, claiming, among other things, descent from Arthur. In order for the claim to be valid, Arthur – fairly obviously – had to be dead. Although it seems strange to a modern sensibility, proving that Arthur was actually dead and not mysteriously still alive was very important to Henry. A Welsh polemical poem, *Armes Prydein* ('The Prophecy of Britain'), written in about 930, predicted the return of Cynan and Cadwaladr, two Welsh heroes of the past, who would unite the Celtic nations against the English and drive them back across the seas to where they came from and belonged. In 1113, some French priests were travelling in Cornwall, and one of their servants foolishly contradicted a Cornishman who stoutly bore witness that King Arthur had not died like other men, but was still alive; there was a vigorous and physical exchange of views which almost became a serious diplomatic incident. To this very day the Cornish Gorseth, the assembly of Bards (of which I am honoured to be a member), following the Welsh example, sings these words at its annual ceremonies:

Py kefer Myghtern Arthur? Ny wor den-vyth an le;
Whath nyns yw marow; ef a vew, hag arta ef a dhe!
('Where is King Arthur to be found? No one knows the place;
Still he is not dead; he lives, and he will come again!')

Arthur came to represent the Celtic spirit; he was an emblem of Celtic resistance to the Anglicization of Britain. Arthur was sleeping with his knights beneath the hills, and at the call of the trumpet he would return alive and in person, leading the Celts to victory and the restoration of the British kingdom. To say that Arthur was dead would be to say that the Brythonic Celtic nations were dead. When my fellow Cornish Bards sing those words, they are asserting Cornwall's Celtic nationhood, and Arthur is still their emblem, their symbolic leader and inspiration.

To produce his proof of Arthur's death, Henry announced that a Welsh minstrel had betrayed the secret of Arthur's resting place: it was the burial ground of Glastonbury Abbey. In 1190 the monks searched for the remains and found a grave (or so they reported) covered by a stone slab, and a cross inscribed in Latin thus: *Hic iacet sepultus inclitus rex Arturius in insula Avalonia* ('Here lies buried the renowned King Arthur in the Isle of Avalon'). (Although the cross itself no longer exists, it was supposedly faithfully copied. A drawing of it was published in William Camden's *Britannia*, published in 1607.) Alongside the skeleton of a tall man were found smaller bones, supposedly of a woman, and even wisps of yellow hair. So, Henry argued, here was indisputable evidence that Arthur was indeed dead, and this was his and Guinevere's grave. Glastonbury Abbey, close to Bath (Mons Badonicus?) and South Cadbury (Camelot?) was a very plausible final resting place for Arthur, and many of today's visitors to the Abbey accept Arthur's grave site as genuine.

We have no way of telling whether there was any historical truth behind the propaganda. Could the monks have lied about their discovery? There are lots of good reasons to believe they might. When Henry's son, Richard I, succeeded to the crown, he produced a sword which he claimed was Excalibur. (He later gave it to Tancred of Sicily during one of the crusades, and nobody knows its final whereabouts.) On the other hand, the Glastonbury grave really may have contained Arthur's bones, and Richard's sword really may have been six hundred years old, although that does seem much harder to believe. What we do know is that Arthur's legend had become so important by the twelfth century that even kings were forced as a political necessity to acknowledge it and to lay claim to it.

ARTHUR AS CELTIC KING

We have already established several of the qualities expected in an early Celtic tribal king or queen: physical perfection without blemish; beyond that, handsomeness or beauty, particularly largeness of stature; experience in battle; exemplary courage; the power of correct utterance and adherence to truth; respect for natural law; a highly developed sense of personal honour; skill in the arts, particularly the noble arts, such as *fiachell* or chess, and oratory; fertility or fecundity. The legendary Arthur clearly possesses these qualities in abundance. But Arthur, real and embellished, also has many qualities which are Roman: political skill; ability in military tactics, notably the effective use of cavalry; concern beyond the territorial or social and political boundaries of the tribe. Lastly, Arthur the historical commander and King Arthur the legendary knight both have qualities which are specifically Christian, although it is the Arthur of legend in whom these are most clearly discernible: devoutness; determination to resist heathen influence; compassion, and even humility; respect for women of any rank, particularly for mothers; dedication to a higher cause, no matter how great the personal sacrifice; a love of fellowship in worthy deeds. These qualities (notwithstanding one or two minor contradictions), when amalgamated, form a virtually complete image of the ideal knight of chivalry, as described endlessly in mediaeval romance.

Yet the image, which seems purely mediaeval, is not actually that far removed from its Celtic original. Indeed, not only is much of the subject content of the Matter of Britain reworked from earlier Celtic stories, much of its morality and significance is also still clearly descended from earlier Celtic beliefs. The tale of the Fisher King, with its underlying themes of sexual innocence, guilt and impotence (the king wounded in both thighs), appears to have much more to do with Chrétien de Troyes' mediaeval French preoccupations with original sin than with anything Celtic, but most of the Arthurian stories, even the obviously late and highly developed ones, seem to relate directly to a Celtic background. Even for Chrétien, most of the stories he wrote can be traced back to material in the Welsh *Mabinogion*, and his prologues frequently acknowledge earlier Celtic sources.

In some cases, the relationship is explicit. The Arthurian legend of the hunting of Twrch Trwyth, for example, has an exact parallel in the Irish Fenian legends. In the Book of Invasions, there is a king, transformed into a boar, whose name is Torc Triath – the name is identical, apart from the difference in Brythonic and Goidelic spelling. A ninth-century Irish story also refers to *oenach Tuirc Threith*, 'the assembly of Torc Triath'. Arthur and Finn both fight giants, magic creatures and lords of the underworld. The Irish tales of beheading, obviously directly related to the head-hunting cults and practices of the early tribal Celts, have a spectacular counterpart in the Arthurian tale of Sir Gawain and the Green Knight, written from Celtic sources by an unknown English author sometime before 1400, which became one of the most popular books in early mediaeval English literature. The story of Tristram and Yseult, or Tristan and Isolde, is paralleled by the very similar Irish tale, *The Pursuit of Diarmaid and Grainne*.

For some of the legendary elements in the Arthurian tales, it is not clear whether the origin was Celtic or not. For example, we know that Arthur's unusual birth circumstances are definitely Celtic; tale after tale in the Celtic mythology has the hero either born out of wedlock, or of an incestuous relationship, and there seems to have been some deep-seated connection between

The leaden cross supposedly found during the excavation of Arthur's grave at Glastonbury Abbey. From a drawing by William Camden, 1607.

such recurring themes and actual social practices, such as fosterage, temporary marriage and concubinage. However, when we look at the legends surrounding Arthur's mysterious half-sister, Morgan le Fay, the origins are more obscure. Some writers have tried to relate her name to that of the Irish wargoddess, the Morrigan, but that is clearly a simple mistake. Morrigan has two elements: *mor* is 'great' and *rigan* is 'queen'. Morgan also has two elements, but the first, *mor*, is Brythonic for 'sea', and the second, *gan*, means 'born'. In Geoffrey of Monmouth's history, Morgan is described as one of nine sisters who preside over *insula pomorum que fortunata vocatur* ('the island of apples which is called blessed', i.e. Avalon). An early French manuscript refers to her as *Morgain le deesse* ('the goddess'). Giraldus Cambrensis later refers to her as *dea phantastica* ('goddess apparition'), and she is called in *Sir Gawain and the Green Knight* simply 'Morgne the goddes'. It seems highly likely that all these representations of Morgan as a supernatural being are merely reflective of the literally hundreds of Celtic goddesses of ancient tradition, but clear and specific parallels are harder to draw.

Nevertheless, many of the Arthurian themes and motifs, even from the later mediaeval material, can be seen to have their origins in the religious beliefs, mores and practices of the ancient Celts. The heroic warrior code is virtually unchanged: a short life if necessary, but filled with honour. The rules for hospitality are strict; in *Culhwch and Olwen*, the hero is promised 'meat for thy dogs and corn for thy horse, and hot peppered chops for thyself and wine brimming over . . . a woman to sleep with thee, and delectable songs before thee' when Arthur receives him as a guest. The ancient Celtic law of *fir fer*, or 'fair play', is invoked in spirit if not in name in tale after tale. Some of Arthur's named warrior companions are Celtic gods lifted directly from the pantheon: Mabon mab Modron (Son son of Mother), Manawydan mab Llyr (son of Lear) and Llwch Llauynnaug (Lugh the Longhanded) among them. The enchanted islands and magic castles in which various Arthurian heroes find themselves as guest or prisoner are all variants of Tir na n'Og, the Land of the Ever Young, or Avallen, the apple orchard of eternal summer, respectively the Goidelic and Brythonic versions of Paradise. In the seemingly bizarre tale of Twrch Trwyth, the king magically transformed into a boar with a comb and scissors in his mane, we see obvious parallels to the original Celtic preoccupation with hair as the outstanding attribute of physical beauty, as well as the theme of shape-shifting, which also occurs very frequently in early Celtic mythology. In the tale of Arthur's judgment given to Gwythyr mab Greidiawl and Gwynn mab Nudd, that they shall fight each May Day until the Day of Judgment for possession of the beautiful maiden Creiddylad, we see the ancient Celtic seasonal myth, which, like the very similar Greek legend of Persephone, begins with an intended rape and ends with an arrangement which balances the seasons harmoniously. A very similar story appears in Caradoc of Llancarfan's *Life of St. Gildas*, in which Guinevere is abducted by Melwas of Somerset (Malory calls him Mellyagraunce) and taken to Glastonbury, from which she is rescued by Arthur. (In the Welsh triads, it is Medraut or Mordred who abducts Guinevere, which leads to the Battle of Camlann, and Arthur's death.)

In the story of the Grail, which would appear to be most obviously Christian rather than Celtic, the Celtic origins are actually even more clearly discernible. There are very frequent references throughout early Celtic literature to magic cauldrons and vessels of plenty. There are cauldrons which produce food endlessly, so that no guest need ever be turned away unsatisfied. There is the cauldron of Tyrnoc, which, like the cauldron of Annwn (the Underworld), will not cook food for a coward. In an early Welsh poem called *The Spoils of Annwn* (date and author unknown), Arthur sails in his magical ship *Prydwen* to the underworld to seize this magical cauldron. The cauldron is decorated with pearls, and kindled by the breath of nine maidens. Its hiding place is variously called Caer Wydr ('The Fortress of Glass'), Caer Feddwid ('The Fortress of Feasting') and Caer Siddi ('The Fairy Fortress'). While many of the later Grail stories abound in Christian images and references, this underlying pagan idea of the 'vessel of plenty' is never entirely absent.

The otherworld, which appears throughout Celtic literature as a place of literally infinite charm, because no one grows old there, or has to toil, and food, drink and entertainment are always magically supplied, is also a place of danger for mortals, precisely because it is so attractive. Many of the Arthurian tales involve the hero (usually a knight) wandering into an enchanted forest, or a castle made of glass, or an island, and there doing battle with mysterious creatures, or being tempted by magical seductresses. The early Celtic name for Glastonbury was Ynys Wedren, 'The Isle of Glass', which places it firmly in the Celtic otherworld tradition. In the main legend of Arthur himself, the otherworld and otherworldly magic are constantly recurring themes: Arthur is conceived by magical shape-shifting; he reveals his right to the throne by drawing the sword from the stone, a superhuman feat; his sword Caledfwlch or Excalibur possesses magical qualities; and so on. In the otherworld there is no death, and no time. The hero is a hero because he can enter this otherworld and return safely to the mundane world; in other words, he can cheat death. The same idea is widespread in classical mythology: Theseus penetrates the labyrinth and destroys the Minotaur; Jason sails in the Argo to Aeëtes and brings back the Golden Fleece; Hercules kills the dragon which guards the golden apples of immortality in the Garden of the Hesperides. What makes the Celtic versions distinctive is the immediacy of the otherworld, the sense that it is close at hand. Caesar describes Celtic warriors making agreements that if they were to die in the coming battle they would settle their cash debts in the next world; he was impressed by how easily and automatically they assumed an immediate and real afterlife.

The origin of the Celtic hero's ability to penetrate the otherworld and return is probably shamanic. The shaman, or priest-magician, was a familiar figure in many early societies; it was his or her task to travel (in trance, or in a state of altered consciousness induced by various means, including drugs) to the otherworld and make intercessions on behalf of the living, and then return. The story of Christ descending to Hell to release the souls held in torment there (usually called the 'harrowing' of Hell) is actually quite similar in idea to these earlier shamanic and pagan journeys to the otherworld. A distinctively Celtic theme in these journeys is shape-shifting, changing into a swan, or a dog, or another human, then changing back again. Although shape-shifting does also appear in classical mythology, it is found so frequently in Celtic mythology that it could be described as an identifying feature.

The unusual circumstances of Arthur's conception and birth place him clearly in the Celtic tradition. In many Celtic tales, the hero's father is a god, animal or creature from another race, while the hero is born as a result of incest, rape or deception. Even Celtic saints follow the same pattern: St. Finan's mother was made pregnant by a salmon in Loch Lein, St. David and St. Cynog were the products of rape, and so on. Arthur is also the product of a kind of rape, since Uther Pendragon had deceived Ygraine into thinking that he was her husband, Gorlois. For the Celts, the unusual birth allowed for the release of unusual energy or ferocity. The ordinary mortal, born of ordinary parents in ordinary circumstances, can never achieve the necessary magical energy to become a hero.

The mediaeval monks who committed the Arthurian stories to parchment had a hard time with many of these pagan sexual themes and ideas. They made great play of Perceval's virginity, for example, and much of the later Arthurian material contains a strange mixture of original Celtic lustiness overlain by almost obsessive Christianized themes of abstinence, continence and sexual purity. The Questing Beast, which is a late addition to the stories, represents the Christian terror of incest. A princess makes sexual advances to her brother; she is impregnated by the Devil; the brother is eaten by a pack of dogs; the princess gives birth to the monstrous Questing Beast, which is made up of many different animal parts, and from whose belly the sound of yelping dogs can be heard.

For a king, the required sexual energy and potency is enormous. The king has to have the power to mate with the entire land, and evidence of possession of such power is a frequent theme in Celtic mythological literature. In several versions of the Arthurian legend, Modred forges a letter saying that Arthur has been killed in France. Guinevere grieves his loss, but the nobles (or druids) tell her that she must marry Modred immediately. Modred's lust for Guinevere, like Uther Pendragon's lust for Ygraine, is unbearable, uncontainable, vastly greater than ordinary sexual lust, because it is the lust for kingship, not merely for fleshly pleasure. Guinevere represents the land of Britain itself, with which the king must mate. Modred's day of birth is given as May Day, which identifies him with Bel, the young sun god, and by implication identifies Arthur with Bran or Lugh, the autumnal or father god.

In many ways, the same parallel is even clearer with Lancelot and Arthur.

The ancient Celtic mythological pattern is of the eternal, unchanging goddess (the land, the kingdom, the nation, Madron, the mother) who gives birth to her son (the people, Mabon, the son), who becomes the father of succeeding generations, but then is overtaken by them. The father-king must die so that the son-king may replace him, in an endless repetition of abdication, in order to ensure the continuing fertility of the land. The love triangle of Arthur, Lancelot and Guinevere is very human and modern in its emotional appeal, but it is also representative of an ancient archetype. In the mythological sense, the kingdom falls into dissolution after Arthur's death not so much because Modred is no longer alive, but rather because Lancelot, the Bel figure to Arthur's Bran figure, cannot possess Guinevere, who is Britain. The variant tale of Melwas or Mellyagraunce abducting Guinevere, and of Arthur rescuing her, is almost identical to the Persephone legend, and has the same connotations of a seasonal mystery.

Similarly, many of the chivalric qualities which emerge in the Matter of Britain have their origins in much more ancient Celtic archetypes. The chivalric ideals included courage, generosity, honesty, loyalty, courtesy and honour. The idea that correct or true utterance has sacred power is druidic in origin. Although the gloss is frequently Christianized in the mediaeval literature, the frequent verbal contracts, oaths of allegiance, or public undertakings to perform certain deeds which recur throughout the Arthurian stories have their origins in this ancient druidic teaching. The power of the chivalric ideal can be seen in a real-life incident: King John II of France was captured by the English at the Battle of Poitiers in 1356. He was allowed to return to France to try to raise the ransom money demanded by the English, and his son, Louis of Anjou, took his place in the London gaol. When Louis escaped from London, John voluntarily returned to prison in London, in order that his honour should not be stained by his son's breaking of his word. In fact, the word 'parole', which we now use for early release of prisoners, means 'word' in French, and is descended from the chivalric tradition that an honourable prisoner could give his *parole* or word that he would return to prison if the terms for his release were not subsequently honoured. The Celtic practice of fosterage, in which oral contracts had such significance, also contributed to this ideal of the power of the spoken word.

Arthur's drawing of the sword from the stone is reminiscent of the legends surrounding the Lia Fail, or Stone of Destiny, which was reputed to shriek when, and only when, it was touched by the true and rightful High King of Ireland. According to the semi-legends of misty history, the Lia Fail was taken by Irish settlers to Scotland, where it became known as the Stone of Scone (pronounced 'Skoon'); to cement the hegemony of English kings over Scotland it was brought by Edward I to Westminster Abbey, where it resided for many centuries under the coronation throne; it was stolen from the Abbey by Scottish Nationalists in 1950, and not recovered until 1952; and it has recently been returned to Edinburgh. The Irish would claim, however, that the Lia Fail never left Ireland at all.

The preoccupation with blows to the head, and with severed heads, which is apparent throughout Arthurian literature, is also directly descended from Celtic beliefs. The Celts venerated the head as the seat of the individual personality, and practised head-hunting, including the construction of shrines in which captured heads could be displayed. It is interesting that Arthur dies from a blow to the head. One of the supposed pieces of convincing evidence given by the monks of Glastonbury that the body they had found was Arthur's was a deep gash in the skull. Similarly, Gawain, who is given Arthur's invincible sword Excalibur during the battle against Lancelot, is finally overcome in a subsequent battle not because anyone defeats him, but because an old head wound bursts open, and he dies. The cult of the head, and of the soul residing in the head, explains why there is so much gory head hacking in the early Celtic vernacular texts, and subsequently in Arthurian literature generally.

Gawain, interestingly, is described as Arthur's heir (rather than Modred) in some of the legendary material, and this is derived directly from actual Celtic social practice, in which a man's nephew, his sister's son, had a special right of inheritance. The name Gawain, originally spelled Gawan or Gawen, is derived from Welsh *Gwalchmei* ('Hawk of May'), or possibly from *Gwri Golt Adwyn* ('Man of the Shining Hair'). The variant Gavin derives from the French variants Gauvain and Gavain. There may have been a real Gawain. For kings born without issue, the sister's son may well have been next in line for the kingship, although this is not verifiable. However, it is a pattern which is found elsewhere in the Arthurian tales: Tristram is King Mark's nephew, and Perceval is the nephew of the Grail King. In the legends, Gawain's strength increases as the day goes on, reaching its peak at noon, when it begins to fade, which obviously identifies him with Bel and other sun-god types.

The story of Gawain and the Green Knight begins on New Year's Day, when a strange knight, dressed all in green, with green hair and skin, arrives at Camelot and challenges Arthur's knights. Gawain accepts the peculiar challenge, which is to deliver a single blow to the knight's head in exchange for a return blow a year and a day hence. Gawain beheads the Green Knight, who promptly picks up his severed head and rides out of the court, reminding Gawain of his promise. Gawain keeps his word, and a year and a day later he rides to the Green Chapel in the forest. Here he is met by Sir Bercilak, his beautiful wife, and an old hag (who is Morgan Le Fay in disguise). Sir Bercilak's wife attempts to seduce Gawain, who resists the temptation, although he does accept a green silk girdle from her. When the day of the return blow comes, the Green Knight's axe delivers only a slight nick to Gawain's skin (a token of his slight sin in accepting the girdle). The Green Knight transforms into Sir Bercilak, and explains that the whole magical episode was devised by Morgan in an attempt to discredit the Round Table. While the themes of chastity, resistance to temptation, and keeping one's word even in the direst circumstances all seem transparently Christian, the underlying motifs are pagan Celtic. The beheading game, or the theme of the returned blow, occurs in several earlier Celtic legends, notably in the Irish tale of *Bricriu's Feast*, where the hero is Cu Chulainn. In this version, the giant brings the axe down on Cu Chulainn's neck with the blunt side down, as a token of respect for his courage for submitting to the blow in the first place. The challenger is genuinely from the otherworld, not merely a mortal temporarily transformed by witchery, and the virtue rewarded is the warrior's virtue of undaunted courage, rather than the chivalric knight's virtue of chastity, but many of the stories' elements are very similar.

Even the Siege Perelous, which seems indisputably late and Christian in origin, may have pagan Celtic antecedents. The legend of the Round Table was tremendously popular, and it is not difficult to see that it represented both a universal idea, namely the roundness of the whole earth, or whole universe, but also a more specific historic image, that of Christ and his disciples together at a table for the Last Supper. The Siege Perelous, the empty seat which can only be taken by a knight who is morally perfect and absolutely pure in heart, is the positive counterpart of Judas Iscariot's negative place at the Last Supper. The universe can only be made whole when the place of the sinner and traitor is taken by a saint, the Grail hero, Galahad. Earlier legends had Arthur ordering the construction of the table at Merlin's suggestion, but in later versions it is brought to Arthur as a marriage gift from Guinevere. In both versions, and in all subsequent elaborations, the Round Table is deeply symbolic of harmony, and mutuality of purpose. However, there is plenty of evidence to suggest that the notion of people in a circle representing harmony and common purpose is much older than Christianity; the hundreds of stone circles still standing in Britain and Ireland are obvious testimony to that. It is highly likely that processions and assembly in circles were normal routines in druidic ceremonial practice. The modern Welsh, Cornish and Breton *gorseddau* always form a large circle for their gatherings.

Merlin, who figures so prominently in the legendary material, may have been a genuine historical figure, although probably not contemporary with the real Arthur. His original name was Myrddin; some writers have suggested that Geoffrey of Monmouth changed the name to Merlin because Myrddin was too reminiscent of the Norman-French word *merde* ('shit') for his important new character to attain the necessary dignity. The whole story of the original Myrddin is pursued very entertainingly by Nikolai Tolstoy in *The Quest for Merlin,*[7] which I warmly recommend to the reader. Carmarthen (*Caer Myrddin,* 'Myrddin's Fortress') in Wales is said to be named after the original bard and prophet on whom Geoffrey's Merlin was based, although the name could also signify 'Sea Fortress'. Myrddin was associated with the Battle of Arfderydd, which is now Arthuret, north of Carlisle. At this battle, Myrddin's king, Gwenddolau, was defeated and killed by Rhydderch Hael, King of Strathclyde, and Myrddin was so distressed by the carnage that he became insane, and for many years wandered the Caledonian Forest in the Scottish Lowlands as a kind of lunatic seer, developing a reputation as a wise man of the woods who could foretell the future. There is an ancient Welsh poem, *Afallenau* ('Apple Trees'), attributed to Myrddin, which lists the poet's sorrows and loneliness in his mad exile in the forest, and which includes the line, 'Death has taken everyone; why does it not call me?' Some writers have interpreted this sentiment as the origin of the notion that Merlin lives time backwards, or is immortal.

The Arthurian legends have had a profound impact on western culture generally, and on British culture in particular. When Henry VII's first son was born, the king made sure that he was born and christened at Winchester (identified as the site of Camelot), and that he was named Arthur. Arthur II would restore Britain's Golden Age, and bring a longed-for peace after the harrowing strife of the Wars of the Roses. In the event, Arthur died young, and Britain got Henry VIII instead (who turned out, as it happened, to have many Arthurian qualities). There has never been a historical King Arthur since then. Perhaps the name is too dangerous, not least because it would raise many expectations which were created in the powerful stories of the legendary King Arthur. Of the real Arthur, we still know very little, but his inheritance is vast. Like Boudica, he has become a symbol of tragic greatness, but the stirring tales in which the facts of his existence were transmogrified into legend have extended his story across the whole world. It is a story which appeals to all ages. John Milton considered writing a great epic poem about Arthur, but changed his mind and wrote *Paradise Lost* instead. Tennyson based his hugely popular epic poem *Idylls of the King* on the Arthurian legends. There have been many notable versions of the legends in modern fiction, and no doubt there are many more to come.

Notes

1   *A History of the English Speaking Peoples*, pp. 60–61.
2   *Historia Brittonum*, 56.
3   See Geoffrey Ashe, *All about King Arthur*, pp. 111–112.
4   Introduction to the Penguin Classics edition, p.18.
5   *History of the Kings of Britain*, IX.2.
6   *All about King Arthur*, p. 69.
7   Published by Hamish Hamilton, London, 1985; in Coronet edition, 1986; and by Hodder and Stoughton (Sceptre imprint), 1988.

NINE

THE HIGH KINGS OF IRELAND TO THE MIDDLE AGES

AS WE observed in Chapter Five, separating myth from historical fact in early Irish history is at least as difficult as distinguishing the real Arthur and the legendary King Arthur. When we come to look specifically at the lineage of the High Kings of All Ireland, the Ard Righe, our most immediate problem is deciding where to start. King Bres ('the Beautiful'), born of a Fomorian father and a Danaan mother, who acted as surrogate for Nuada after the latter had lost his arm in battle, is still clearly a purely mythological figure. So too (in all probability) is Eremon, one of the three leaders of the Milesians, who became (at least in legend) the first High King of All Ireland after defeating his brother Eber Finn in battle.

There follows a procession of Milesian High Kings, about whose actual existence little can be said. Tighernmas, seventh in the Milesian line, is said to have first smelted gold and introduced gold ornaments to Ireland. The twenty-first Milesian king is said to have been Ollam Fodla, a great poet and seer (the name is an epithet, translated by early Irish historiographers as 'Doctor of Wisdom'), who reputedly established the very first *feis Temro* ('Feast of Tara'), at which the High King was affirmed. The word *feis* is derived from Old Irish *fo-aid* ('sleeps with'), signifying that at this gathering the High King 'slept with' or mated with the land in a ritual marriage.

Several of the early High Kings are obvious personifications of this ancient notion of ritual marriage between the king and the land, or the presiding goddess of the land. King Ailill Olam of Munster, for example, dared to attempt the rape of Aine, a goddess of love and fertility descended from the sea god Manannan Mac Lir. The goddess destroyed him with her magic. Knockainy ('Aine's hill') in County Kerry is named after the goddess, and was the site of Midsummer Eve celebrations in her honour well into the nineteenth century. Another Ailill, this one the brother of the High King Eochaid, made the mistake of falling in love with his brother's wife, Etain. Etain was also a goddess, one of the Tuatha de Danann. Ailill's unrequited love for Etain brought him into a wasting disease, and finally death. In both stories, the goddess represents the agricultural fertility of the land, and the inappropriateness of the would-be lover or king leads eventually to his death. A third King Ailill, this one King Ailill Mac Mata of Connaught, was the weak and ineffectual husband of Queen Medb. As a result of her taunts, he agreed to go to war with Ulster over the Brown Bull of Cuailgne (Cooley), the story of which forms the basis for the great epic, the *Tain Bo Cuailnge* ('Cattle Raid of Cooley').

One of the Milesian High Kings was a queen: Macha Mong Ruad ('Macha of the red hair'). Macha was the daughter of Aod Ruad ('Aod the Red'). When her father died, she fought off one king, Dithorba, killing him in battle, and married another, Cimbaoth, to secure the throne. After Cimbaoth died, she ruled alone. The ancient capital of Ulster, Emhain Macha ('the twins of Macha'), was named in honour of her sons. Macha's foster-son, Ugani Mor ('the Great'), is said to have led the first Irish raids against Britain.

Conaire Mor supposedly reigned in the first century BC, driving out his four foster-brothers, who returned with a British force and destroyed Meath and killed Conaire, an event which is recorded in the ancient folk tale *Bruighean Da Derga*. There is a legend of birth in peculiar circumstances for Conaire, as with many of the Celtic heroes. His mother's story is a little reminiscent of the story of Snow White. Her name was Mes Buachalla ('foster-child of the cowherd'), and she was the daughter of Cormac, king of Ulster. However, Cormac was so disappointed at having a daughter instead of a son that he ordered the baby girl thrown into a pit in the forest. The servants could not bring themselves to kill the infant, so they gave her instead to a poor cowherd, who raised her with tender care. She grew to be so beautiful that, despite her apparently lowly origins, the High King Eterscel decided to marry her. On the very eve of her wedding, however, Mes Buachalla slept with the bird-god, Nemglan. The son born of this union was Conaire Mor, whom Mes Buachalla passed off as the son of Eterscel. Throughout his life, the great Conaire was under a *geis* or taboo that he must never kill a bird.

The legend which describes Conaire's accession to the High Kingship is typically Celtic, and again reminiscent of Arthurian legend. After Eterscel died, Ireland fell into disarray. The druids assembled and agreed to follow the ancient custom of *tarbhfhess*, the bull-sleep. The sleeper was chosen, and ate his meal of fresh beef and broth from a newly slain bull. The druids chanted over him as he slept. When he awoke, he announced his vision: the next High King would be found walking on the road towards Tara, stark naked, carrying a bird sling in his hand. The druids set out on foot to find him. In the meanwhile, Conaire Mor, riding his chariot towards Tara, was suddenly surrounded by a flock of birds. Since he was hungry, he took out his sling and made ready to fire at them. The birds immediately shed their feathers and became warriors, launching a ferocious attack on Conaire. They were stopped, however, by their leader, who stepped forward and introduced himself as Conaire's father, Nemglan. The god reminded Conaire of the *geis* against him, and Conaire was ashamed. He accepted his father's punishment, which was that he should abandon everything he owned, even his clothing, and walk barefoot back to Tara, carrying only the sling to remind him of his sin. The druids found him shortly thereafter, and he was received at Tara as the High King.

Another of these great early Milesian kings was Conchobhar or Conor Mac Nessa, who reputedly reigned during Christ's lifetime. To Conchobhar's court belong the tales of the deeds of the hero Cu Chulainn, to which we shall return in Chapter Eleven. Conchobhar himself was supposedly the son of Fachtna Fathach ('Fachtna the Giant') and Nessa, although Nessa in fact slept with a druid on her wedding eve (just as Mes Buachalla had slept with a god) and the child was raised as though it were Fachtna's. Conchobhar had the misfortune to fall in love with Deirdre or Derdriu, usually known as Deirdre of the Sorrows. When Deirdre was born, the druid Cathbad gave a prophecy that she would be the most beautiful woman in Ireland, she would marry a king, and she would cause death and destruction throughout the land. She fulfilled the prophecy by marrying Conchobhar when he was an old man, and then leaving him for the younger Naoise, precipitating terrible wars between Conchobhar and Naoise's king, Fergus Mac Roth. Conchobhar eventually died of a 'brain ball', a magical ball made by Conall from the brains of a slain Leinster king, which Fergus threw with a sling to lodge in Conchobhar's skull. When Conchobhar fell into a rage in his old age, the ball exploded and killed him.

In the first century AD, according to the legends, the Milesian dynasty was temporarily broken by a rebellion led by Carbri Cinn Cait ('Carbri Cat Head' – Kincaid or Kincead are modern variants of the same name), whose reign produced famine and disease, because he was a usurper, not a rightful High King. Some years later, the Milesian dynasty was restored when Tuathal Feachtmar ('Tuathal the Desired One') returned from exile in Britain and won (by repute) 133 battles in order to secure the High Kingship. It was Tuathal who established Meath as the fifth fifth of Ireland, the province of the Ard Righ, and re-established the *feis Temro* at Tara. He also built palaces in the other four provinces, at Tlachtga in Leinster, at Uisnech in Munster, at Cruachan in Connaught, and at Taillte in Ulster. (A stone fort called the Grianan of Ailech, which stands inside an ancient hillfort in County Donegal, is supposed to have been a separate capital for the kings of western Ulster. Emhain Macha, the capital of Ulster according to many of the tales, was sited at Navan Fort in County Armagh.) Five arterial roads radiated outwards from Tara: the Slighe Midluachra, or Northern Road; the Slighe Cualann, which ran in the direction of modern County Wicklow; the Slighe Asail, which ran south; the Slighe Dala, which ran southwest; and the Slighe Mor ('Great Road') which ran westward to Galway.

Alwyn and Brinley Rees identify a number of features which are common to many of the heroic and semi-mythic High Kings: the king's advent and future greatness have been foretold; his arrival brings death or misfortune to a presiding power, often a relative; his mother has to overcome great difficulties before he can be born; his birth circumstances are unusual, often involving incest, siring by a god or supernatural being, or an unusual fostering arrangement; his coming is heralded by events in the natural world; certain totem animals are associated with his birth or upbringing; he displays amazing qualities in earliest youth; he is often given an unusual name.[1] We shall return to the gods and mythic archetypes in more detail in Chapter Eleven.

By the time of Tuathal, it may be that we are dealing with real, historical personages rather than figures of pure mythology, but the dividing boundary is extremely difficult to discover. The next two High Kings of significance, Cathair Mor and Conn of the Hundred Battles, appear to have been genuine historical leaders. Cathair is said to have left a detailed will at his death, and copies of this document were made through succeeding ages. Conn, as his name suggests, did a lot of fighting. It was Conn's enemy, Mogh, who returned from banishment in Spain and established dominion in the south of Ireland, so that the island came to be divided into two halves, the northern half being Leth Cuinn, or Conn's Half, and the southern kingdom being Leth Mogha, or Mogh's Half. The two southern kingdoms, Leinster and Munster, fared differently, with Leinster being the weaker partner. For centuries, the early chronicles tell us, the people of Leinster were forced to pay the *boroimhe* or cattle tribute to the Ard Righ, a duty which they greatly resented and occasionally rebelled against. The story of the Battle of Dun Bolg tells how Leinster warriors were smuggled into Tara hidden in baskets loaded on three hundred teams of twelve oxen each, then burst out of their hiding places, like the Trojans from the Wooden Horse, to overcome the High King's warriors.

However, even in the lives of these High Kings, who appear to have been genuine historical figures, there are interwoven tales of adventure which clearly belong to the world of mythology. For example, Conn of the Hundred Battles is reputed to have taken as his mistress the goddess Becuma Cneisgel ('Becuma the Healer'). Becuma was jealous of the attention Conn showed to his son, Art, so she contrived to have him sent off on a journey to the Land of Wonder to seek out Delbchaem ('Fair Shape'), a feat which Art achieved after several perilous adventures. The tale is highly reminiscent of the Arthurian stories of knights pursuing almost impossible quests in dangerous, enchanted lands.

Another High King who undertook magical journeys was Ferghus Mac Leda of Ulster, who owned a pair of magical shoes which allowed him to travel underwater. The shoes had belonged to King Iubdan, a king of the faery folk, who gave them to Ferghus in exchange for his release from captivity. With them, Ferghus explored the lakes and rivers of Ireland (all places of high magic in druidic tradition) and acquired all the strength which comes to the hero who dares to venture into otherworld places. In Loch Rory, however, he met a river-horse of such terrifying ferocity that his face became permanently distorted by fear. Now blemished, he could no longer rule as High King. Ferghus abdicated, and returned to Loch Rory to fight the monster which had brought him such sorrow. He slew the river-horse, and his face regained its original beauty, but in the course of the battle he lost the magic in his water shoes, and he drowned.

Cormac Mac Art was Conn's grandson. His father Art, who had pursued the Delbchaem, had been called Art the Lonely, because his brothers Connla and Crionna had both been killed in battle. Cormac, whose reign is tentatively assigned from AD 227 to 263, is said to have rebuilt and greatly extended the palace at Tara, including the great banqueting hall, over 235 metres (760 ft) long, known as the Teach Mi Chuarta. He was reputedly a great and wise High King, frequently compared with Solomon. He also has a tale of strange birth, his mother Etain having fallen asleep after bearing the child, and a she-wolf taking him away to raise with her cubs. The Fenian tales, the saga of Fionn or Finn Mac Cool, belong to the court of King Cormac. The Book of Leinster records that Cormac had a retinue of over three thousand, and that his court had a decidedly international flavour: it was frequented by Gauls, Romans, Franks, Friesians, Caledonians, Picts and Saxons. It is very difficult to imagine such diverse visitors at Tara all at one time, but that is what the Book of Leinster says happened. Cormac is said to have introduced the first watermill to Ireland. His reign ended when his son, Cellach, had insulted a woman of the Deisi clan, and the clan leader or petty king, Aonghus, put out the High King's eye in a fight; the High King could no longer reign if there was any blemish in his person. In his retirement, from 263 to his death in 267, he is said to have written several books, including *Teagasc an Riogh* ('The Teaching of a King'), a kind of manual on how to be an effective monarch, although the genuine authorship is attributed by most historians to a much later author, in part because of its linguistic style. The Book of Acaill, also attributed to Cormac, was an important source for later law treatises, including the Brehon laws. The following extract from *Teagasc an Riogh* confirms the great importance of correct utterance and the telling of truth in the Celtic tradition:

> By the king's truth great people are ruled.
> By the king's truth great mortality is driven off from his people.
> By the king's truth great battles are sent into the territory of the enemy.
> By the king's fair truth fair weather comes in each proper season, with
> winter fine and frosty, spring dry and windy, summer warm with
> showers, autumn with heavy dews and fruit.
> For it is the king's falsehood which brings ill-omened weather on wicked
> people and dries up the fruits of the earth.

Frequently in the vernacular tales a false utterance or judgment is followed by some natural catastrophe: cattle cease to give milk, the streams and wells run dry, the fruit withers on the vine, the fish disappear from the rivers and lakes. In one tale, the part of the palace of Tara where a High King delivered a false judgment collapsed and could not be rebuilt.

After Cormac, there followed several generations of High Kings, among whom Muiredeach Tireach is especially notable for his reign of twenty-seven years, during which there was considerable strife between Ulster and the rest of Ireland. For a short while, part of Ulster became a new and separate kingdom, Oirgialla or Oriel.

Throughout these successions, there is a pattern of queenship which is historically unclear, but which makes mythographic sense. Queen Medb of Connaught, herself a daughter of a king of Tara, is said to have been wife to King Conchobhar, but is said also to have mated with Tinda Mac Connra, with Eochaid Dala, and with Ailill Mac Mata, each of whom became King of Connaught. Another Medb, Queen Medb Lethderg of Leinster, daughter of Conan of Cuala, was (according to the legends) the wife of nine High Kings in succession, including four generations of father and son, ending with Art and Cormac Mac Art. Although the historical reality may have been different, the meaning of the story is clear: the kingship is a marriage to the goddess of the land, or to her personification, and without the approval and consent of the queen or goddess, the High King cannot rule: 'Great indeed was the power of Medb over the men of Ireland, for she it was who would not allow a king in Tara without his having herself as wife.'[2] The name Medb (also Mebh and Maeve) is closely related to the Brythonic word *meddw* (Welsh) or *medhow* (Cornish), meaning 'drunk', and to the English word *mead*. Medb is 'the intoxicating one'. She is the Queen of Plenty.

The first High King whose historical existence is absolutely undisputed is Niall Noigiallach, or Niall of the Nine Hostages, grandson of Muiredeach Tireach. Niall was one of the Scotti, the bands of raiders who made frequent incursions into Britain. We have precise dates for his raids on Chester and Caerleon (395) and his death at sea (405). His descendants, known as the Ui Neill, ruled as High Kings of Ireland for almost six centuries. Even some of the saints claimed ancestry from him: Colm Cille, or St. Columba, was of the Ui Neill, and was nephew to a High King, Muircetach Mac Erca.

Niall's father, Eochaid Muighmedon, became High King somewhere around AD 350. Niall's mother was Carthann, a British queen. Eochaid subsequently remarried and his new queen, Mong Fionn ('Fair Hair'), bore him four further sons. There is a legend that when Niall and his half-brothers were still youths, Eochaid set fire to a smithy in which they were shoeing horses to see how each son would cope. Brian saved the chariots; Ailill saved a sword and a shield; Fiachra picked up the trough; and witless Ferghus picked up a bundle of firewood. Only Niall had the sense to pick up the anvil block and the tools, and his father recognized immediately that Niall would be the next Ard Righ. Another legend tells of the five brothers out hunting, working up a great thirst, and coming to a clear stream, where a withered, hideous hag told them that any of them who wanted to drink must first kiss her and lie with her. Only Niall did so. Immediately, the hag turned into the most beautiful of maidens, and made the four half-brothers swear loyalty to Niall as High King. This legend is an obvious variant of the traditional notion of the rightful king marrying or mating with the kingdom. The hag-maiden is Eireann herself.

The small colony of Scotti who had sailed from Antrim across the water was soon beset by Picts from the north and east. Niall crossed the Irish Sea to defend the colony, drove the Picts backwards, and established Argyle and Cantire as Scottish (Irish Alban) territories. (This Irish/Scottish kingdom, known as the Dal Riada after its founding king, Carbri Riada, was finally declared an independent kingdom at the Convention of Drimceatt or Drum Cett in 575.)

The legend says that Niall was killed in Gaul by a fellow-Irishman, King Eochaid of Leinster, who ambushed him, but the general agreement among historians is that his death was more mundane: his ship capsized in a sea battle, and he was drowned along with the rest of the crew, in AD 405.

Niall died about fifty years, or two generations, before Patrick came to Ireland. By the time Diarmait Mac Cerbaill (Diarmuid O'Carroll) was crowned Ard Righ in 558, or thereabouts, two generations after Patrick's arrival, Ireland was changing from a deeply religious pagan country to a deeply religious Christian country. In a devastating plague in 548, two great monastic founders, Finnian of Clonard and Ciaran of Clonmacnoise (both later canonized), had died. Christian families bequeathed large estates in their memory, and the large monastic foundations began growing rapidly during the second half of the sixth century. Many of the abbots belonged themselves to leading families, or could claim indirect kinship with noble and even royal houses. It became a tradition for at least one son from each noble household to join the church, usually by going to the monastery at which one of his fore-bears or kinsmen was a noted founder or early luminary. These large monas-tic foundations thrived with very little interruption until the ninth century, when Viking incursions began breaking up the system.

The claims and counterclaims of High Kingship now become confused not because, as earlier, we are struggling to separate myth from reality, but because the geographical and territorial issues start to become very complex as we look at how the Ui Neill spread their influence wider. The sea voyages and incursions continued, and small kingdoms came and went in more rapid succession. By the time the Vikings arrived, the situation was even more volatile and confused. Between 832 and 870 the Viking incursions presented the greatest threats to the monastic settlements, which had become very wealthy; an abbot or a scribe of great talent was sometimes a more lucrative hostage than a petty king or nobleman. Moreover, the battles were not always between Irishmen and Norsemen: they were far more frequently between Irishmen and Irishmen, with the Vikings taking advantage of the frequent dis-putes and intertribal battles. Even if a High King was declared, the title was rarely, if ever, undisputed.

Part of the kingdom of Dal Riada still lay back across the water, in Ireland, although it gradually grew apart from the new Scottish Dal Riada. The two kingdoms fought in alliance against Domnall Mac Aed, King of Tara, but were defeated at the Battle of Mag Rath (Moira) in 634. From that date onward, the name Dal Riada tends to refer to the Scottish kingdom only.

The other part of the old kingdom of Ulaid, or Ulster, was now called Dal Fiatach, after the legendary ancestor of the clan, Fiatach Find. It was a king of Dal Fiatach, Baetan Mac Cairill by name, who first subdued Ellan Vannin, the Isle of Man. (The Manx language, now moribund, is very closely related to the Goidelic languages of Ireland and Scotland. There is evidence that both Brythonic and Goidelic were known in the island in the fifth and sixth centuries, but Manx came to resemble Scottish Gaelic most closely.) Baetan died in 581.

In the seventh century, a complex alliance of the Scottish Dal Riada and the northern Britons (who were being pressured northwards by Aethelfrith of Northumbria) began to shape what eventually was to become Scotland. A key figure was Aedan Mac Gabrain, King of Dal Riada, who made great incursions into the northern and southern Pictish kingdoms. From this period onwards, the story in the north of Britain is of Celtic Britons retreating before Anglian advances into the territory south of Strathclyde which still bears their Celtic name, Cumbria, and of the Goidelic Celts north of them forming into the earliest Scottish houses and clans. From the middle of the fifth century onwards, there were also Irish settlements established on the northern and western seaboard of Wales.

Meanwhile, in Ireland itself, the increasingly powerful Christian church found itself in occasional conflict with the Irish kings, including the High Kings. Colm Cille, or St. Columba, had secretly made a copy of the Psalms from his master, Finian of Moville. Finian demanded the surrender of the copy, and made a formal claim for judgment from the High King, Diarmuid O'Carroll. Diarmuid gave the famous judgment, 'Le gach boin a boinin' ('To each cow its calf'), which meant that the owner of the original, namely Finian, was also the rightful owner of the copy. The judgment led to the Battle of Cuildremne in Sligo, at which many lives were lost, and Colm Cille was sent into exile in the following year, 562. He went to the Isle of Iona, in the Scottish Dal Riada, where he founded his famous monastery.

In 577, the advancing Anglo-Saxons defeated the British at the Battle of Deorham, and Welsh and Cornish began their separate linguistic journeys. By 593, Northumbria had become the strongest of the English kingdoms. Both events further isolated the Irish from British influence. In 615, the British were defeated by Aethelfrith of Bernicia at the Battle of Chester, and the Angles penetrated to the Irish Sea, massacring a large number of monks in Bangor. In 620, the king of Northumbria conquered the Isle of Man. Now the sea routes to Ireland were closed.

In 635, St. Aidan founded Lindisfarne Priory, and in 640 he began missionary work in Northumbria. The gradual Christianization of Britain, begun by St. Augustine in 597, eventually made commerce with Ireland possible again, but it was a slow process. By 716, St. Columba's church on Iona accepted the Roman Easter, which the English churches had accepted at the Synod of Whitby in 664. Bede produced his great ecclesiastical history in 731.

In 843, the Pictish and Scottish kingdoms united in resistance to attacks from the Danes. Scotland's first king, Cinnead (Kenneth) Mac Alpin, died in 860. In 866, the Danes seized York, and in 870 they conquered East Anglia, killing St. Edmund, its last king. In 916, the Danes renewed their attacks on Ireland, and seized control of Munster. The succession of High Kings is very unclear during this period, principally because the available chronicles deal mostly either with local events, or with the Danish incursions. The changes in alliances during this period are also very rapid. For example, by 937 the army which met Aethelstan at the Battle of Brunanburh consisted of Danes, Scots and Strathclyde Britons all fighting together on the same side against the English king (with some success – the Scots annexed Cumberland and Westmorland in 945).

The first High King who showed some resistance to the tide of Norse invasions sweeping across Britain, Ireland and northern Europe was Maelsechlainn (Malachy) II, who defeated a Danish army at Tara in 979. (Brian Boru later accused him of complicity with the Danes – see below.) We know very little else about him, however, although the unusual name does recur in early mediaeval Irish history, which suggests that it may have gained some popularity. (There was, for example, a cleric called Malachy of Armagh who first brought the Canons Regular of St. Augustine to Ireland in the twelfth century and built in 1140 a stone oratory at Bangor which the locals condemned because 'we are Irish not Gauls'.) There was a Maelsechlainn or Malachy I to precede Maelsechlainn II, and there was also a Malachi Mor, whose son Colman became a saint of Lower Austria after his martyrdom in 1012.

The Northmen were unstoppable for any length of time. In 980 they raided Chester, and in 982 they raided Dorset, Portland and south Wales. In 994, Olaf Trygvason of Norway and Sweyn of Denmark besieged the city of London. By 1016, Cnut (Canute) the Dane was King of All England. In 1020, the Faroes, Shetlands and Orkneys recognized Olaf Haroldson of Norway as their king. However, another Irish king – whether he could be considered a High King was originally moot – emerged during this period to defend Ireland against the Viking invasions. This was Brian Boru, who defeated the Northmen at the Battle of Clontarf in 1014, and whose name is still commemorated in Irish folklore as the mightiest of all Ireland's warrior kings.

Brian has since become such a common name in the English-speaking world that it is easy to forget that it was a Gaelic name originally. The second part of the name, Boru, is also written Boroma or Boroimhe, since it is derived from Gaelic *boroma*, meaning 'cattle tribute'. The legend goes that Brian was standing with one of the favourite poets of his court, one Mac Liag, watching a vast herd of cows which had been paid to the King in tribute from Ulster and Leinster. The poet, in admiration, composed a song of praise to Brian for the great flocks and herds which had come to him. The King, deeply moved by the poet's sincerity, gave him the whole herd, worth an immense fortune. Thereafter, Brian was called Brian Boroimhe ('Brian of the Cattle Tribute'), or Brian Boru.

Brian was born in Munster in 926, the son of Cenneidigh ('Fair Head', the same as the Scottish name Cinnead, modern Kenneth or Kennedy). Cenneidigh was a nobleman of the royal family, chief of Tuaith Muin, or Thomond, the northernmost of the three principalities of Munster, but not king of the province. In the ninth and tenth centuries, Munster was constantly ravaged by invading Danes, and Cenneidigh was one of the principal leaders of the resistance to the Danish incursions. In 951, when Brian was still a young man, his brother Mathgamhain (Mahon) became king of Thomond. Some time later, Mathgamhain became king of the whole province. We know that Brian was an active warrior against the Danes, and with his brother as king his own social status and wealth must have been considerable.

In 976, when Brian was already 50 years old, King Mathgamhain was murdered. Brian avenged the murder, and after a two-year period of inter-tribal conflict, he was himself declared king of Munster. Despite Brian's years – 50 was a very ripe old age at the end of the first millennium – his ambition stretched beyond Munster. Ireland had been so riven by Viking invasions and settlement that the only clear way towards the High Kingship, to which Brian aspired, was by conquest not only of the Northmen, but also of the other provinces.

Brian began by bringing Leinster under his control, and extracting oaths of submission to his sovereignty from the kings and nobles of that province. In addition, he drove into Wicklow, and into Dublin itself, and defeated the Danes who had settled there, burning their homesteads and forcing them to flee westwards. Secure now in both Munster and Leinster, he turned inwards to Meath. The reigning High King was Maelsechlainn, towards whom Brian felt particular bitterness because there was suspicion that the Ard Righ was a secret collaborator with the Danes. After years of campaigning, in which he suffered several setbacks and reverses, Brian defeated Maelsechlainn and was himself finally declared Ard Righ of all Ireland in 1002. He was now 76 years old.

Nevertheless, he was compelled to continue fighting in battle, leading his forces in person, until Connaught and Ulster had also yielded and sworn allegiance to him, which they did in due course. He ruled another twelve years as High King, showing wisdom and strength, despite his great age. The Danes continued to press for permanent control of Dublin and Wicklow, and there were constant internal feuds, battles and even interprovincial wars, all of them exacerbated by the presence of the land-hungry Northmen.

Finally, on the afternoon of 23 April 1014, Brian Boru's army inflicted a mighty defeat on the Danish forces at the Battle of Clontarf. The High King, who swung his own sword in the front line of the battle, was now 88 years old. After the battle, however, the old king was murdered while he lay sleeping in his tent. He was buried at Armagh. One of his original charters, signed in his own hand, is still preserved at Trinity College in Dublin. Ireland has had many military heroes, but Brian Boru is still widely regarded as the greatest of them all.

The extraordinary courage and tenacity of this most famous of all the High Kings led to a special significance for the name O'Brian, which originally indicated descent from his family. Spelled O'Brien, it was the family name of the earls and marquesses of Thomond for generations (the earldom from 1543 to 1741, and the marquessate from 1800 to 1855), all of whom claimed descent from the great king Turlough O'Brien (c. 1009–1086), king of Munster and High King, himself descended from Brian Boru. The Irish bagpipes used in battle were known as Brian Boru pipes, in honour of the great High King.

Turlough O'Brien attracted the notice of Lanfranc, Archbishop of Canterbury, for his adherence to traditional patterns and laws of marriage, most of which were pagan in origin. In 1074 Lanfrance wrote to Turlough urging him to rid Ireland of its 'evil customs'. This tension between the Christian Church and the High Kings continued for another century. At the Synod of Kells in 1152 four archbishoprics were recognized: Armagh, Cashel, Tuam and Dublin. Gradually, a pattern of dioccsan organization, much closer to the general European model, replaced the old monasteries, and abbots found themselves ousted by bishops and diocesan priests.

In 1169, the Anglo-Normans invaded Ireland, and within a few generations Ireland was changed for ever, with the High Kings consigned to history. The Pope granted possession of Ireland to Henry II of England in 1172. The English colonization reached its peak about 1275, and was followed by a brief resurgence of Gaelic hegemony, culminating in the wars of 1315–1318, which had been caused by resentments at the use by the English kings of Irish resources for non-Irish purposes. It was said that almost half of the funds used by Edward I to build his castles in Wales had been purloined from the Irish. The anti-Irish Statutes of Kilkenny were enacted in 1366. These were designed to prevent any further spread of Irish customs among the English: settlers were forbidden to use the Gaelic tongue, or to hire Irish minstrels, and even hurling was banned in English areas. In the fifteenth century, the English King's dominion was effectively restricted to the settler-occupied area known as the Pale (from which the expression 'beyond the Pale', meaning uncivilized or unacceptable, is derived) and the three areas controlled by the Anglo-Irish lordships, namely Ormonde, Desmond and Kildare. The first Protestant Reformation Parliament met in Dublin in 1536, and twenty years later the Plantations began, with the English crown granting confiscated land to Irish settlers.

To end this chapter, there follows a speculative list of the best known among the High Kings of Ireland. There are many names included which are clearly those of gods or heroes, not terrestrial kings; there are many gaps;

there are kings whose claims to be High King of all Ireland are not clear; and many of the dates are very tentative, but I have attempted to put the list in chronological order:

Bres the Beautiful, of mixed descent, Fomori and Tuatha de Danann

Eremon, the first Milesian High King

Tighernmas, seventh in the Milesian line, introduced gold-working to Ireland

Ollam Fodla, great scholar and poet, established first palace at Tara and the *feis Temro*

Aod Ruad ('the Red'), reigned alternately with Dithorba and Cimbaoth

Macha, daughter of Aod Ruad, the only queen (goddess) to be given the title Ard Righ

Ugani Mor, foster-son of Macha

Laegaire Lorc, son of Ugani Mor

Labraid Loingseach, born dumb so could not rule, later recovered speech

Ferghus Mac Leda, underwater shoes

Rory Mor of Ulster

Eterscel

Conaire Mor, first century BC

Crimthann Niad Nair ('Shy Hero'), famous for foreign expeditions

Eochaid Feidlech, father of Medb

Conchobhar Mac Nessa, during Christ's lifetime, great-grandson of Rory Mor

Carbri Cinn Cait, not of Milesian stock, brought famine and disease

Feradach Finn-feactnach ('the Fair-righteous'), of Pictish stock

Fiacha of the White Cows

Elim of Ulster, reigned twenty years

Tuathal Feachtmar ('the Desired One'), restored Milesian dynasty, founded Meath

Feidlimid Rechtmar ('Lawgiver'), son of Tuathal

Cathair Mor, left a detailed will and catalogue of royal possessions

Conn of the Hundred Battles, son of Feidlimid

Airt or Art the Lonely, son of Conn

Ferghus Blacktooth of Ulster

Cormac Mac Art, Conn's grandson, possibly 227 to 263, rebuilt and extended Tara

Cairbre Lefchaid, son of Cormac

Fiachi or Fiacha Mac Cairbri, beginning of the fourth century

Colla Uais, nephew of Fiachi, slew his uncle and seized the throne

Muiredeach Tireach, son of Fiachi, overthrew Colla and reigned 27 years

Eochaid Muighmedon, son of Muiredeach Tireach, reigned c.350

Crimthann, brother-in-law of Eochaid

Niall Noigiallach ('of the Nine Hostages'), grandson of Muiredeach, died 405

Dathi Mac Fiachra of Connaught, nephew of Niall Noigiallach

Laoghaire, son of Niall Noigiallach, began reign in 428

Ailill Molt of Connaught, son of Dathi

Muircertach Mac Erca, reigning at time of birth of his nephew St.
    Columba, 521

Ainmire, father of Aedh

Diarmait Mac Cerbaill or O'Carroll, c.558, exiled St. Columba to Iona
    in 562

Aedh Mac Ainmire, tried to ban poets from Ireland at Convention of
    Druim Cett in 575

Baetan Mac Cairill, King of Dal Fiatach, first conquest of Isle of Man, died
    in 581

Domnall Mac Aed (Donal Mac Aoda), King of Tara, defeated Dal Riada
    armies in 634

Diarmuid Ruadnaid ('the Ruthful'), blessed by St. Carthach to whom he
    had shown mercy

Ceann Falad, died 677

Fionnachta the Festive, reigned c.690

Aed Finnliath, c.850, made alliance with Vikings

Cormac Mac Cullinan of Cashel, great scholar and linguist, killed in
    battle 903

Muirchertach (Murtogh) of the Leather Cloaks, fought Danes 918 to 943

Maelsechlainn (Malachy) I

Maelsechlainn (Malachy) II, defeated Vikings 979

Malachi Mor, son St. Colman martyred in 1012

Brian Boroimhe or Boru, lived 926 to 1014, defeated Vikings in 1014
    aged 88

Turlough O'Brien, lived c.1009 to 1086

Roderic O'Connor, last fair of Taillte (Teltown) 1169, last High King

During their times, the High Kings of Ireland continued and developed a
uniquely Celtic pattern of governance. However simple, bloody and ruthless
they may have been in reality, they are remembered in Irish lore as exemplars
of the Irish spirit. Tara now may be no more than a hill among muddy fields,
but the High Kingship which Tara represented is inseparably tied to the Irish
sense of nationhood, as Thomas Moore's justly famous elegiac poem records:

> The harp that once through Tara's halls
> The soul of music shed,
> Now hangs as mute on Tara's walls
> As if that soul were fled.
> So sleeps the pride of former days,
> So glory's thrill is o'er,
> And hearts that once beat high for praise
> Now feel that pulse no more!

No more to chiefs and ladies bright
The harp of Tara swells;
The chord alone that breaks at night
Its tale of ruin tells.
Thus Freedom now so seldom wakes,
The only throb she gives
Is when some heart indignant breaks,
To show that still she lives.[3]

Notes

1   Alwyn Rees and Brinley Rees, *Celtic Heritage*, p. 75.
2   *Celtic Heritage*, pp. 223–4.
3   From *Irish Melodies*, quoted in *A Library of Poetry and Song*, ed. William
    Cullen Bryant, pub. J.B. Ford & Co., New York, 1874.

TEN

THE WELSH AND BRETON ROYAL DYNASTIES

THE ORIGINS OF WALES

S WAS mentioned in Chapter Four, the name Wales is derived from an Anglo-Saxon word *weahlas*, meaning 'foreigners'. The native British who were driven westwards or contained within their western territories called themselves originally merely by their tribal names, but later, when the 'English' presented a common enemy, they began to use the collective term *Cymri* ('fellow-countrymen') for themselves. The term, derived from an earlier form *Combrogi*, originally applied to all British-speaking tribes on the western Atlantic seaboard (the southwest peninsula was known as West Wales for many centuries), and still survives in the name of Cumbria. Gradually, however, as the British states collapsed, the Cymri became identified with the territory which they still call *Cymru*, but which the English call Wales.

Unlike Ireland, which had a long and uninterrupted period of self-rule before the first Viking invasions, Wales has been affected by successive waves of invasion, interaction and direct rule, from the Romans, through the early English, the Anglo-Normans, the mediaeval English and, many would argue, the modern English. Despite all these influences, Wales has retained a very strong sense of her national, Celtic identity, not least because the Welsh language has survived and even flourished in some respects, in the face of intense competition from the pressures of English and American English.

It would be unfair to ignore the fact that some of the early invasions were Celtic. In the previous chapter, I mentioned the Irish (Scotti) incursions and settlements on the Welsh Atlantic seaboard. Dyfed was ruled by a dynasty originally from Ireland. Gwynedd is interpreted by some as the Welsh form of the Irish name Feni, the dynastic family to which many of the mediaeval Welsh households are supposed to have traced their ancestry. The Feni were displaced from northwest Wales by the Gododdin, under their leader Cunedda, who came to Gwynedd with his eight sons and one grandson when the kingdom of Manaw Gododdin, east of Strathclyde, collapsed during the end of the Roman occupation. The great poem *The Gododdin*, its author Aneirin and the equally famous poet Taliesin were almost certainly from what is now northeastern England or southeastern Scotland, the ancient territory of Manaw Gododdin, but now are all of them intensely identified with Welsh culture.

There has been much debate about when these movements took place, even about whether Cunedda actually existed. The Roman leader, Magnus Maximus, known in Welsh legend as Macsen Wledig ('the Powerful'), abandoned the legionary garrison at Segontium in AD 383, which has led quite a few historians to speculate that Cunedda may have reached Gwynedd during the period 380 to 400. Most later writers, however, place the migration around 440, which would make Cunedda a contemporary rather than a predecessor of Vortigern.

During the period when the earliest English kingdoms were shaping themselves towards a kingdom of England, so too were the kingdoms of Wales forming dynasties, sometimes on the model of the Irish Ard Righ, with a High King, like Hywel Dda (see below) for example, exercising authority over many smaller kingdoms or chieftainships, sometimes making treaties and alliances with the English, sometimes openly at war with them. In the end, as with Ireland, the Norse and, finally, the English imposed overlordship on the Celtic state, but for some centuries there was a succession of Welsh dynastic royal families.[1]

THE EARLY KINGDOMS

First, however, as with Ireland, we have to trace briefly the story of a king who is clearly mythological rather than real, although mediaeval Christian scholars made great claims for his historical authenticity. This is Bran, the son of the British sea god Llyr. The name Bran means 'Crow' or 'Raven'. In the vernacular literature he is just as frequently called Bendigeidfran, 'Bran the Blessed'. Bran gave his sister Branwen in marriage to the Irish king Matholwch, but failed to obtain the consent of her half-brother Efnisien. During the wedding feast in Wales, Efnisien, slighted because his permission had not been sought, cut off the lips, ears and tails of Matholwch's horses. By way of apology for Efnisien's crime, Bran sent Matholwch a magic cauldron, which had the property that dead warriors put into it would emerge alive, although without the power of speech. Back in Ireland, Branwen was cruelly treated by Matholwch. Although she had borne him a son, Gwern, she was forced to work as a scullery maid in the kitchens. To rescue his sister from this insulting treatment, Bran raised a great army and sailed to Ireland, and

there was great bloodshed on both sides. Bran returned with only seven survivors. On the journey, Bran himself died of an infected wound. He told his
companions to cut off his head, which they did. The head miraculously
remained fresh and alive, speaking to them. The group was later called the
Assembly of the Wondrous Head. Bran warned his companions that they
must never turn to look towards Cornwall, but, after many years of peaceful
company together (which to them had seemed like only hours), one of the
companions forgot, and the head began to die also. Bran ordered his men to
bury his head beneath White Hill in London (where the Tower of London
now stands), from where he would always offer protection. (The ravens at the
Tower are a token of Bran's continued presence.)

Although the legend may be no more than that, the historical events of
the second, third and fourth centuries certainly supply the necessary background: there were, indeed, frequent raids from Ireland against Wales, and no
doubt some retaliatory expeditions from Wales to Ireland. The burial of the
head in London presupposes that Bran was the ruler of all Britain, or at least
the southern part of the island, but there is no classical evidence of any such
figure, and archaeological evidence would be very difficult to assign to a particular individual. According to the legend, Bran's son was Caradawg or
Caradoc, who was overthrown by Caswallon. The historical Caradoc, or
Caratacus, described in Chapter Seven (see pages 148–149), may have given
his name to the legendary prince.

Cunedda, mentioned above, is supposed to have left Manaw Gododdin
in the early fifth century and founded the northern dynasty of Gwynedd. The
early manuscripts often refer to 'three royal tribes' of Wales, and these are
generally held to be represented by the northern dynasties of Gwynedd and
Powys, and the larger but more amorphous southern kingdom of
Deheubarth. Giraldus Cambrensis tells us that the kingdoms were agreed by
three sons of Rhodri Mawr in the ninth century, but there are at least four
hundred years and perhaps twelve generations between Maelgwn Fawr, first
recognized king of Gwynedd, and Rhodri Mawr.

The name Deheubarth, for the southern kingdoms, is derived from Latin
dextralis pars, literally 'the right-hand part'. A Celtic term *Gwyr y Gogledd*,
literally 'men of the left-hand', came to signify the north of Wales generally,
a meaning retained to this day. The pattern was of small, tribal kingdoms,
similar to those in Strathclyde, Manaw Gododdin, Cumbria, and earlier in
Gaul and in Britain generally – the ancient and original Celtic pattern of royal
tribe, sept and clan. Some of these little kingdoms survived independently for
a remarkably long time while the great marches of history went on all around
them. The unification of Wales does not begin to show any real signs of
achievement until the time of Merfyn Vrych and his son Rhodri Mawr in the
ninth century, and the great Hywel Dda ('the Good') in the tenth century, and
even then there were some small kingdoms which could claim an independent
history of half a millennium.

The kingdom of Powys developed independently, its tribal base being the

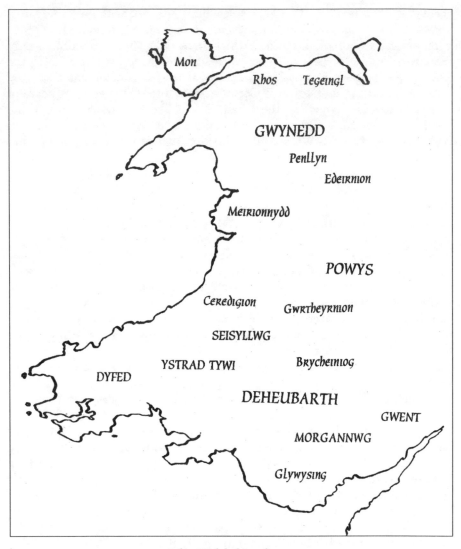

The Welsh kingdoms.

powerful Cornovii (literally 'horned people') whose territory had included the valleys of the Severn and the Dee from pre-Roman times. The kingdom probably took its name from the Latin *pagus* ('country district', origin of the word pagan). By the early Middle Ages the tiny kingdoms of Builth and Gwrthrynion on the upper Wye River had become part of Powys. Gwrthrynion is derived from Gwrtheyrn, which is a later variant of the name Vortigern. King Fernmail, who reigned in Builth *c*.AD 930, the same time Nynniaw or Nennius was writing his chronicles, claimed uninterrupted descent from Vortigern.

Between Gwynedd and Powys lay the smaller kingdoms of Meirionnydd, Penllyn and Edeirnion. In the southeast, where the Roman influence had been strongest, there were several small kingdoms, among them the royal house of Gwent, which took its name from the garrison of Caerwent. Dyfed, which had been settled by Irish immigrants, as attested by its many stones inscribed in Ogham, continued to attract further Irish immigration after the Roman departure, and remained separate in language (Q-Celtic as opposed to P-Celtic; see page 10) as well as in custom. Both Dyfed in the southwest and tiny Brecknock in the south retained their independence from the fifth century to the tenth century.

The other early southern kingdoms, including Ystrad Tywi, Gwyr (Gower) and Brycheiniog, also went their own ways. Morgannwg (Glamorgan), which remained a separate kingdom until the eve of the Norman Conquest, developed from its strong Roman traditions a long Christian tradition and included, as well as the old Roman fortified cities of Cardiff, Caerleon and Caerwent (within the smaller kingdom of Gwent), the important monastic centres of Llancarfan, Llandaff and Llanilltud.

We know that the critical period, during which not only was Wales forming, but also the Gaelic north was turning into the beginnings of Scotland and the Germanic east was turning into the beginnings of England, was from about AD 400 to 600. Unfortunately, this is a period for which reliable historical evidence is thin on the ground, which has made it a favourite arena for historical controversy and point-scoring between professors. The monk Gildas wrote *De Excidio Britanniae* ('Concerning the Fall of Britain') in about 540, but this is a crabby work, filled with polemic, written in dense and verbose Latin, and riddled with sometimes confusing biblical quotations. The earliest of the saints' lives, *The Life of St. Samson*, was probably written during or soon after the period, but it is obviously limited in scope. The poems of Taliesin and Aneirin, not found in manuscript until after 1250, were probably composed about 600, but, as was noted above, it is highly probable that both poets were originally inhabitants of what is now southeastern Scotland rather than Wales. Bede's *Ecclesiastical History of the English*, which is a magnificent work, appeared about 730, but Bede was deeply prejudiced against the Welsh. It was only much later that the Welsh genealogies seemed of any importance, so that much of the reconstruction of the earliest Welsh kingdoms was based on late evidence and therefore speculative. The *Annales Cambriae*, on which we largely rely for what little evidence there is, were probably written around 960 at the request of Owain ap Hywel Dda. A further complicating factor is that the early mediaeval Welsh chroniclers, often anxious to generate genealogies and pedigrees to support claims of inheritance, filled in the gaps with invented kings, usually deriving their names from place names, like Meirion or Marianus from Meirionnydd, Ceredig from Ceredigion, Edeyrn or Aeternus from Edeyrnion, and so on. As with Geoffrey of Monmouth's interpolations of fictitious names, the effect is pernicious: all the names become suspect.

We have already looked at the story of Vortigern (Chapter Six), whose period of greatest influence was *c.*420 to 450. In the Welsh form of his name, Gwrtheyrn, he is noted in the early genealogies as an ancestor of the kings of Powys, although later Welsh chroniclers were less keen to grant him that status because of the poor reputation he acquired after the disastrous invitation to Hengist and Horsa. In the power vacuum left behind after the Romans, it is probable that petty kingdoms were the rule. Welsh has the word *rhi* as a cognate for the Irish *ri* or *righ* ('king'), but the early Welsh also used the word *brenin*, which seems to have denoted more specifically a petty or tribal king, and in modern Welsh all the vocabulary surrounding royalty, such as *brenhinfainc* ('throne'), *brenhindod* ('royalty'), *brenhinaidd* ('regal'), etc., is clearly derived from the latter term.

After Vortigern, the first figure of note is Maglocunus, properly Maelgwn ap Cadwallon Llaw Hir ('of the Long Hand'), known in Welsh tradition as Maelgwn Fawr ('the Great') or Maelgwn Gwynedd. He cannot be thought of as a true King of Wales, since his sphere of influence was originally confined to Gwynedd. His seat was the fort at Degannwy, where archaeological excavation has revealed evidence of imported goods from as far abroad as southern France, Athens and the Black Sea.

Maelgwn, much like Arthur, was later glorified as the epitome of the warrior-hero king, but, as with Arthur, the reality of his life is very difficult to ascertain. His seat was at Aberffraw, on the southwestern shore of the island of Anglesey, facing Caernarfon Bay. Maelgwn is reported to have died of the great Egyptian plague in 549, which would make him a contemporary of Arthur (assuming that both of them actually existed). There is evidence that some of the legal concepts in the early law books can be traced back to Maelgwn's time and influence. He was a man of culture, who had minstrels and poets at his court. In the same way that later kings of Britain felt the need to trace their ancestry back to Arthur, so also did later Welsh kings and princes feel the need to show their descent from Rhodri Mawr, and, through him, all the way back to the great Maelgwn. For example, when Llywelyn called an assembly to receive the homage of lesser kings of Deheubarth in 1216, he chose Aberdyfi as the meeting place because, reputedly, it was at Aberdyfi that Maelgwn Fawr's kingship had been acknowledged seven centuries earlier.

Between 550 and 650, the English (whom the Welsh called *Saeson* or Saxons) took control of most of southern Britain. They captured Salisbury in 552, and Aylesbury in 571. As noted in the previous chapter, the Battle of Deorham or Dyrham in 577, at which the English killed three British kings and captured Bath, Cirencester and Gloucester, marked the point at which the Celts north of the Severn were separated from their countrymen to the south and west, so that the Cornish and Welsh languages began to develop separately from that date onwards. The ancient Celtic kingdom of Dumnonia (modern Cornwall, Devon and parts of Somerset) continued to survive for some time, however. There was a Celtic king in Devon as late as 710, and the latest reference to a Celtic king in Cornwall is not until 878. Even though Cornwall was formally absorbed into the kingdom of Wessex in 950, it remained Celtic-speaking for at least six more centuries, and Celtic in culture and spirit for three centuries more, and is considered by its staunchest supporters (myself included) a Celtic nation to this very day.

The dynasty of Maelgwn was Christian, and the church of Llangadwaladr ('Cadwaladr's monastery'), which still stands near Aberffraw, houses a Latin inscription to King Cadfan, a close descendant of Maelgwn: *Catamanus Rex sapientissimus opinatissimus omnium regum* ('King Cadfan, the wisest and the most famous of all kings'). In 633 Cadfan's son, Catguollaun or Cadwallon II, killed Edwin I of Northumbria, the first English king to invade Wales, and went on to kill Edwin's successors, Osric of Deira and Eanfrith of Bernicia. Cadwallon pursued the defeated Northumbrians northwards, but was himself killed in battle in 634.

The last English kingdom to develop was Mercia, which was most powerful from about 640 to 800. It was the expansion to the west of Mercia, England's midland kingdom, which effectively defined the eastern border of Powys and hence, eventually, of Wales. The capital city of Powys, Pengwern, was captured and destroyed by the Saxons in 642, a loss commemorated in elegiac Welsh poems written about two hundred years later. The Welsh (strictly speaking, we should rather say the Celts of Powys at this time) made consistent and determined efforts to reclaim their ancient territories until, probably some time between AD 780 and 796, King Offa of Mercia built a series of fortified earthworks collectively known ever since as Offa's Dyke (meaning 'ditch'). The dyke is actually a few miles longer than the much more famous Hadrian's Wall, although it is visually far less impressive. It was clearly intended more as a border than as a fortification. It was built of earth rather than stone, it was not regularly garrisoned, and there were several gaps where either dense forest or the winding River Severn served the purpose of demarcating the border sufficiently. The remains are still unbroken from Treuddyn in Flintshire to the River Arrow in Radnorshire. South of the Arrow the dyke disappears, but traces reappear between Monmouth and the Severn Estuary, where it reaches the coast in the Beachley peninsula. It has been suggested that the dyke was constructed with the collaboration of some of the kings of Powys and Gwent. For example, the course taken at Rhiwabon appears to have been designed to leave Cadell ap Brochwel, King of Powys, in possession of his fortress at Penygardden. Gwent, in particular, appears to have cut some kind of special deal with Offa, since the dyke deliberately veers east of the natural boundary of the Wye valley, and the continuation down into the Beachley peninsula appears to have been intended to allow the people of Gwent continued access to their traditional harbours on the estuary.

Offa was killed at the Battle of Rhuddlan in 796. Although his dyke remained unfinished, it effectively marked the eastern border of the territory which was eventually to become known as Wales. By this time, the Welsh language was distinctively Welsh, and no longer Brythonic. One of the significant changes (which, incidentally, also happened in English) was the loss of grammatical terminations, like the Latin *-us*, *-um*, *-i*, *-o*, and so on, which formerly indicated whether the word was in the nominative, accusative, genitive or dative case. As a result, Roman name forms like Maglocunus or Caratacus began to appear as Maelgwn or Caradoc. (A further complication is that these names became and remained popular for generation after generation, so that not only are there countless instances of the names Williams or Jones or Davies in a modern Welsh telephone book, there are also dozens if not scores of Maelgwns and Llewelyns and Cadells and Gruffudds (Griffiths) in the royal genealogies, so that telling one from another is very difficult: like Jones the Post or Williams the Bread, we have to start talking about Gruffudd ap ('son of') Rhys of Deheubarth as opposed to Gruffudd ap Rhys of the House of Gwynllwg, whose grandfather was Gruffudd ap Ifor Bach.)

About fifty years after Offa's death appeared the first king who might be thought of as a Welsh king rather than a Brythonic king. He was a direct descendant of Maelgwn Fawr, and he was called Rhodri, later honoured with the title Rhodri Mawr ('the Great'). Rhodri acquired his title, status, and a kingdom which stretched from Anglesey in the far north to Gwyer or Gower in the far south through a very complicated series of marriages and inheritances which brought the great houses of Gwynedd, Powys and Seisyllwg (formerly Ceredigion and Ystrad Tywi) into one blood line. One of his ancestors was Coel Hen, a dynastic king of the north known better in later folklore as Old King Cole. Rhodri's father was Merfyn, King of Gwynedd. His mother was Nest, of the house of Powys. His wife was Angharad of the house of Seisyllwg. Rhodri acquired all three kingdoms in succession: Gwynedd when his father, Merfyn, died in 844; Powys when his uncle, Cyngen, died in 855; and Seisyllwg when his brother-in-law, Gwgon, died in 871. But Rhodri became known as Rhodri Mawr not only because he ruled a greater geographical territory than any Welsh king before him, but also because he was a mighty warrior against the Northmen, as Brian Boru was to become in Ireland a century later. In 856, Rhodri secured a great victory over the Danes, defeating their leader, Horn, and recovering possession of the island of Anglesey, which had for a thousand years been thought of as a central seat of Celtic druidism. It was a symbolic victory, which gave great delight to the Irish and to the Franks, but also did much to restore the Celtic spirit of the Romanized Britons who were now rapidly becoming the Welsh. Rhodri had battles with the English, too, particularly in Powys. As the English kingdom of Mercia declined, the English kingdom of Wessex ('of the West Saxons') grew rapidly in power and influence and began making inroads into Powys. Rhodri Mawr and his son, Gwriad, died in battle against the West Saxons in 877.

His immediate successor was his son, Cadell, but it was his grandson, Hywel, who achieved far greater power and recognition than even his grandfather had achieved. Because of the difficulty with names mentioned a few paragraphs ago, it is worth being a little more deliberate about which Hywel we are discussing here: this was Hywel ap Cadell ap Rhodri, most commonly known as Hywel Dda ('the Good'). Hywel was King of Seisyllwg. His wife was Elen, sister of Llywarch ap Hyfaidd, King of Dyfed. When Llywarch died in 904 (killed by order of Hywel, according to some commentators), Hywel became King of Dyfed as well as of Seisyllwg. It appears that he also became King of Brycheiniog at the same time. It was this group of southern kingdoms which afterwards came to be known collectively as Deheubarth. The King of Gwynedd and Powys at this time (about 930) was a relative of Hywel's, another grandson of Rhodri Mawr, namely Idwal ab Anarawd ap Rhodri. In 942, Gwynedd, Powys and Deheubarth were united under Hywel's rule, and for the first time we have a king whom we might justifiably call King of Wales. The only piece missing from the jigsaw puzzle was Gwent and Morgannwg (Glamorgan) in the southeast. The kings of Glamorgan were also descended from Rhodri Mawr through his daughter, Nest.

Hywel acquired his epithet 'the Good' principally because of his association with the early establishment of law in Wales, rather than because of any outstanding personal qualities. In 928 he made a pilgrimage to Rome, where, so legend has it, he took copies of his laws to be blessed by the Pope. He also spent a good deal of time at the English court. Hywel's codification came to be known as the Law of Wales, and the site of its first promulgation is traditionally given as Whitland, close to the border between Dyfed and Seisyllwg. Although the earliest surviving manuscript (written about 1230, copied from a text compiled about 1175) is written in Latin, the original language of the Law (and of most of the surviving copies) was Welsh. Amendments, explanations and case examples were constantly added and incorporated into the texts over the course of many years, so that Hywel's Law continued to exercise a very great influence long after he was dead. Although there is not space here to describe the Law of Wales in detail, one part of it is worth special mention: unlike canon law, which did not allow for dissolution of marriage, the Law of Wales recognized nine different forms of marriage union, and also gave detailed guidance on inheritance and distribution of property if the marriage came to an end. In that respect, at least, Hywel's Law seems to be much closer to an earlier, Celtic model than to Roman or Christian law.

When Hywel died in 950, the ancient division between north and south reopened. His son Owain succeeded him as King of Deheubarth, but Gwynedd and Powys returned to the line of Idwal ab Anarawd. In the next generation after Owain, his sons Einon and Maredudd (Meredith) were both kings. From 986 to 999, Maredudd ab Owain rebuilt and restored his grandfather's original kingdom, or at least approximately the same territorial hegemony, but his was a troubled reign. The Vikings had established firm strongholds in Dublin and the Isle of Man by now, and from them they launched attack after attack on Wales, particularly on the coastal settlements, many of which to this day bear names which are of Nordic rather than Celtic origin, such as Anglesey, Bardsey, Caldey, Fishguard and Swansea.[2] Nordic marauders invaded Anglesey in 987 and captured over two thousand of its inhabitants to be sold into slavery. In 989, Maredudd raised a penny poll-tax to generate money with which to bribe the Northmen to stay away, but their raids continued unabated. In 999, they attacked St. David's and murdered Morgenau, the bishop.

At the turn of the millennium, there was no clear pattern of identity or unification in Wales, and it was not until the advent of Gruffudd ap Llywelyn, who ruled from 1039 to 1063, that a united kingdom of Wales, this time including Morgannwg in the southeast, emerged. Indeed, Gruffudd was the only Welsh king ever to rule over the entire territory of Wales. Gruffudd's lineage, not surprisingly in this rat's nest of tiny kingdoms within larger dynastic houses, is complicated. As his name tells us, his father was Llywelyn. This Llywelyn was Llywelyn ap Seisyllt, who had married Angharad, daughter of Maredudd ab Owain. So, through marriage, Gruffudd could claim Maredudd as his grandfather and, through him, descent all the way back to Hywel Dda and Rhodri Mawr. Gruffudd seized the throne of Gwynedd and Powys in 1039 by killing Iago ab Idwal, great-grandson of Idwal ab Anarawd. He fought for control of Deheubarth with Gruffudd ap Rhydderch ap Iestyn, whom he finally defeated in 1055. In 1056 or 1057, he seized Glamorgan and drove out its king, Cadwgan ap Meurig. So, for a period of about seven years, from 1057 until Gruffudd's death in 1063, Wales was, for the first and only time, a single kingdom ruled by a single king. Gruffudd was undoubtedly a brutal leader and a man of intense personal ambition. Not only did he consolidate the Welsh kingdoms, he also launched attacks against the English, notably defeating Leofric, earl of Mercia, in 1039, and, in alliance with Leofric's son, Aelfgar, burning Hereford and seizing for Welsh repossession many of the borderland territories which had been in English control for two or three centuries. Harold, earl of Wessex and later King of England, seeking revenge for these attacks, pursued Gruffudd in a series of battles, and eventually Gruffudd was killed somewhere in Snowdonia in the high summer of 1063 – by his own men, according to some reports.

After Gruffudd's death, Wales reverted to its traditional pattern of disunity, with the three large kingdoms of Gwynedd and Powys in the north and centre and Deheubarth in the south. King Harold of England left the Welsh comparatively unmolested, so long as they remained disunited. Gwynedd came first into the possession of a boy-king, another Gruffudd, of Irish-Norse descent, and then Gwynedd and Powys fell to Bleddyn and Rhiwallon, the half-brothers of Gruffudd ap Llywelyn. Deheubarth fell to Maredudd ab Owain. Gwent and Gwynllwg were seized by Caradog, the son of Gruffudd ap Rhydderch. The rest of Glamorgan reverted to Cadwgan ap Meurig. Then, in 1066, three years after Gruffudd's death in Snowdonia, William of Normandy landed at Hastings, defeated and killed King Harold, and introduced Norman rule to Britain.

The Normans treated Scotland with far greater respect than they did Wales, although they readily recognized the cultural and historical identities of both nations. They despised the Saxon English, whom they rapidly reduced to servile status. For a while, they maintained much more courtly relations with the Welsh, and there were several significant alliances by marriage between Welsh and Norman houses. In particular, largely because of their own long literary traditions and love of troubadours, the Normans had a great deal of respect for Welsh language and literature, especially Welsh poetry. They were also deeply impressed by the long tradition of secular law in Wales, that had begun all the way back with Hywel Dda.

Soon, however, the pettiness of the Welsh kings and their sporadic ambitions came into direct conflict with the Norman ideal of a settled, regulated state with feudal responsibilities and roles clearly established. From 1066 to 1081, William merely watched from the sidelines while various Welsh kings took turns in killing each other, seizing petty kingdoms, and then themselves being killed. In 1081, however, two stronger leaders emerged from the carnage: these were Gruffudd ap Cynan of the House of Gwynedd, and Rhys ap Tewdwr of the House of Deheubarth. William sent a group of barons to take control of the borders: his kinsman William Fitzosbern to Hereford, Roger de Montgomery to Shrewsbury, and Hugh le Gros ('the Fat') of Avranches to Chester. By 1086, there were Norman castles at Caerleon, Chepstow and Monmouth. Hugh the Fat captured Gruffudd ap Cynan and imprisoned him for twelve years. The *Domesday Book* records that Rhys ap Tewdwr paid William an annual tribute of £40.

When William died in 1087, his second son, William Rufus, became King of England. The border barons took advantage of his weakness to press further into Wales, seizing territory as they went. In 1093, Rhys ap Tewdwr was killed trying to resist Bernard of Neufmarche. Brycheiniog, Penfro and Glamorgan all fell to the barons. In the south, they pressed their advantage all the way west to Dyfed: Pembroke Castle, one of the most outstanding of the Norman fortifications, was built during this period.

For the next five hundred years or so, the pattern continued of a 'buffer zone' between the Celts of true Wales and the Anglo-Normans or English. The zone, which changed frequently, came to be known as the Welsh Marches, and the earls who maintained their castles and households there came to be known as the Marcher Lords, or the earls of March. There were similar Scottish Marches. The Welsh earls of March were descended from Roger de Mortemer. His son Ralph figures largely in the *Domesday Book* as the holder of huge estates in Shropshire and Herefordshire. His grandson Hugh, who spelled his name de Mortimer, founded the priory of Wigmore in Herefordshire. Roger de Mortimer (1286–1330), the 8th earl, was knighted by Edward I and appointed Lord Lieutenant of Ireland by Edward II in 1316. Another Roger de Mortimer (1374–1398), 4th earl of March and Ulster, was also appointed Lord Lieutenant of Ireland, at the tender age of 7. The earldom of March eventually became merged in the crown of England, when

Edmund de Mortimer, 5th earl of March and Ulster, died in 1425 without issue. These Marcher Lords established separate rights and privileges for themselves which, ironically, later helped maintain the separation between England and Wales.

The royal Welsh houses in inner Wales, the true Wales inside the Marches, continued to exist until about 1400, with their complex separate genealogies and confusing names. The House of Powys, for example, produced a succession of kings called either Madog or Gruffudd over a period of about two centuries. The House of Deheubarth produced a series of kings called either Maelgwn or Rhys, with a couple of Owains and Maredudds, a Llywelyn and a Thomas. The House of Gwynedd also had Llywelyns, Maredudds and Gruffudds, another Thomas, a few Owains and Cynans, and a Rhodri.

From two of these houses was descended the last of the great Welsh warrior kings, the last Welsh hero of the ancient type, Owain Glyn Dwr, often Anglicized as Owen Glendower. Glyn Dwr's mother was Elen or Helen, daughter of Thomas, descended from the Lord Rhys of the House of Deheubarth. His father was Gruffudd Fychan II, son of Madog, of the House of Powys. Through both parents, therefore, he could claim descent from the ancient Welsh kings. Glyn Dwr was born about 1359, probably at his father's estate of Glyndyrdwy in Merioneth. He was sent to Westminster to study law, and for a short while was squire to the earl of Arundel. The greatest title that anyone at the English court would ever deign to give to a Welsh king like Glyn Dwr would be 'prince', but even that would be hard to come by, so it is not all that peculiar to see someone who would be called 'king' in Wales (especially with a pedigree as immaculate as Glyn Dwr's) called 'squire' or 'seneschal' or some such title in the English court. Glyn Dwr later joined the service of Henry of Bolingbroke, the future Henry IV.

The House of Glyndyrdwy had a longstanding feud with their English neighbours, the Greys of Ruthin. In 1400, Reginald Grey, following feudal custom, should have called Glyn Dwr to armed service in a court expedition against Scotland. Grey deliberately neglected to give Glyn Dwr that call, and then accused him of treason for failing to appear. Welsh sympathies had been on the side of Richard II, and therefore against Henry, so what was essentially a family quarrel now joined forces with a national trend, and Glyn Dwr found himself the champion of a Welsh rebellion against the English king. When Henry returned from Scotland in the September of 1400, he found north Wales in insurrectionary turmoil. He led an expedition into Wales in person, but the campaign was ineffectual. By the spring of 1401, Glyn Dwr was leading raids into southern Wales, so Henry mounted another expedition, which also ended in failure. During the winter of 1401–02, Glyn Dwr forged alliances with the Irish, the Scots and the French. He had powerful secret allies in the English court in the persons of Henry Percy (Hotspur) and Percy's brother-in-law, Sir Edmund Mortimer. In the spring of 1402 he attacked Ruthin, taking Grey prisoner, which represented a sweet personal revenge as well as an important strategic victory for the Welsh. In the summer, he defeated the men of Hereford, who were under the command of Sir Edmund Mortimer. When tales of how kindly Mortimer was being treated as a prisoner got back to the English court, Henry began to realize the gravity and importance of the Welsh rebellion. Within months of being taken prisoner, Mortimer was released and married Glyn Dwr's daughter. In the autumn of the same year, Henry was driven back a third time by Welsh forces. Glyn Dwr now openly declared himself King of Wales, established a government, and called a parliament of Welsh nobles at Machynlleth. The French, honouring their alliance, sent troops to his aid, and in 1404 he captured the important strategic castles of Harlech and Aberystwyth. He was within a hair's breadth of restoring the kingdom of Wales, which had existed only once before, for those seven short years under Gruffudd ap Llywelyn, almost four centuries earlier.

In the spring of 1405, however, Henry's fortunes at last improved. He recovered Aberystwyth in 1408, after a long siege. In February 1409, the English recaptured Harlech, and Glyn Dwr's wife, children and grandchildren were taken prisoner. There is doubt about how Glyn Dwr himself came to his death. According to the *Chronicle* written by Adam of Usk, he died in 1415. According to Welsh legends, he used magical powers to remain in hiding from the English court, and lived a peaceful old age with his sons-in-law, eventually dying and being buried at Monington in Herefordshire.

Modern political debate about Wales has been about devolution, rather than independence, but for all those who discuss such questions, the name of Owain Glyn Dwr has acquired a special status. While Maelgwn, Rhodri Mawr and Gruffudd ap Llywelyn can be said to have achieved greater things, it is Owain Glyn Dwr who has become the Welsh national hero, revived and amplified in legend and folklore as the incarnation of the national Celtic spirit of Wales.

THE BRETON KINGDOMS

The northwestern corner of Gallia Comita, 'Long-haired Gaul', had come to be known as Armorica during the Empire. During the fifth century, while Niall Noigiallach and the Irish Scotti were making raids against the British coastal settlements, some restless Britons were also setting out on maritime adventures. Some of them crossed from Dumnonia to Armorica, and established small British settlements and enclaves. Their language, still Brythonic rather than Cornish or Welsh, would have been fairly similar to the Romanized Gallic of Armorica, but not exactly the same, nor even necessarily mutually intelligible. By AD 450, much of the territory north of the Loire was ruled by British or Breton petty kings, although many of the indigenous peoples were of Gallic stock. We know very little about this early period of Breton history.

In the fifth, sixth and seventh centuries, these small British enclaves were hugely increased in size and numbers by floods of refugees from mainland Britain, fleeing before the onslaughts of the Angles, Saxons and Jutes. In time, these waves of immigration created the separate Celtic nation of Breizh, Bretagne or Brittany, which, like Wales and Scotland, has had a long history of independence and semi-independence, and, like the other Celtic nations, still retains a strong linguistic and cultural identity to this day.

The largest, and possibly earliest, of the Breton kingdoms was Domnonia in the north, which obviously took its name directly from the kingdom of Dumnonia in Britain. In 530, Domnonia annexed the province of Leon in the northwest, which until then had remained independent. In the *Life of St. Samson of Dol*, the earliest of the Breton accounts of saints' lives, Domnonia is called Prettonaland. Prydein (early Welsh), Pretton, Breton, Bretagne and Britain are all variants of the same name. The legendary founding king of Prettonaland was Riwal, of the royal house of Gwent. Riwal could just as easily be a title or epithet as a real name: the *Ri-* element is probably the early Welsh for 'king', cognate with *ri* or *righ* in Irish.

Cornouaille, to the south of Domnonia, seems obviously to have taken its name from Cornovia or Cornwall, but the connection is actually rather difficult to prove, since neither name appears before the ninth century. Nor do we have any historical accounts of its governance or royal families before the ninth century; all we have are disconnected or episodic references in the various lives of the Breton saints.

The third of the early kingdoms was Bro Waroch ('Waroch's Land'), which occupied more or less the same territory as the ancient tribal area of the Veneti or Venuti, who were allies of Rome during the occupation. Waroch, who gave his name to the kingdom, was a sixth-century king or chief who defied the Franks. The Veneti were a seafaring people, who had frequent interactions with the British Celts, and it has been suggested, quite plausibly, that they may have given their name to Gwynedd. As noted in Chaper Six, the King Vortigern of history and legend mysteriously reappears in Bro Waroch as St. Gwrthiern.

The early histories of these Breton kingdoms concentrate almost exclusively on saints and saints' lives, and it only takes a little thought to understand why. The colonists who fled from the heathen Angles, Saxons and Jutes were peace-loving Christians, whose natural leaders were the clerics, scholars and physical as well as spiritual guides for their journeys. It seems likely that there was no great military resistance to their settling in large numbers, partly because of the longstanding Armorican connections with the British mainland, but also because the newcomers appear to have been content with poor heathland and virgin forest for their settling grounds, which again is consistent with the notion of people united by faith rather than by tribal allegiance or territorial ambition. Saint Meën, for example, is said to have come from

Archenfield in southeastern Wales, and to have established a monastery in the Forest of Broceliande in the eastern part of Brittany. Meën was of royal stock in Wales, and maintained a close friendship throughout his life with King Judicael of Domnonia, but his story is not one of conquest, or of royal intrigue, but rather of the establishment of a small monastery deep in the heart of the forest, away from the affairs of men. The patron saint of my home town of Camborne in Cornwall is St. Meryasek or Meriadoc, reputedly a Welshman who also lived and worked as a bishop in Brittany, where there is still a community named after him. The *Life of St. Malo* describes how the saint found a golden statue of a ram while he was clearing the land, and took it to the court of King Childebert asking for its value and for tenure, which the Frankish (French) king granted. All of these tales reinforce the notion that, while the original British and Welsh stock from which the Breton settlers came may have had very traditional Celtic patterns of kingship and tribal governance, the settlers themselves were led differently, and conducted their affairs with men of learning as their representatives, closer in style to the model of druidic leadership.

The earliest Breton king for whom we have any significant historical evidence is the sixth-century King Cunomor or Cunomorus of Pou-Castel. The name has two Celtic elements: *Cun-*, which means 'dog' or 'hound', and *-mor*, which could mean 'of the sea' but is more likely to mean 'great'. The same name is found on a stone inscription in Cornwall, which suggests that it may have been a common royal name. Cunomor's original stronghold was Pou-Castel (modern Carhaix), in Poher, from which he cast his net wider and ended up ruling the whole kingdom of Domnonia, as well as Poher and Leon, from approximately 540 to 554. The Breton histories portray him as a usurper and tyrant, and rejoice in his death, reportedly at the hands of his own people in his native Poher.

When the Frankish or Merovingian kings came to power in Gaul, leading eventually to the formation of the country named after them, France, they resented Breton claims of independence. They refused to allow any of the Breton kings to use the ancient title *rix* or king; instead, they insisted that each should use the term *conte* or count, which they used for their provincial officials. The Breton kings resisted. Notable among them was King Waroch, who gave his name to Bro Waroch, mentioned above. In 587 he invaded Nantes, and in 590 a Frankish army was defeated by his son Canao.

The Breton chiefs maintained their struggle for independence for another three hundred years, defying even the mighty Charlemagne, who sent no less than three full expeditions to suppress them. By the middle of the ninth century, however, the French hegemony was too powerful to resist any longer. Salomon, son of Erispoe, paid homage to Charles the Bald of the Franks, and was executed in 874 when he tried to renege on his oath of loyalty. It was the last attempt at formal Breton independence. Informally, however, Brittany has maintained a cultural and linguistic independence to this

day, and there are still aspirations for some measure of political independence. These were greatly strengthened in recent historical times by the vin-
dictive practice of the *sabot* – a teacher tying a clog around the neck of a child
heard speaking lowly Breton instead of polite French in school – and the
equally volatile question of young Bretons resisting conscription into the
French army and receiving long gaol sentences for their refusal.

Notes

1   Much of the information on the Welsh early kingdoms and royal houses in
    this chapter was gleaned from John Davies's magnificent *History of Wales*,
    originally published in Welsh as *Hanes Cymru* in 1990, English edition 1993,
    and from Myles Dillon and Nora Chadwick, *The Celtic Realms* – see
    Bibliography.
2   *A History of Wales*, p. 98.

ELEVEN

THE KINGS AND QUEENS OF MYTHOLOGY

THE LITERARY SOURCES

WHILE we have learned much about Celtic kingship from the classical authors, from archaeology, and from the chroniclers and historians of the Middle Ages and beyond – in other words, from all the usual historical sources – there is one other rich and fascinating source of information, namely the body of Celtic literature written in the vernacular Celtic languages. Since so much of the material is mythological or folkloric, it tells us very little about historical kings and queens, and what little it does tell us is highly suspect. However, while studying the literary sources may not tell us much more about real individuals, it does tell us a great deal about kingship in Celtic society in general.

There are two Celtic literary traditions, the Goidelic and the Brythonic, which, generally speaking, might just as easily be called the Irish and the Welsh. Some tales and legends were obviously generated in other Celtic countries – for example, the story of Tristan and Isolde in the Arthurian cycle is almost certainly Cornish in origin – but the vast majority of the material is either Irish or Welsh. Moreover, there are definite and easily observed correlations between the Irish material and the Welsh material, and even some story lines in common, so that we can meaningfully use phrases like 'the Welsh version of the tale', and so on. Speculation about which versions came first is fairly pointless, since all the material, from both sides of the Irish Sea, suffers from the identical problem: these tales were carried by oral tradition for many centuries before ever they were written down, and the date of the writing down does not necessarily tell us much about the date of the story's origin. Some of the stories are of the purely mythological type, and, therefore, timeless, while others contain references to (supposedly) historical personages, although these references can be so jumbled or obscure that they tell us very little and, of course, many of them are later interpolations. One of the most curious aspects of the vernacular literature is the clashing of warrior-society material, clearly pagan and archaic in style and content, with later Christian glosses or interpolations: because the writing down was done by Christian clerics, we find a curious jumble of dragons, warriors, saints, gods, demons, Celtic paradises and a Christian Hell, goddesses, fighting queens and invocations to Jesus Christ.

The Irish material is usually classified into four groups. The *Mythological Cycle*, set largely in the Boyne Valley, concerns the earliest gods and tribes, the Fomori, the Tuatha de Danann, and so on, and the faery folk or *tuatha sidhe*; this is probably the oldest of the four. The *Ulaid* or *Ulster Cycle* is set around the time of Christ, and tells the stories of the Ulaid or Ulstermen; some of the material must be historical, but it is very difficult to separate the fact and the fiction. The *Kings Cycle* contains that amorphous collection of tales about the earliest (supposedly) historical kings, like Bres, Conn, Eochaid, and so on, whom we met in Chapter Nine. The fourth cycle, which did not become popular until the twelfth century and may indeed be more recent in original composition also, is the *Fenian* or *Finn Cycle*, which describes the exploits of the hero Fionn Mac Cumhaill (Finn McCool). While these classifications are helpful, they are also artificial. The same characters sometimes appear in more than one of the cycles, and frequently – as one would expect from material generated by a long oral tradition – there are cross-references to characters or incidents that the original storyteller would no doubt have expected his audience to understand without difficulty. If World War III were to happen tomorrow, and the descendants of the survivors five hundred years from now had pursued an oral tradition, that tradition would contain a jumble of references to Mickey Mouse, John F. Kennedy, Superman, the Pope, and so on, and sorting out the real from the mythological would be very difficult.

We think that the Irish stories were first written down some time in the eighth century. There are references to a text called *Lebor Druimm Snechtai*, which included versions of *The Wooing of Etain*, *The Destruction of Da Derga's Hostel* and *The Birth of Cu Chulainn*. Unfortunately, the Vikings – who were not great readers – destroyed most of the early manuscripts. *Lebor na Huidre* (The Book of the Dun Cow), dating from the twelfth century, contains some of the same stories, plus *Bricriu's Feast* and partial versions of *The Intoxication of the Ulaid* and *Tain Bo Cuailnge* (pronounced Toyn Baw Kooling-uh) or *The Cattle Raid of Cooley*, but the manuscript is only a fragment. We know that the scribe was a monk named Mael Muire, who was killed by raiders in the Clonmacnoise cathedral in 1106. *The Book of Leinster* dates to about 1160. It contains versions of some of the same stories, including a more complete *Tain*, as well as additional material like *The Labour Pains of the Ulaid* and *The Tale of Mac Da Tho's Pig*. *The Yellow Book of Lecan*, which includes the most complete account of *The Wooing of Etain*, dates to the fourteenth century.

The Welsh material is found mainly in two texts: *Llyfr Gwyn Rhydderch* (The White Book of Rhydderch), which dates from about 1300, and *Llyfr Coch Hergest* (The Red Book of Hergest), which dates from about 1400. As with the Irish material, the composing of the tales was much earlier than the writing down. To judge by content, the oldest of the stories appears to be *Culhwch hag Olwen*, and the subject matter of these tales may well go right back to the very beginnings of Celtic society. When Lady Charlotte Guest put together an edition of these stories in 1838, together with the poem *Hanes Taliesin*, she mistakenly took the Welsh word *mabinogi* ('story, tale', derived from *mabinog*, a boy or apprentice bard) and invented a plural for it, *mabinogion*, intending to mean 'tales', and gave her collection that title. Even though the name is actually a mistake, it has stuck, and the tales have been known collectively ever since as the *Mabinogion*.[1]

THE UNUSUAL BIRTH

We saw in the story of Arthur, and of many of his knights, frequent references to unusual birth circumstances. This is a very common Celtic theme. The success of the *tarbhfhess* or bull dream to discover the next rightful king, or the drawing of the sword from the stone, or any of the variants of that theme, are predicated on the notion that the rightful king already exists – he simply has to be found. The question as to whether there was any interaction between early druidism and early Pythagoreanism is highly speculative, but there does seem to be in Celtic mythology at least some suggestion of the idea of an eternal, immutable soul which may undergo transmigrations from one existence to another. Even the begetting of the child seems predetermined, as, for example, in the case of Uther Pendragon's sudden and insatiable lust for Ygraine, which produces Arthur. In the Tain, there is a similar predetermined moment:

> Nes the daughter of Eochaid Salbuide of the yellow heel was
> sitting outside Emain with her royal women about her. The druid
> Cathbad from the Tratraige of Mag Inis passed by, and the girl said
> to him:
> 'What is the present hour lucky for?'
> 'For begetting a king on a queen,' he said.
> The queen asked him if that were really true, and the druid swore
> by god that it was: a son conceived at that hour would be heard of in
> Ireland for ever. The girl saw no other male near, and she took him
> inside with her.
> She grew heavy with a child. It was in her womb for three years
> and three months.
> And at the feast of Othar she was delivered.

The child born of the union is Conchobor (pronounced Kon-chov-or or Kon-chor), otherwise known as Conchobhar Mac Nessa, High King of Ireland. The unusual gestation period amounts to thirty-nine months; that number, with factors 3 and 13, held particular significance in druidism.[2] Another king, Noidhiu Noimbreathach ('of the Nine Judgments') is born of his mother Fingel after she has been impregnated by a sea spirit and has carried the child for 9 years and 9 months.

From this willingness to accept and even welcome the inevitable coming of the king or hero there developed the decidedly unChristian practice, later much abused in Scotland as the *ius primae noctis* ('right of the first night'), *mercheta mulierum* or Laird's Right, of allowing the king or lord to sleep first with any newly married girl. It happens with Conchobhar, too:

> Ulster grew to worship Conchobor. So high was their regard for him
> that every man in Ulster that took a girl in marriage let her sleep the
> first night with Conchobor, so as to have him first in the family. . . .
> Any Ulsterman who gave him a bed for the night gave him his wife
> as well to sleep with.

There are different versions of the story of the conception and birth of Cu Chulainn (pronounced Koo-hull-in). Conchobhar travels with his sister (or daughter) Dechtine (or Dechtire) in pursuit of a flock of birds which has grazed the plain of Emain to destruction. They take shelter from snow in the newly built house of a young couple. That night, the host's wife gives birth to a son. At the exact same moment, a mare outside the house drops two foals, which the man presents to the child as a gift. In the morning, the mysterious birds, the house, and the host couple have all disappeared: only the child and the two foals remain. Conchobhar and Dechtine bring them back to Emain. Here the child dies. Dechtine, stricken with grief, drinks from a copper vessel, and a tiny creature leaps from the drink into her mouth: it is the child again. She becomes miraculously pregnant with the little creature and calls him Setanta (pronounced Shay-dan-da) meaning 'Miracle'. However, Conchobhar now betrothes her to Sualdam Mac Roich:

> She was ashamed to go pregnant to bed with her husband, and got sick
> when she reached the bedstead. The living thing spilled away in the
> sickness, and so she was made virgin and whole and went to her
> husband. She grew pregnant again and bore a son, and called him
> Setanta.

Although the story is laughable to a modern, scientific sensibility, the under-lying mythological point is very clear: this hero spirit, the Setanta or Miracle who is to become the great warrior Cu Chulainn, is so eager to be born into the real world and fulfil his destiny that he is willing to be conceived three times, rather than the normal once.

(Cu Chulainn acquired his heroic name, meaning 'Culainn's Hound', because, while still a child, he killed Culainn's ferocious guard dog, which could only be restrained by three chains, with three men on each chain, and then, to make amends for the deed, agreed to guard Culainn's flocks until a replacement guard dog could be reared and trained.)

The king's or hero's physical appearance is also frequently unusual, although there is sometimes a very fine difference between what constitutes noble distinctiveness and what might be considered a blemish. The description of Cu Chulainn's handsomeness includes the following:

> In each of his cheeks
> a spot red as blood,
> a green spot, a blue spot
> and a spot of pale purple.
>
> Seven lights in his eye –
> he is not one to be left sightless.
> It has the ornament of a noble eye;
> a dark, blue-black eyelash.
>
> A man known throughout Eriu
> is already good; and this one has
> hair of three different colours
> this young beardless lad . . .

(The hair of three different colours was probably achieved with herbal dyes and limewash.)

We have already mentioned the stories of Cormac being born on a wood pile and taken away to be raised by a she-wolf (see page 176), and of Mes Buachalla, 'foster-child of the cowherd', who slept with the bird-god Nemglan and produced the hero Conaire Mor, destined to be High King of Ireland (see page 176). In *The Wooing of Etain*, the heroine is transformed into the shape of a fly and falls into the cup of the wife of Etar, an Ulster hero. Etain is subsequently born of the wife, and called Etar's daughter.

Many of these stories imply individual reincarnation – the hero is born at the precise moment of his father's death – but even when the connection is not that precise, the underlying theme is very consistent. The true king or hero is destined to fulfil his role. He comes from a timeless place by a magical or mysterious process, does the work he has to do among mortals, and then returns to the timeless place from which he came. He is not born of a regular marriage, like ordinary men, because he has to have qualities which are beyond the ordinary; therefore, he is the product of incest, or adultery, or intercourse between humans and gods, especially gods in animal form.

Interestingly, many of the Celtic saints also have stories of unusual birth circumstances. St. Alba, St. Bairre and St. Ciwa are all suckled by wolves.

St. Brendan the Navigator is suckled by a wild doe. St. Colm Cille's mother is visited during her pregnancy by an angel, who brings her a cloak which then floats away to Heaven. St. Finian's mother is impregnated by a salmon while bathing in Loch Lein. St. Cadoc, St. David and St. Cynog are all born of an act of rape. St. Beuno is born of elderly parents, who have not had sexual intercourse for twelve years previously. The saint's birth is often foretold by another saint, by an angel, or (apparently incongruously) by a pagan druid. Very often, the saint's mother is given a vision of the saint's future character and greatness, in the form of a star, or a ball of light, or even as an image of the saint as a fully grown man or woman, bathed in a glowing radiance and with a halo about his or her head.

THE WARRIOR KING

Not surprisingly in a society which held warfare and battle skill in such esteem, it is the fighting qualities of the king or potential king which are first reported in many of the tales. As we saw in the stories of Vercingetorix and Vortigern, and to some extent of Arthur, the king is first and foremost the military leader. Like Maelgawn or Brian Boru, he has to swing his sword in battle even if he is 80 years old or more; wisdom, experience or title alone are not sufficient unless the king is also a warrior in every sense.

Cu Chulainn's training includes the Pierced Flagstone, which, as the name suggests, consists of a holed flagstone set over a fire with bellows; he performed on it 'until his soles were blackened and discoloured'. He also learns how to climb a spear and stand on its point without making his feet bleed. He conquers the test of the Pupils' Bridge by going into his famous rage or 'warp-spasm' and performing the 'salmon-leap'. The warp-spasm or *riastradh* (literally, 'contortion') was a battle rage of such proportions that he was no longer recognizable:

> His shanks and his joints, every knuckle and angle and organ from
> head to foot, shook like a tree in the flood or a reed in the stream. His
> body made a furious twist inside his skin, so that his feet and shins and
> knees switched to the rear and his heels and calves switched to the
> front. . . . His face and features became a red bowl: he sucked one eye
> so deep into his head that a wild crane couldn't probe it onto his cheek
> out of the depths of his skull; the other eye fell out along his cheek. . . .
> His cheek peeled back from his jaws until the gullet appeared, his lungs
> and liver flapped in his mouth and throat. . . . His heart boomed loud
> in his breast like the baying of a watch-dog at its feed or the sound of
> a lion among bears. . . . The hero-halo rose out of his brow, long and
> broad as a warrior's whetstone, long as a snout, and he went mad
> rattling his shields. . . . Then, tall and thick, steady and strong, high as

the mast of a noble ship, rose up from the dead centre of his skull a straight spout of black blood darkly and magically smoking like the smoke from a royal hostel when a king is coming to be cared for at the close of a winter day.

The kinds of physical feats or tests which Cu Chulainn underwent as part of his training reappear much later in the Arthurian literature, sometimes connected with chivalric motives; Lancelot, for example, has to crawl along a bridge of razor-sharp sword edges to prove his love for Guinevere. He suffers terrible wounds, but is met with indifference by her, which drives him to madness.

This is the list of war feats which Cu Chulainn learns from his teacher, Scathach ('the Shadowy One', who is a woman):

> . . . the apple feat – juggling nine apples with never more than one in his palm; the thunder-feat; the feats of the sword-edge and the sloped shield; the feats of the javelin and rope; the body-feat; the feat of Cat and the heroic salmon-leap; the pole throw and the leap over a poisoned stroke; the noble chariot-fighter's crouch; the *gae bolga*; the spurt of speed; the feat of the chariot-wheel thrown on high and the feat of the shield-rim; the breath-feat, with gold apples blown up into the air; the snapping mouth and the hero's scream; the stroke of precision; the stunning-shot and the cry-stroke; stepping on a lance in flight and straightening erect on its point; the sickle-chariot; and the trussing of a warrior on points of spears.

Some of these are more obscure than others. The *ga bolga* appears to have been a special kind of spear with spiral hooks, designed to eviscerate the victim as it was withdrawn.

The Tale of Mac Da Tho's Pig, from *The Book of Leinster*, is a ridiculous tale which barely makes any sense to a pacific modern sensibility, but its revelry in wild boasts, pointless violence and mayhem absolutely typifies the warrior spirit which a Celtic king was supposed to embody. Mac Da Tho deliberately invites the men of Ulster and the men of Connaught to his hostel on the same feast night, knowing there will be fighting. He presents for their main dish the eponymous pig, which has been nourished by sixty cows for seven years and comes to the table with forty oxen laid across it. There is meat enough for all, but that is not the point. The warriors argue over who has the right to cut the first slice, the hero portion, and a series of insulting matches begins. Conall of Connaught finally cuts the first slice, and what follows is obvious:

> Everyone hit someone. Blows fell upon ears until the heap on the floor reached the centre of the house and the streams of gore reached the entrances. The hosts broke through the doors, then, and a good

drinking bout broke out in the courtyard, with everyone striking his
neighbour. Ferghus pulled up a great oak by the roots . . .

To complete the entertainment, Mac Da Tho unleashes his ferocious hound
to see which side it will choose. *Bricriu's Feast* tells a very similar tale, except
that there is also a beheading match like that in the story of *Gawain and the
Green Knight,* and even more is made of the insulting, with Bricriu frequently referred to as Nemthenga ('Poison Tongue').

THE WARRIOR QUEEN

There is a legend concerning the well of St. Keyne, in Cornwall. When a
couple are newly married, whoever drinks first from the well will rule the
household throughout the remainder of the marriage. It is a charming piece
of folklore, which has generated some amusing poems and songs. The well is
said to have attained its power from St. Keyne, a fifth-century female hermit
who tortured her body for the good of her soul. At her death, according to
the legend, forgiving angels came down and removed the hair shirt which she
had worn for years and replaced it with a heavenly white robe. In fact, Keyne
was a queen before she was a saint, and it may be that the legend comes more
from remembrance of her as a warrior queen than as a Christian hermit. She
was the daughter of King Brycham of Brecknock, the tiny kingdom in the
south of Wales which maintained an independent line of succession all the
way from the fifth century to the tenth century. As with so many of the early
Celtic saints, there is very little evidence for the historical facts of her life,
since all the hagiographies are extremely fanciful and unreliable. However,
we do know that Brecknock survived many attempts at conquest or violent
assimilation, and we can reasonably infer that the royal dynasty of Brecknock
would have been very familiar with the arts of war. It would be very interesting to go back in a time machine and see how Princess Keyne of the royal
family of Brecknock in Wales ended up living the desperately poor and lonely life of a hermit in the remoteness of Cornwall. Her legend – which is virtually all we have left of her – seems to suggest that she was a woman of great
power at some time in her life.

Celtic queens were clearly expected to demonstrate just as much physical
fortitude as Celtic kings. Even those who did not become commanders in war,
like the well-attested Boudica and Cartimandua, were expected to have
warrior-like qualities. When the Irish goddess Macha gives birth to her
famous twins, it is in the most strenuous physical circumstances:

Soon, a fair was held in Ulster. . . . Crunniuc set out for the fair with the
rest . . .
'It would be as well not to grow boastful or careless in anything you

say,' the woman [Macha] said to him.

'That isn't likely,' he said.

The fair was held. At the end of the day the king's chariot was brought onto the field. His chariot and horses won. The crowd said that nothing could beat those horses.

'My wife is faster,' Crunniuc said.

He was taken immediately before the king and the woman was sent for. She said to the messenger:

'It would be a heavy burden for me to go and free him now. I am full with child.'

'Burden?' the messenger said. 'He will die unless you come.'

She went to the fair, and her pangs gripped her. She called out to the crowd:

'A mother bore each one of you! Help me! Wait till my child is born.' But she couldn't move them.

'Very well,' she said. 'A long-lasting evil will come out of this on the whole of Ulster.'

'What is your name?' the king said.

'My name, and the name of my offspring,' she said, 'will be given to this place. I am Macha, daughter of Sainrith mac Imbaith.'

Then she raced the chariot. As the chariot reached the end of the field, she gave birth alongside it. She bore twins, a son and a daughter. The name, Emain Macha, the Twins of Macha, comes from this. As she gave birth she screamed out that all who heard that scream would suffer from the same pangs for five days and four nights in their times of greatest difficulty. This affliction, ever afterward, seized all the men of Ulster who were there that day, and nine generations after them.

The tale is reminiscent of American Indian legends about Apache women giving birth on horseback while the rest of the tribe kept on going. There is a similar theme of a scream as an omen in the story of Derdriu or Deirdre of the Sorrows, whose scream from the womb before her birth presages great evil. Derdriu's death is also as wilful and violent as any warrior's:

'What do you see that you hate most?' Conchobor said.

'You, of course,' she said, 'and Eogan mac Durthacht!'

'Go and live for a year with Eogan, then,' Conchobor said.

Then he sent her over to Eogan.

They set out next day for the fair of Macha. She was behind Eogan in the chariot. She had sworn that two men alive together in the world would never have her.

'This is good, Derdriu,' Conchobor said. 'Between me and Eogan you are a sheep eyeing two rams.'

A big block of stone was in front of her. She let her head be driven against the stone, and made a mass of fragments of it, and she was dead.

Cu Chulainn's trainer in arms, mentioned above, was Scathach, a female warrior and prophetess. Even more ferocious than Scathach is Aife, 'the hardest woman warrior in the world', who challenges Scathach to single combat, which Cu Chulainn accepts in Scathach's place. Even so, Cu Chulainn has to use trickery to win the fight, not to mention a handhold which modern wrestling would certainly not approve:

> Cu Chulainn went up to Scathach and asked her what Aife held most dear above all else.
>
> 'The things she holds most dear', Scathach said, 'are her two horses, her chariot and her charioteer.'
>
> Cu Chulainn met and fought Aife on the rope of feats. Aife smashed Cu Chulainn's weapon. All she left him was a part of his sword no bigger than a fist.
>
> 'Look! Oh, look!' Cu Chulainn said. 'Aife's charioteer and her two horses and the chariot have fallen into the valley! They are all dead!'
>
> Aife looked around and Cu Chulainn leaped at her and seized her by the two breasts. He took her on his back like a sack, and brought her back to his own army.

When Queen Medb is reviewing her armies with her consort, King Ailill, she is concerned about the Galeoin, a troop of three thousand men of Leinster. When Aillill asks what fault she finds with them, she answers that she finds none, and then lists their excellent soldierly qualities. The problem, she says, is that if they go with them they will get all the credit:

> 'But they are fighting on our side,' Ailill said.
>
> 'They can't come,' Medb said.
>
> 'Let them stay, then,' Ailill said.
>
> 'No, they can't stay either,' Medb said. 'They would only come and seize our lands when we are gone.'
>
> 'Well, what are we going to do with them,' Ailill said, 'if they can neither stay nor come?'
>
> 'Kill them,' Medb said.
>
> 'That is a woman's thinking and no mistake!' Ailill said. 'A wicked thing to say.'

In the event, the Galeoin are scattered to different parts of the army, but the point has been made that a warrior queen can be even more ruthless than a warrior king, and much less susceptible to trivial questions about honour or loyalty.

The most powerful examples of the warrior queen are the Irish battle-goddesses, the Morrigan, Badbh, Macha (who gave birth to the twins, mentioned above) and Nemhain. In the tales, the goddess appears as a washer-woman at a river ford, washing the hero's weapons and armour in preparation for his departure from this life. She, or they (this is one goddess with many aspects), can shape-shift at will. Her favourite form is that of the crow or raven, picking among the corpses when the battle is done, the limbs are twitching, and the blood is growing cold and black on the ground. Nemhain, whose name means 'Frenzy', kills a hundred warriors just by shrieking her hideous scream at them. The Badbh, frequently called Badbh Catha or the Battle Crow, appears in the *Tale of Da Derga's Hostel* as a hideous, crow-black hag, bleeding, and with a rope around her neck, to foretell Conaire of his death. The Morrigan or Great Queen is an instigator of war, a bringer of death and destruction as well as, seemingly incongruously, a powerful goddess of fertility. She is fickle: loving and supporting the warrior-hero when she favours him, vicious and destructive when he is out of favour. When Cu Chulainn finally dies, the Morrigan is seen perched on his shoulder.

The 'banshee', which is the English pronunciation of Irish *bean sidhe* ('faery woman'), is a generic type of the war goddess or death goddess. Her wailing cry, which foretells death, is called in Irish the *caoin*, pronounced 'keen', which is the origin of the English use of 'keen' to mean 'mourn' or 'weep for'. There are various Irish folk legends about the *bean sidhe*. One is that she leads ghastly funeral processions, with an immense black coach drawn by four headless black horses, and that if any residents of a house are foolish enough to open the door when the *bean sidhe* knocks at it, they will receive a bowl of blood thrown into their faces.

THE RIVALS

One of the constantly recurring kingship themes is that of succession, the new king replacing the old. In the context, already established, of kingship being seen as a kind of symbolic mating or marriage between the king and the land, or the goddess representing the land, the relationship between old king and new king takes on an added dimension. In the gods Bel and Bran we see two archetypes: Bel is the young sun-god, the May god, god of the waxing year, Mabon or Maponus, the son, the aspirant, the lover; Bran is the old thunder-god, the god of autumn, god of the waning year, the father. When Bran dies, Bel takes his place, and, of course, eventually becomes Bran: the cycle goes on endlessly. This theme appears in many different forms in Celtic mythology. The tales of rivalry often involve shape-shifting and magic, which led in turn to stories about duelling wizards or druids, but the fundamental battle has a much more basic psychology: it is the battle between father and son for possession of the mother, who here represents not only her sex, but the nation itself.

The most famous of these shape-shifting battles in Celtic literature is not actually between the young god and the old god; rather, it is between the young god and the goddess. In the Welsh story of *Taliesin*, Cerridwen, the witch-goddess, is brewing the broth of knowledge and inspiration in her magic cauldron. The boy, Gwion, left to stir the pot, sucks his thumb when a drop of the hot liquid splashes on it. He is instantly filled with the knowledge of all things, past, present and future. In symbolic terms, he has acquired the power of the goddess, he has conquered death, he is now the king. Cerridwen pursues him. He changes into a hare, so she becomes a greyhound; he shape-shifts into a fish, so she becomes an otter; he becomes a bird, she becomes a hawk; he hides in a barn as a grain in a heap of wheat, so she becomes a black hen and pecks him up, ending the chase. The message of the legend, not difficult to unravel, is that it is the goddess who always triumphs, no matter how cunning or courageous the hero; the queen-goddess of the land who survives, no matter how powerful the king. There is also an underlying sexual mythography here. The goddess's magic cauldron is the womb, from which all life is born. Cerridwen's swallowing of Gwion as a grain of corn brings him back inside her, and is reminiscent of the many other instances in the Celtic legends where the swallowing of an insect or tiny object is associated with impregnation. In this particular story the symbolism becomes quite explicit, since the next thing that happens is that Cerridwen becomes pregnant by the grain of corn and Gwion is born again, and then goes off on another set of adventures.

The notion of the ritual mating of the king with the land is sometimes graphically explicit. In the Irish tales, the Dagda ('Good God'), a club-wielding Hercules-type figure, straddles the river-goddess Boann for a nine-month-long night of pleasure. This god in particular, whose appetites are so gargantuan that he sometimes takes on a kind of buffoonish character, is frequently represented as being in pursuit of food or sex, or both. He is not always a buffoon, however. One of his matings is with the Morrigan, the great goddess of war and death, and that is not such a light undertaking. Some of the rival-king myths, particularly the Irish ones, involve sexual encounters which seem remarkably casual; it is only in the later legends, particularly the Brythonic stories that went via Brittany eventually into the Matter of Britain, that the encounters become more mysterious, courtly and romantic, and the male rivalries more subtle and complex.

Sometimes the rivals are brothers, rather than father and son. In the Welsh tradition, Arawn, King of the Underworld, and Amaethon or Amathaon ('Husbandman' or 'Ploughman'), the god of agriculture, are both children of the great goddess Don. Amaethon steals from Arawn a hound, a deer and a bird. As a result, a great battle is fought between them, known as the Cad Goddeu, or Battle of the Trees. The poem *Cad Goddeu*, which tells the story of the battle, is complex, elliptical and filled with deeply obscure references, and it has been a favourite hunting ground for scholars of early Welsh literature for centuries now, but it appears to be about the capture of a holy oracular shrine by the guessing of a god's name. Robert Graves relates it to the possible fourth-century BC arrival of Belgic Brythons in the British Isles, and their capture of a religious site, perhaps Avebury, which they subsequently dedicated to the ash-tree god, Gwydion (the counterpart of Odin or Woden in Teutonic mythology), instead of the former god, Bran or Arawn.[3]

In the *Tain*, the whole saga hinges around the pursuit of a sacred bull, the Brown Bull of Cooley, but the bull was originally one of a pair of rivals, whose tale is told in *The Quarrel of the Two Pig-Keepers*. Two faery kings, Ochall Ochne of the Connaught *sid*, and Bodb of the Munster *sid*, are rivals. Their rivalry is transferred to their two swineherds, Friuch ('Bristle') and Rucht ('Grunt'). Both are dismissed and begin a battle of shape-shifting. They become birds of prey, Ingen ('Talon') and Eitte ('Wing'); they fight for two years under the sea as Bled ('Whale') and Blod ('Seabeast'); they become two stags, each destroying the other's herd of does and making a shambles of the herd's dwelling place; they become two warriors, Rinn ('Point') and Faebur ('Edge'); they become two phantoms, Scath ('Shadow') and Sciath ('Shield'); they become two dragons, and pour snow on each other's lands; they drop down out of the air and become two maggots, Cruinniuc and Tuinniuc; one of the maggots is eaten by a cow drinking from the River Cronn in Cooley, which duly delivers it as the Donn Cuailnge or Brown Bull of Cooley, while the other maggot is swallowed by a cow belonging to Queen Medb and King Ailill and is duly delivered as the Finnbennach Ai, the White Bull of Ai Plain.

In the *Tain* itself, the father–son rivalry is explicit: Cu Chulainn kills his own son, Condlae or Connla, the son of Aiofe. The story ends with Cu Chulainn disembowelling his son with a stroke of the *ga bulga* (see page 35), then carrying his limp body from the shore where they fought amidst cries of lamentation. But Cu Chulainn himself is curiously dispassionate about the death, at least to a modern sensibility. He knows full well that it is his own son whom he is about to kill, and Emer pleads with him that 'neither fair nor right is it to rise against your son of great and valorous deeds,' but the battle lust still rises full in him, to the extent that even his speech is semi-coherent, as Jeffrey Gantz's accurate translation conveys:

'Silence, woman! It is not a woman's advice I seek regarding deeds of bright splendour. Such deeds are not performed with a woman's assistance. Let us be triumphant in feats. Sated the eyes of a great king. A mist of blood upon my skin, the gore from the body of Condlae. Beautifully spears will suck the fair javelin. Whatever were down there, woman, I would go for the sake of the Ulaid.'

There is a very interesting sexual reference right towards the end of the *Tain*. The battles have been fought up and down, thousands of warriors have been slaughtered, we have listened to account after account of individual combat and death, and then, at last, Cu Chulainn and Queen Medb meet for the final single combat, the climax of the whole story. At precisely this moment, Medb's period begins, or, as the text puts it, 'Medb got her gush of blood', and she asks her champion, Ferghus, to keep guard while she relieves herself. 'By god,' says Ferghus, 'you have picked a bad time for this,' to which Medb replies,

'I can't help it, I'll die if I can't do it.' So the final showdown between Cu Chulainn and Medb ends in this strange anticlimax, with Medb attending to the ablutions of her menstruation, and Cu Chulainn sparing her life, even though, as he says, 'If I killed you dead, it would only be right.' The sudden onset of Medb's period is a curious detail to have survived so long and through so many tellings of the tale, and it can only be supposed that it must relate to the underlying theme of the rival kings, in which, of course, only the kings die, and the queen, who is the land and the nation, continues to live and be court-ed. There can be no more direct and unequivocal image of the queen's fertil-ity than her menstruation, the absolute sign of her ability to bear children.

The Dream of Oenghus, one of the Irish legends, tells the story of Oenghus (Angus), also called Mac Oc ('Son of Youth'), who is the Bel or Mabon archetype. He actually appears in two other stories, but in this tale he is the protagonist. He is given a vision of a beautiful maiden, and pines with love for her. She is Caer Ibormeith ('Caer of the Yew Berry'). To the Celts, and in general folklore ever since, the yew was associated with death, so Caer represents the challenge that every young king must meet: to face death and the otherworld without fear. The Bran figure or archetype is Ethel Anbhual, Caer's father. He is the King of Sidh Uamain, in other words a faery king. He refuses to allow Caer to be wooed by Oenghus. To escape from Ethel, Caer and Oenghus shape-shift into swans at the festival of Samhain. Samhain was the time of year when movement between this world and the otherworld was especially easy. In Caer's case, it was the only time of year when she could shape-shift. The symbolism of the swans is twofold. First, swans are famed for their faithfulness to each other; swans mate for life. Secondly, swans were very frequently associated with death, as evidenced by the many portrayals or models of funerary waggons drawn by swans which have been found at Celtic archaeological sites. Midhir and Etain, in their parallel legend, are also transformed into swans. Finally, Caer and Oenghus fly to Brugh na Boinne, Oenghus's palace, a place sanctified by his mother, the goddess Boann who gave her name to the River Boyne. Although the tale is a romance, it contains many elements of the rival king pattern.

Perhaps the most complex of the rival theme legends is the story *Math, son of Mathonwy*, from the *Mabinogion*. Math, a king of Gwynedd, and Gwydion, his nephew (actually, his sister's son, which has a special relevance since in Celtic law of succession the throne passes to the sister's son if the king has no issue of his own), are two magicians of great power. The first part of the story is essentially a wizard duel, like that between Friuch and Rucht in *The Quarrel of the Two Pig-Keepers*. Gwydion provokes a war between north Wales and south Wales. Now a new character enters the story: this is Gwydion's sister, Arianrhod ('Silver Wheel'). Math tests her virginity by requiring her to step over his magic staff. She immediately delivers two objects, a child and 'a small something'. The first, a boy, immediately runs into the sea and is given the name Dylan Eil Don ('Sea Son of Wave'). The second, the 'small something', Gwydion wraps in a handkerchief and hides in a chest

*Bronze sculpture of the dead hero Cu Chulainn, cast in 1916 by
Oliver Shepherd, which now stands in the main Post Office in Dublin.
The raven on his shoulder is the Morrigan, the goddess queen of death.*

at the bottom of his bed. It grows into a boy, and keeps on growing at a prodigious rate. Gwydion brings the miraculous child to meet his mother at her castle, Caer Arianrhod. (The Welsh give the name Caer Arianrhod to the northern constellation Corona Borealis.) The rest of the story tells of the exploits of the prodigious child, who is called Llew Llaw Gyffes ('Llew, or the Lion, of the Steady Hand'). His mother places several spells on him, one of which is that he shall never taken a human woman to wife. Math and Gwydion then create for him a wife made out of wild flowers, and call her Blodeuwedd (*blodau* means 'flowers'). While Lleu is away, his flower wife takes a lover, Gronw Pebyr, and plots with him how to kill Lleu. To complicate matters, another of Arianrhod's spells was that Lleu could only die in very precise and peculiar circumstances: he had to be neither within a house, nor outside; neither on horseback, nor on foot; neither on water nor on dry land. Blodeuwedd contrives to have Lleu demonstrate how these irreconcilable conditions can be met, and he ends up with one foot on the back of a he-goat, the other on the edge of a bath, under a canopy of thatch on the bank of the River Cynfal. As soon as he is in position, Gronw throws a spear at him. Lleu, wounded, immediately shape-shifts into an eagle and flies up into a tree. After some time has passed, Gwydion searches for his nephew by following a sow which escapes from her sty every night. He finds the sow feeding on rotting flesh and maggots at the foot of a tree. Gwydion sings a powerful charm or *englyn*, and an eagle flies down. Gwydion touches the eagle with his wand and it transforms into Lleu, in piteous condition, nothing but skin and bone. Gwydion brings Lleu back to Caer Dathyl for healing, then pursues Blodeuwedd. He turns Blodeuwedd into an owl (the name means 'Flower-face'). Gronw is brought back to meet his punishment, which is the punishment of the return blow. He must stand where Lleu stood, and receive the spear as Lleu received it. He asks for a stone to be placed between him and Lleu, which is agreed. Lleu's spear passes straight through the stone, leaving a hole in it, and Gronw dies.

This charming and richly complex tale clearly has many symbolic themes running though it, but one of them is obviously the theme of the rivals. It is also interesting that the key relationship of sister's son, the relationship of royal inheritance, appears twice in the story: Gwydion is Math's nephew (or successor) and Lleu Llaw Gyffes is Gwydion's nephew (or successor). Gwydion and Arianrhod are children of the goddess Don, who is the Brythonic counterpart of the Irish Dana, whose children are the Tuatha de Danann. There is a strong suggestion of Nordic influence in the tale, not least because Gwydion is the Brythonic variant of the name Odin or Woden, who is a northern Teutonic god. Lleu is often compared with the Irish god Lugh, and both are compared with the classical Hermes or Mercury.

One other element in this particular legend is of interest. Math, son of Mathonwy, can only stay alive by resting his feet in the lap of a virgin, unless it is a time of war, and then the need disappears. The virgin is a symbol of untapped sexual energy, of the life force to which the king is 'wedded'; this rather peculiar image is really only a variant of the sacred marriage idea, although a rather unusual one. What is interesting is that the ceremonial relationship disappears in wartime, perhaps because at such times the king is staring timelessness full in the face, and the ritual marriage with the land becomes temporarily redundant.

THE KING AS SAGE AND LAW GIVER

Of Conchobhar Mac Nessa it was said, 'There was no wiser being in the world. He never gave a judgment until it was ripe, for fear it might be wrong and the crops worsen.' The power of correct utterance was immense, and so was the responsibility that went with it. False utterance would lead to sterility, corruption, failed harvests, disease and death.

In Pwyll, Prince of Dyfed, from the Mabinogion, Pwyll is sitting at a feast with his betrothed, the goddess Rhiannon. In walks a stranger, who announces that he has a boon to ask, and Pwyll magnanimously says, as befits a generous host, 'Whatever boon thou ask of me, so far as I can get it, it shall be thine.' The stranger promptly demands to sleep with Rhiannon; he is the hideous suitor whom she has been trying desperately to avoid. By speaking thoughtlessly and carelessly, Pwyll has precipitated a diplomatic catastrophe, which is only averted by Rhiannon's cunning and magical skills. As she says to Pwyll, 'Be dumb as long as thou wilt. Never was there a man made feebler use of his wits than thou hast.'

In the Irish tales, frequent mention is made of *imbas forasnai*, usually translated as 'the light of foresight'. This power, which is mystical rather than a quality acquired through wisdom or profundity of character, can be given to both men and women. The prophetess Fedelm, who has the *imbas forasnai*, foretells the destruction of Medb's army in the *Tain*, and when Medb demands that she change her vision, she intones unchangingly, 'I see it crimson, I see it red, I see it crimson, I see it red.' Scathach, Cu Chulainn's teacher of warfare, has the same power of vision and tells him of his life ahead 'full of triumph and women's love'. In the same way that the king or queen is predestined to come from the place of timelessness and to return there after death, he or she is also frequently given the power to see ahead in time to the future, which is, after all, only time past seen from a different place. In the Arthurian stories, this *imbas forasnai* is separated out into the character of Myrddin or Merlin, but in the earlier Celtic literature it is found not only in the druids and prophetesses but also in the kings and queens themselves, who have an uncanny sense of their own destiny.

One of the recurring images of the time-bound, or mortal, king pursuing the timelessness of destiny, or the otherworld before and after life, is that of a horse-rider pursuing another horse-rider but never gaining on him or her. An example occurs in *The Destruction of Da Derga's Hostel*, with Conaire Mor as the pursuer:

> After that, as Conaire was making along the Slighe Chualainn, he perceived three horsemen up ahead making for the house. Red tunics and red mantles they wore, and red shields and spears were in their hands; they rode red horses and their heads were red. They were entirely red, teeth and hair, horses and men.
>
> 'Who rides before us? Conaire asked. . . . .
>
> He went after them then, lashing his horse, but they remained a spear-cast ahead; they did not gain on him, and he did not gain on them.

The red colouring confirms that these riders are from the otherworld. Red and white were the Celtic colours of death, not black. The hounds of Hell, who appear in the Brythonic tales, are white with red eyes and red tips to their ears. There is a virtually identical horse pursuit in the Welsh stories, when Pwyll, Prince of Dyfed first meets the goddess Rhiannon. Day after day, Pwyll sends riders after a beautiful woman seen riding at Arberth. Swift as they are, none can catch up with her. Finally, Pwyll makes the attempt himself, on the fastest horse in he kingdom:

> Pwyll mounted his horse, and no sooner had he mounted his horse than she passed him by. He turned after her and let his horse, mettled and prancing, take its own speed. And he thought that at the second bound or the third he would come up with her. But he was no nearer to her than before. He drove his horse to its utmost speed, but he saw that it was idle for him to follow her.
>
> Then Pwyll spoke.
>
> 'Maiden,' said he, 'for his sake whom thou lovest best, stay for me.'
>
> 'I will, gladly,' said she, 'and it had been better for the horse hadst thou asked this long since.'

The point of Rhiannon's chiding remark is to remind Pwyll of the deeply revered Celtic and druidic notion that correct and truthful utterance is every bit as powerful as deeds, and sometimes more so.

The name Rhiannon is related to the Welsh word *rhiain*, which means 'virgin', and it has been suggested that her name is a simplification of *rhiain Annwn* ('virgin of the Underworld'). The name may also be related to the goddess name Rigantona ('Mighty Queen'), found in several inscriptions. In this same story, Rhiannon is given an unusual penance to perform: she has to carry guests on her back, like a horse. She is a manifestation of the horse-goddess, worshipped throughout the Celtic world as Epona, and frequently depicted as a white mare. Giraldus Cambrensis recounts an Ulster myth in which the initiate king copulates with a white mare, which is then sacrificed, carved and boiled. The king bathes in the broth and drinks directly from the bath, and he and his retinue eat the meat. The initiate is now the king. He has become one with Epona. The account has been contested as an invention and unwarranted attack on the Irish by Giraldus, who was a Welshman, born in Pembrokeshire, but there is good evidence to support it, and, if Giraldus is telling the truth, the ritual would still have been performed in his time (his dates are *c.* 1146 to 1220).

The king acquires his power because of his familiarity with timelessness, the otherworld, or with death. Pwyll, who is Prince of Dyfed, is given the name Pwyll Pen Annwn ('Chief of Hell') because he goes into the otherworld for a year as part of a tryst with its true king, Arawn. Each takes the other's place, including his semblance. Annwn (sometimes spelled Annwfn) is usually translated as 'Hell' or 'Hades', but it is actually a far more pleasant place than either of those. Pwyll is treated royally. He even sleeps with Arawn's wife (who cannot distinguish him from her husband), but does not violate her. When the two kings exchange places again at the end of the year and a day agreed, Arawn makes love to his wife, who tells him how relieved she is to have his lovemaking again after a whole year without it. Arawn immediately understands how steadfast and unswerving Pwyll has been, and blesses his kingdom, which now becomes even more fruitful and prosperous than before. The mythic point of the tale is that the terrestrial king, by entering the realms where ordinary mortals dare not tread, brings fecundity and prosperity to the land.

In the *Mabinogion*, these encounters with the mysterious forces of the otherworld are sometimes told very subtly, in a way that anticipates some of the riches of the later Breton tales and Arthurian literature. Here, for example, is a passage from *Manawydan Son of Llyr* in which the hero, Pryderi, has followed his hunting dogs and a great white boar (white being the colour of death or the underworld) and has wandered into a castle or *caer* which is not of this world:

> When he came to the caer neither man nor beast nor the boar nor the dogs nor the house nor habitation could he see in the caer. As it were in the middle of the caer floor, he could see a fountain with marble work around it, and on the edge of the fountain a golden bowl fastened to four chains, and that upon a marble slab, and the chains ascending into the air, and he could see no end to them. He was transported with the great beauty of the gold and with the exceeding good workmanship of the bowl, and he came to where the bowl was and laid hold of it. And as soon as he laid hold of the bowl, his two hands stuck to the bowl, and his feet to the slab on which he was standing, and all his power of speech forsook him, so that he could not utter one word. And thus he stood.

It is easy to see how many of the mystery elements in the Grail stories can be traced back to earlier tales of bowls and magical cauldrons. In a sense, they are all symbols of the womb, the vessel of great mystery from which all life springs.

When the king is in tune with nature and his destiny, his powers are great. Cu Chulainn instantly tames a magnificent stag and yokes it between the poles of his chariot: 'I swear by the god the Ulaid swear by, I will turn my head and fix the deer with my eye so that it will not turn its head or dare to move.' The king can even distort nature, as well as himself. This is the effect three kings had on the women of Ulster:

> The women of Ulaid suffered three blemishes: every woman who loved
> Conall had a crooked neck; every woman who loved Cuscraid Mend
> Machae son of Conchubur stammered; and every woman who loved
> Cu Chulainn blinded in one eye in his likeness.

(The reference to blindness in one eye describes Cu Chulainn's warp-spasm feat of drawing one eye deep inside his head.)

However, when destiny deserts the ailing or failing king, all nature joins in the rout. When Cu Chulainn is struggling in personal combat with Loch Mac Mofemis, even the animals seem to join in the fight against him. They fight in a stream, and an eel wraps itself around Cu Chulainn's leg to trip him. A she-wolf attacks him, and he blinds it with a stone from his sling. The blinded wolf drives a stampede of cattle against Cu Chulainn, and shape-shifts into a hornless red heifer at the head of the stampede. The eel, wolf and heifer are all aspects of the goddess (in this case, the Morrigan), whom the Greeks might have called Nemesis and the Romans called Fortuna, but the Celtic goddess and tutelary guardian of the land is infinitely less forgiving of the fallen king.

There is a very interesting late variant of this legend of the king at odds with his destiny, or with nature. It is the Irish tale of Suibhne (Sweeney) Geilt. In this case, the king goes through all his trials and tribulations not because he is fighting against the goddess of the land, or the natural creatures whom she commands, but because he has dared to challenge Christian authority. King Suibhne is outraged that St. Ronan, without permission, has built a Christian church on his land. He seizes the saint's psalter and throws it into a lake. The saint curses the king, who becomes insane and spends the next seven years leaping in and out of the trees, convinced that he is a bird, and unable ever to sleep since he is constantly tormented by visions of headless corpses and corpseless heads attacking him from all sides. Finally, a priest takes pity on his torment and converts him to Christianity and Suibhne dies in peace at last. The theme alone tells us that this is a Christianized reworking of an earlier pagan motif.

As well as sage and seer, the king is also expected to act more mundanely as a judge. Although this was a chief function of the druids, and there are many examples in the tales of druids settling disputes (especially disputes between kings), the king also has to be able to make settlements, particularly property settlements, in a way which satisfies honour and is fair to all parties. After Efnisien has maliciously attacked Matholwch's horses, Bendigeidfran or

Bran the Blessed has to think of and announce a suitable restitution which he will offer to Matholwch:

> Make known to him that he shall have a sound horse for each one of those spoiled, and along with that, as an atonement to him, he shall have a staff of silver that shall be as thick as his little finger and as tall as himself, and a plate of gold as broad as his face. And make known to him what kind of man did that, and how it was against my will that it was done, and it was my brother on the mother's side that did it, and how it would not be easy for me to put him to death or destroy him. But let him come to see me face to face, and I will make peace on those terms he may himself desire.

In the event, the peace is not made, and Bran is forced to cross to Ireland to rescue his sister Branwen from the insults which Matholwch has heaped upon her, but the story illustrates in legend what must have been a very frequent and very important role for the historical Celtic kings, that of judge and arbiter in disputes. The closely woven social fabric, and in particular the bonds of fosterage, were helpful to the judicious king and a good safeguard against interminable fighting and death.

THE INAUGURATION

The king or queen would be chosen from a limited pool of applicants. The choosing might be by acclaim, but it might equally well be by divination or augury, such as the *tarbhfess* or bull sleep. Whichever method was chosen, the rightness and fitness of the king or queen would be manifest. He or she would be perfect in physical form, without blemish, imposing in stature, experienced in battle, and so on. Most important of all, the kingship was also a marriage – the Irish actually referred to sovereignty as *banais rigi,* 'royal marriage'. From the marriage, fertility and fecundity would follow, crops would be blessed, there would be fish in the streams and rivers. If any of these conditions were not fulfilled, even if the king or queen were of obvious worth and deeply beloved by the people, something would have to be done. In *Pwyll, Prince of Dyfed*, the hero, Pwyll, whom we met a short while ago, has married the goddess Rhiannon, but the marriage is childless:

> And in the third year the men of the land began to feel heaviness of heart at seeing a man whom they loved as much as their lord and foster-brother without offspring; and they summoned him to them . . .
> 'Lord,' said they, 'we know that thou art not of an age with some of the men of this country, but our fear is lest thou have no offspring of the wife thou hast; and so, take another wife of whom thou mayest

have offspring. Thou wilt not last for ever,' said they, 'and though thou desire to remain thus, we will not suffer it from thee.'

Pwyll negotiates for a further year, during which time Rhiannon delivers a child. The interesting point here is the 'we will not suffer it from thee' on which the people insist. The king is the absolute and undisputed ruler, in ways unfamiliar to the subjects of modern monarchs, but if he does not fulfil the basic kingly requirement, then the people will not suffer it, and out he goes.

The early Celtic kings do not appear to have used a physical crown as a symbol of regal authority, even though the head held such religious significance for them. Anne Ross says that the symbol of the king was a white rod,[4] but a white hazel rod or staff was a druid's emblem, as the literature makes clear, so there seems to be some confusion. The crown, as a symbol of kingship, appears to have developed from the Roman diadem, and although there are historical crowns of considerable interest dating from the sixth and seventh centuries, none of them appears to be Celtic in origin, though some claims have been made for the famous Iron Crown of Lombardy, preserved at Monza, supposedly fashioned in part from a nail out of the Rood of the Crucifixion.

I have argued elsewhere that the most likely day for inauguration ceremonies would have been Midsummer's Day.[5] The August festival is called Lughnasa. The first part of the name is that of the god, Lugh. The second is *nasadh*, the Goidelic for 'commemoration'. This festival was a mourning festival, a celebration of the passing of the Bran-type god or king, the god of oak, who has been replaced by the sun-god, Bel. It is interesting that Christians placed the day of St. John, who foretold the coming of Jesus, on Midsummer's Day. The placement makes perfect mythographic sense; it is the day when the new king comes into his kingship.

Notes

1   To save endless footnotes, quotations from the tales in this chapter are all taken from one of the following editions: Jeffrey Gantz (trans.), *Early Irish Myths and Sagas*, Penguin Classics, 1981; Thomas Kinsella (trans.), *The Tain*, Oxford University Press, 1969; Gwyn Jones and Thomas Jones (trans.), *The Mabinogion*, Dent, Everyman's Library, 1949 and 1974.
2   For further details, see my book *The Celtic Druids' Year*, Blandford Press, 1994, pp. 151–160.
3   *The White Goddess*, p. 124.
4   *Everyday Life of the Pagan Celts*, p. 160.
5   *The Celtic Druids' Year*, pp. 119–140.

TWELVE

✳

THE ROYAL CELTIC LEGACY

S O FAR we have looked at the historical Celtic kingdoms and their underlying social, religious and political backgrounds, and at the notions of kingship revealed in Celtic myths and legends. Now, in this final chapter, we will briefly examine how these ideas have spread through space and time, and what legacy they have left, on the world in general and on the Celtic nations themselves.

There are great riches here. The Celtic spirit, so dynamic and distinctive, has continued to exert a powerful influence in the world, even though the early kingdoms in which it had its birth are long since gone. Ireland would not be a politically independent republic without that legacy. Wales and Scotland would be very different places without that legacy. Even England, which has been so enriched by Celtic culture, would not be the same without that legacy. The Celtic migrations to America, Canada, Australia, New Zealand and elsewhere have carried that legacy across the whole world. I have eaten a steaming, home-made Cornish pasty in Michigan as well as in Camborne or Penzance. I have listened to traditional Irish singing and fiddling in Boston as well as in Killarney and Tralee. I have had conversations in Cornish with natives of Moonta, New South Wales, Australia, and conversations in French with families of Breton extraction on Cape Breton Island in Nova Scotia, Canada (where there are also Scots Gaelic kirks, a Gaelic-language summer school, and Canadian Highland Games).

In 1508, the anonymous Spanish romance *Amadis of Gaul* was published. It captured the mediaeval imagination and became immensely popular. Jean Baptiste Lully and Johann Christian Bach both wrote opera versions of the story, as did Handel, under the title *Amadigi di Gaula*, also sometimes called *Oriana*. Jules Massenet's opera on the same theme is called *Amadis*.

Robert Southey, the Poet Laureate of England, wrote an epic poem based on the story, which was published in 1803. But where does the story come from? The briefest glance at the plot and themes tells us immediately:

Amadis, called the Lion Knight for the device on his shield, also Beltenbros ('darkly shining Bel' or 'Bel of the shadows') for his swarthy handsomeness, is the illegitimate son of Perion, King of Gaula (Wales, rather than Gallia or Gaul) and Elizena, Princess of Brittany. At his birth, his mother conceals him in an ark and launches him in a stream which carries him to the Scottish coast. He is found by the knight Gandales and called 'Child of the Sea'. The boy grows into a handsome youth of devastating physical prowess. He falls in love with Oriana, but to win her he has to undergo a series of tests, including the Arch of True Lovers and the Forbidden Chamber, required by King Apolidon, ruler of the magical island to which they have come to prove their love. Amadis passes the tests, and the couple produce a child of great beauty, called Esplandian.

Even without the giveaway place names, it is crystal clear that this is a Celtic royal myth, even though it appears in late mediaeval Spain. Many of the elements with which we have become familiar are obviously present: the hero's illegitimate birth; his rite of passage by water as an infant; his raising by a kindly foster-parent; his taking of a god's name (Bel) as an epithet; his rivalry with an older king to win his queen; the couple's fertility after the young king has passed the tests and proved himself worthy to generate the succession.

The principal agent for this widespread dissemination of Celtic ideas and themes was the Matter of Britain, the Arthurian legends, although, as we noted earlier, there are many commonalities and connections between the Irish and Welsh material, so it would be wrong to exclude the Gaels entirely from this influence. In fact, the Fenian stories, in all probability composed quite a bit later than the other Irish cycles, appear to have influenced the development of the Arthurian material directly. There are tales in which Arthur fights witches, or mythical beasts, or giants in almost identical fashion to Fionn Mac Cumhaill. The story of Tristan and Isolde, which, as mentioned earlier, was probably Cornish in origin, has a kind of parallel in the Irish *The Pursuit of Diarmaid and Grainne*. The frequent theme of the hunt or quest in wild places, deserts and empty forests is certainly also very prominent in the Fenian legends.

The migrations which brought Celts to all parts of the world belong to a later part of this chapter, but world voyaging itself begins very early in Celtic history. Many of the early voyage stories, as with so much of early Celtic material, present a mixture of fact and myth which it is very difficult to untangle.

THE EARLY VOYAGE LEGENDS

Voyages on the sea and on land, and tales of lands that have sunk beneath the sea, play a large part in Celtic cosmology. Avallon, the Brythonic paradise, or Tir n'an Og, the Gaelic land of eternal youth, are to be found by sailing across a western sea. Lyonnesse, the Isles of the Blessed and Hi Brazil, ancient variants of Atlantis, are Celtic lands which sank beneath the sea. The gods and saints who made epic and often fantastic voyages encountered many mysterious islands. Celtic literature and art are suffused with images of flux and transformation, of marshes and estuaries, the shore of the river-ford, islands and tidal causeways, where land and water meet. The magician sea-god Manannan Mac Lir turns the ocean into a meadow, the waves into trees. Sometimes the sea is made of crystal, or of lead, and the islands of glass. Glastonbury, associated with Avallon, with Joseph of Arimathea and Jesus, with Arthur, and with a host of ancient Celtic associations, was called in Brythonic *Ynys Wedren*, 'the Isle of Glass'. The Celts are not thought of as great seafarers, like the Phoenicians or the Vikings, but it appears there may have been at least some real individual voyages of note.

Part of the difficulty lies in the fact that visits to the otherworld play such an important part in Celtic mythology. Voyages to strange lands and visits to the otherworld can easily become confused or merged. The Irish had two different words to describe such tales. *Eachtrai* were experiences or adventures. *Imrime* were journeys (*imrim* literally means 'riding' and *Domhnach na hImrime*, 'Sunday of the Riding', is the name given by the Irish to Palm Sunday). But *eachtra* in modern Irish, as well as meaning 'experience' (*do chuid eachtrai a aithris* means 'to say what happened to you'), can also mean 'adventurous journey' or 'expedition'. It is related to the adjective *eachtartha*, meaning 'outlying' or 'foreign'. The Voyage of Bran Mac Febal is listed as an *eachtra*, but in the text itself is called an *imrim* (or *immram*, in the older spelling).

Apart from the *eachta* of Bran, the Irish chronicles list seven tales of voyages, only three of which are known to us: the *Voyage of Maelduin*, the *Voyage of the Ui Chorra* and the *Voyage of Snedgus and Mac Riagla*.[1]

The voyage made by Bran Mac Febal (*Immram Brain*, probably late seventh century) appears to belong purely to the world of myth. His journey begins when he finds a silver apple branch covered with white flowers. He gathers his kinsmen together, and a young woman suddenly appears dressed in a gleaming cloth. She sings to Bran's people a song of the wonders to be found in the islands of the otherworld beyond the sea, where beautiful maidens dwell and there is no sickness, sorrow or death. The maiden vanishes, taking the magic silver branch with her, even though Bran was holding it tightly with both hands. The next day, Bran, his three foster-brothers and twenty-seven companions sail westwards. They meet Manannan Mac Lir, god of the sea, who rides across the waves in his chariot. In a long and beautiful poem, Manannan explains how for him, god of the sea, the ocean is a

meadow, with flowers, shrubs and fruit-bearing trees. The meadow is called
Mag Mell:

> Speckled salmon leap from the womb
> of the white sea, on which you look;
> they are calves, they are coloured lambs
> with friendliness, without mutual slaughter.
> Though you see but one chariot-rider
> in Mag Mell of the many flowers,
> there are many steeds on its surface,
> though you do not see them.
> Along the top of a wood
> your coracle has sailed, over ridges;
> there is an orchard of beautiful fruit
> under the prow of your little boat.

That same day, Bran's boat reaches the Isle of Laughter, where his companions experience such joy and merriment that they are hardly able to stand. In
the evening they reach the Isle of Women. The men are afraid to come to
shore, but the women's leader throws a ball of thread which sticks to Bran's
hand, and she reels them in. They find soft beds and delicious food, and stay
for what appears to be a year, although, in fact, many years pass. Finally,
Bran is persuaded by one of his homesick crew to sail home, but is warned
by the goddess that he and his companions must not set foot on Irish soil. As
the boat approaches the Irish shore, Bran discovers that nobody recognizes
him, and that his voyage of a little over a year has actually lasted centuries.
One of the kinsmen is foolish enough to disregard the warning given by the
goddess, and as his foot touches the shore he crumbles instantly into a pile of
dust, as though he had been dead for centuries (which, indeed, he has). Bran
writes his story in Ogham script on wooden sticks, which he flings into the
sea for the tide to bring to shore, then he and his companions sail off for ever,
and what becomes of them nobody knows.

The *Voyage of the Ui Chorra* is set in Christian times. The Ui Chorra are
three brothers who have made a pact with the Devil and have been plunder-
ing the churches of Connaught. The eldest brother is miraculously granted a
vision of Heaven and Hell, after which the brothers repent their ill-doing, and
repair and restore the churches. As a final penance, they put themselves in a
boat, row out to sea, then throw away the oars to see where destiny will take
them. Alwyn and Brinley Rees point out that setting someone adrift at sea
was quite probably a historical form of punishment. The *Life of St. Padraig*
refers to the saint punishing a tyrant by chaining his feet, throwing away the
key, then putting him in a coracle without oar or rudder to go wherever God
intends him to go.[2]

The *Voyage of Snedgus and Mac Riagla* is also a story about punishment
by setting adrift. The men of Ross have killed a tyrannical king. The king's

brother condemns them to be burned alive, but St. Colm Cille or Columba of Iona persuades him instead to let them be set adrift on the sea in small boats. Two of the saint's clerics, Snedgus and Mac Riagla, undertake voluntarily to set themselves adrift in coracles also. They travel to many magical islands. On the sixth island they find the men of Ross, all alive and living without sin in the company of Enoch and Elijah. Clearly, this tale is simply a Christianized version of the pagan tales of the Isles of the Blessed.

The *Voyage of Maelduin* (*Imram Curaig Mailduin*) is found both in the *Lebor na hUidre* and in the *Yellow Book of Lecan*. It is a very curious tale indeed. The earliest text is attributed to Aed Finn ('the Fair'), 'chief sage of Ireland' in the eleventh century, but the story is probably from the eighth century originally. Maelduin, the foster-son of a queen, discovers in manhood that his mother was a nun who had been raped by a chieftain of the Aran Islands. When he goes to seek his father, he discovers that he has been murdered. He sets sail to find the murderer and avenge his father's death. On the advice of a druid, he takes seventeen men with him on the voyage, no more and no less. His three foster-brothers swim out to the boat after it has set sail, and thus create an unpropitious number of passengers, which leads to complications further on in the story. The travellers visit thirty-one islands in all, where they meet a variety of extraordinary creatures and sights: ants as big as ponies; giant horses; flaming pigs; sheep which change colour from black to white, or white to black; shouting birds; an island of women, like the one visited by Bran; a fortress with a glass bridge; an island where the people are divided by fences of gold, silver, brass and crystal into four groups – kings, queens, warriors and maidens.

The story of the voyage of St. Brendan the Navigator, which appears to have been heavily influenced by the story of Maelduin, commemorates a

St. Brendan meets a mer-king, from a fourteenth-century woodcut illustration.

sixth-century saint who may actually have existed. His story is full of similar wondrous encounters, but with a Christian gloss: a whale appears on Easter Day so that Brendan and his followers can climb on its back to hold their Easter service; one of the companions dies after seeing the pain of Hell, but Brendan restores him to life; and so on.

Very recently, there have been attempts to vindicate the Brendan voyage in particular, and to demonstrate that the early Celts were far more accomplished seafarers than previously supposed. Vessels with timber frames and hide hulls have been shown to be more seaworthy than one might think. The New England Antiquities Research Association has periodically published in its journal discussions of the idea that the original western explorers of the American eastern seaboard were not Christopher Columbus and his sailors, nor even Leif Eriksson and other Vikings, but seafaring Celts, and these discussions have included references to (admittedly highly disputed) lithic inscriptions which appear to be in Ogham.[3]

SAINTS AND MISSIONARIES

St. Padraig and St. Colm Cille exerted a very profound influence on Irish Christianity, which in turn has carried the Celtic spirit far and abroad, in a great variety of contexts and settings. Indeed, Irish missionary work continues to this day and continues to bring Irish Celtic values as well as Christian values to various peoples all across the world.

The pagan British, the Picts of Scotland, and the Angles, Saxons and Jutes were the first to experience the missions of the Celtic Church. When Oswald, the English King of Northumbria, needed sanctuary, he took it in St. Colm's Celtic settlement on Iona, and when he recovered his throne in 634, it was to Ireland that he turned for a bishop. They sent him Aidan, who became the founding saint of Lindisfarne. The English missionary Willibrord, who converted the Friesians to Christianity in 690, was trained in Irish monastic houses.

The early Irish monks also travelled to the continent. St. Columbanus landed in Gaul in 590 and founded a monastery at Luxeuil (which had been a pagan Celtic religious centre for many centuries), and eventually moved on to Bobbio in Italy, where he founded another abbey in 614. St. Gall died in the Alps in 612, and the monastery established around his tomb in 720 went on to become one of the most important seats of learning and scholarship in early mediaeval Europe.

The religious manuscripts of this period, predominantly Irish but also influenced by Pictish and Anglo-Saxon artistic elements, produced works of such staggering beauty that they are rightly treasured to this day. The *Book of Durrow* is probably the earliest of these treasures, dating from around 680. The *Lindisfarne Gospels*, commissioned in sacred memory of St.

Cuthbert, are attributed to Abbot Eadfrith himself, an Anglian monk and leader of the Lindisfarne community, who reputedly spent six years in training in Ireland before returning to Lindisfarne in 698. The great *Book of Kells*, the most famous of these works, was probably created at Iona before the Viking raid of 807 which drove the monks across the water to Ireland. It is heartbreaking to think that the Vikings may well have thrown into the fire dozens and scores of pages of work, and perhaps even some complete books, of equal beauty to the *Book of Kells*, or perhaps even surpassing it. Bede, who probably saw illumination work being done at the monastery of Monkwearmouth and Jarrow in his own time (673–735), said of these magnificent books:

> We have known that when some persons have been bitten by serpents,
> the scrapings of leaves of books that were brought out of Ireland,
> being put into water, and given them to drink, have immediately
> expelled the spreading poison, and assuaged the swelling.[4]

IRELAND 1100–1916

After the last of the High Kings, Ireland underwent many changes. The Vikings had left their mark, including a significant contribution of vocabulary to the Irish language. It was largely through Viking influence and trade that the larger towns were established, notably Baile Atha Cliath ('Town of the Shallow Ford'), later called Dublin ('Black Lake'). The Normans, and even the Anglo-Normans, introduced limited change, many of them becoming Gaelicized themselves, even speaking some Gaelic. The profound changes to Irish society began in the sixteenth century, when Henry VIII and Elizabeth I introduced a far more aggressive English control of Irish affairs. The Reformation exacerbated the situation and established religious labels for an essentially political difference which have remained stumbling blocks to open discussion to this day. Catholic Ireland was now dominated by Protestant England. Hugh O'Neill, Earl of Tyrone, who claimed descent from the Ui Neill, led a rebellion against the Protestant hegemony, but was forced to flee to France in 1607. His territories in Ulster were seized and settled, as a matter of deliberate policy, by Protestants of Scottish and English stock, and the foundation of modern Ulster was laid. The uprising of 1641 led to atrocities against the Protestant communities, which were answered by the even greater atrocities of Oliver Cromwell's campaign, to which much of the present Irish resentment of British rule can still be attributed. The sealing event which created two Irelands, the Catholic Republic of Eire and the Protestant enclave of Northern Ireland, was the Battle of the Boyne in 1690, when the new Protestant King William of Orange, William III of England, or King Billy, defeated the deposed Catholic King James II at the siege of Londonderry.

Under King Billy, the Penal Laws passed between 1702 and 1715 severely restricted the Catholic population. The religious orders were banished. Catholics were barred from public office, from Parliament, from the university, from practising law, even from teaching or keeping a school. By 1714, only 7 per cent of Irish land was owned by Catholics. There was another Catholic uprising in 1798, which ended in dismal failure, and Ireland was forcibly joined with Britain in 1801.

The eighteenth century not only introduced a separate Protestant Ulster, it also introduced a new and different culture to the rest of Ireland. Dublin acquired its Georgian streets and facades. The culture of the Gael, of pre-Reformation Celtic society, was suppressed in favour of neoclassicism. The ancient poetry was rejected as barbaric, and was replaced by a far more genteel and predictable type. The traditional longhouse was replaced by the English-style small farmhouse. Beech trees and limes were introduced in great number and the rambling old farmsteads were tamed into small squares.

Ironically, the potato, which many people think of as so typically Irish that it must have been grown there for ever, was one of the additions to Irish culture during this phase. The plant was probably brought to Munster by Sir Walter Raleigh towards the end of the sixteenth century, but it only achieved widespread popularity during the cultural changes of the last quarter of the eighteenth century. Put even more simply, it was really the English who brought the potato to Ireland. Before then, the Irish had subsisted on the same staples as all the other Celtic nations: barley, wheat and oats, supplemented by meat (salted in winter) and dairy products. The introduction of the potato in extensive plantings interrupted that traditional, Celtic way of life, and the potato famine was one of the direct results.

The population of Ireland in 1801 was five million. By 1840 it had risen to eight million, and when the potato blight struck in the years 1845 to 1847, there was mass starvation. It has been estimated that over a million Irish died in the potato famine, mostly children and the elderly, and another million emigrated. In the hundred years between 1840 and 1940, over five million Irish people emigrated to America alone, as well as others who went, along with the Scots, the Welsh and the Cornish, to Canada, Australia and New Zealand, or to the rapidly growing industrial cities of Britain, like Liverpool, Manchester or Birmingham.

One of the immediate results of the potato famine was a much closer identification of Catholicism with national aspirations. In the late 1700s, it was the Presbyterians of Belfast who were talking about a United Ireland and bringing their ideas to the revolutionary congresses in Philadelphia and Paris. After the famine, it was only the Catholics of the devastated and deserted south who claimed the moral right to speak for ancient Eriu, the Celtic nation. There were further disastrous harvests between 1877 and 1879, which led to a fresh round of emigrations, and to a series of confrontations, known as the Land War, between poverty-stricken tenants and desperate landlords.

One of the results of the Land War was the virtual elimination of the Catholic Irish landed gentry. It meant that the fight for Irish independence, when it came, would be a proletarian one, as indeed it was. One of the early leaders and supporters of the Land League was Charles Stuart Parnell, himself actually of a patrician Anglo-Irish family with estates in County Wicklow. The struggle became known as the struggle for Home Rule. The Easter Rising of 1916, incomplete though it was, saw the first proclamation of a free and independent Irish Republic, although it was to take several more years before any real political independence was achieved, and that independence did not include Irish sovereignty over Ulster. As William Butler Yeats wrote, all was 'changed, changed utterly'.

SCOTLAND: THE CLEARANCES AND BEYOND

Scotland underwent suffering similar to Ireland's, the difference being that if Ireland's woes could be said to have sprung from the humble potato, the woes of Scotland sprang from the simple sheep. In the late 1800s, Catherine MacPhee of Uist wrote the following:

> Many a thing have I seen in my own day and generation. Many a thing, O Mary Mother of the Black Sorrows. I have seen the townships swept and the big holdings being made of them, the people driven out of the countryside to the streets of Glasgow and to the wilds of Canada, such of them as did not die of hunger and plague and smallpox going across the ocean. . . . I have seen the big strong men, the champions of the countryside, being bound on Loch Boisdale quay and cast into the ship as would be done to a batch of horses and cattle, the bailiffs and the ground-officers and the constables and the policemen behind them in pursuit of them. The God of Life, and He only, knows all the loathsome work of men on that day.[5]

Donald Macleod of Sutherland wrote a series of letters, published serially in the Edinburgh *Weekly Chronicle* originally as 'Gloomy Memories' and as a separate volume in 1883, the first of which begins as follows:

> I am a native of Sutherlandshire, and remember when the inhabitants of that country lived comfortably and happily, when the mansions of proprietors and the abodes of factors, magistrates and ministers, were the seats of honour, truth, and good example – when people of quality were indeed what they were styled, the friends and benefactors of all who lived upon their domains. But all this is changed. Alas, alas!
> I have lived to see calamity upon calamity overtake the Sutherlanders. For five successive years, on or about the term day, has scarcely

anything been seen but removing the inhabitants in the most cruel and unfeeling manner, and burning the houses which they and their fore-fathers had occupied from time immemorial. The country was dark-ened by the smoke of the burnings, and the descendants of those who drew their swords at Bannockburn, Sheriffmuir, and Killicrankie . . . were ruined, trampled upon, dispersed, and compelled to seek an asylum across the Atlantic; while those who remained from inability to emigrate, deprived of all the comforts of life, became paupers – beggars – a disgrace to the nation whose freedom and honour many of them had maintained by their valour and cemented with their blood.[6]

The great national tragedy being described here is usually called the Highland Clearances. Ever since the Act of Union of 1707 which removed Scotland's Great Seal and required her to send her ministers to the English Parliament at Westminster, there was political tension between the two countries. The Jacobite rebellions of 1715, defeated at Preston, and of 1745, intended to restore Prince Charles Edward, better known as Bonnie Prince Charlie, to the Scottish throne, ended in dismal failure at the Battle of Culloden in 1746. The Highlands were ruthlessly subjugated by the English in the years following Culloden, and many atrocities were committed by English soldiers on the ordinary folk of the Highlands and Islands. The playing of the bagpipes was forbidden, which led to a curious wordless, rhythmical singing called *puirt a bheul*, or mouth music, which survives as a part of Scottish tradition to this day. Lords Kilmarnock, Lovat and Balmerino were executed for their part in the uprising, but it was not these comparatively straightforward political and military events which led directly to the Clearances: rather, it was the intro-duction of a new breed of sheep, the Great Cheviot.

The clan system had been fairly effectively destroyed in the aftermath of the Jacobite rebellions, and the Scottish nobility, who once would have been proud to trace their ancestry back to Celtic kings, became greedy to emulate their English peers in the south. They were land-rich and cash-poor, how-ever. The glens were overpopulated, despite some early emigration, and the thin Highland soils on the mountains supported black cattle poorly. The sys-tem of tenants and sub-tenants, originally a relic of ancient Celtic practice, had become confused and corrupt, with much rack-renting and profiteering by middle-men. By the late eighteenth century, however, modernizing farmers in the Borders had mixed their stock with Lincoln ewes and Ryeland and Spanish rams, and produced the Great Cheviot, a docile and tractable animal which gave good yields of meat and wool and, most importantly, was suffi-ciently hardy to take the stiff winters of the Highlands. The year 1792 was called *Bliadha nan Caorach* in Scots Gaelic, meaning 'the Year of the Sheep'. A landlord who might have made two pence an acre with cattle could now make two shillings an acre, twelve times as much in a year, with sheep graz-ing the same land. There was a sudden stampede of sheep into the Highlands, and the only way to achieve that was for the local tenants to be evicted, by force if necessary. Force was necessary. The armed gentry employed the Black Watch to suppress local rebellions, many of which were led and fought by women, desperate to keep their homes and feed their families. The work of clearance was frequently put into the hands of English agents, like James Loch, Commissioner to the Marquess of Stafford, who despised the Celtic Highlander as lazy, brutish and ignorant, and not worthy of consideration. The Victorians' solution was to encourage Scottish emigration, which they did, supplying ships in great number. When the Crimean War began in 1854, Whitehall sent to Scotland, as it had done many times before, to raise fighting men, but recruiters who went to the Highlands and Islands were met by angry men who baa-ed like sheep at them, and said, 'Since you have preferred sheep to men, let sheep defend you.'

Another great difference between Ireland and Scotland was that the Scottish clans, many of which had been petty kingdoms in their earliest beginnings, survived in name at least, because the English aristocracy tolerated, or even encouraged, the generation of a conservative Scottish aristocracy to keep the ordinary people at bay: the more archaic and feudal, the better. This led to some ridiculous aggrandizement, most notably the perversion of the simple country plaids and styles of dress into great costumes, with plumes and fol-de-rols, frothy ruffs and polished brass buttons, so that the clan chiefs came to look like the peacocks they were. They often spoke with the lordly drawl of Westminster or Whitehall, too.

Nevertheless, the clan names did survive, and they have done much to keep people of Scottish descent in touch with their ancestry. Some of the names have become familiar in their Anglicized forms or spellings. For example, the name Chisholm derives from the original Gaelic Siosalach, and the proper patronymic for the clan chief is An Siosalach ('The Chisholm').[7] The principal clans are listed, with notes on clan seats, patronymics, plant emblems, etc., in the Appendix on pages 243–249.

THE CELTIC WORLD TODAY

From about 1840 in Ireland, and some decades later elsewhere, there began a revival of pride in Celtic culture and heritage. It expressed itself in different ways. The Young Ireland movement, originally an art movement, began to espouse increasingly specific political aims; indeed, without it, the political movement towards Irish independence might have begun very differently. As the Victorian age was replaced by the Edwardian, Welsh nationalists lauded their ancient culture, promoted their language and literature, and revived the annual *gorseddau* and *eisteddfodau*. Revived Cornish and Breton *gorseddau* were re-established a few years later. On the Isle of Man, Yn Cheshaght Ghailckagh (The Manx Language Society) was formed to try to save the language and rouse it from its deathbed. In 1904, Henry Jenner published his

Handbook of the Cornish Language, the first and most vital step in the astonishing Cornish language revival which continues apace to this day.

William Butler Yeats, Ireland's greatest poet, articulated the essence of the Celtic revival in a book introduction:

> So far as this book is visionary, it is Irish; for Ireland, which is still
> predominantly Celtic, has preserved with some less excellent things
> a gift of vision, which has died out among more hurried and more
> successful nations: no shining candelabra have prevented us from
> looking into the darkness, and when one looks into the darkness
> there is always something there.[8]

The distractions and hustle of modern life, its 'shining candelabra', have certainly encouraged people of Celtic descent, or with an interest in Celtic culture, to explore Celtic history with ever greater enthusiasm. Not least appealing is the profound Celtic belief in a wonderful afterlife, in the naturalness of passing from this world to the otherworld, and of spirits good and wise, as well as awe-inspiring, coming into this world and bringing us powerful magic. In an age full of doubt and grief, as ours is, such connectedness to eternity and its certainties is profoundly comforting.

Celtic romanticism has also created a host of problems, however. Rousseau-like ideas about 'the noble savage' clouded serious historical study of the early Celts, who were often endowed with noble and lofty sentiments and great powers of oratory: the speech of Caratacus or Caradog in captivity is a case in point. Strenuous efforts were made to deny head-hunting and human sacrifice. What was wanted was a sanitized Celt. In the 1760s a writer named James Macpherson wrote a pseudo-ancient text, based on a combination of genuine Irish material and his own vivid imagination, and hawked it around as the work of 'Ossian', an ancient Scottish bard. Not only did the forgery convince a host of his contemporaries and near-contemporaries, including the distinguished historian Sir Edward Gibbon, it even reappears to this day in pamphlets and small press volumes about the Celts. Almost more pernicious than outright forgery has been the sanitization of Celtic myth and legend in book and film; it is sad to see these rich and complex stories reduced to costume versions of swoon-in-June in shoddy fiction, or Disneyfied into sword fights up and down the staircase and slapstick between floppy-haired, purple-spotted dragons.

However, the enthusiasm for matters Celtic is not entirely a matter of bathing in daydreams. Modern Ireland, still very distinctively Celtic, has managed to establish a thriving economy and extensive modernization, and membership of the European Union, without loss of identity. Scotland has very recently (September 1997) voted overwhelmingly for devolution and the re-establishment of a Scottish Parliament, closely followed by a less convincing but nevertheless positive vote for devolution in Wales. All thirty-two of Scotland's voting regions voted for the parliament, with only two – Dumfries and Galloway, and Orkney – narrowly failing also to vote for tax-raising powers. Within hours of the result, the Scottish Nationalist Party was predicting a restoration of complete independence for Scotland, and the party even gave a target date: 2007, exactly three centuries after the Act of Union which took away Scotland's independence. Even the problems of Ulster, completely intractable for thirty years (or four hundred, depending on one's point of view), have seemed in recent times to be capable of some kind of resolution which would afford honour and respect for all sides.

The Celtic identity, in ways more or less subtle, also permeates and influences British culture as a whole. The British Tourist Authority publishes an international magazine called *In Britain*.[9] The May 1996 volume contains the following main features, among which the reader should be able to discern, without any prompting from me, at least five or six major articles on a Celtic theme or topic, or about a Celtic place, or with a definite Celtic connection:

Shipshape and Bristol Fashion: a tour of Bristol.

Letter of the Month: a visit to Stonehenge.

Made in Britain: featuring Welsh and Cornish pewter jewellery; Welsh whisky, mead, wine and cheese; Laura Ashley's factory at Carno, south Wales; the whisky distilleries at Fettercairn in Kincardineshire, Glenturret at Crieff in Perthshire, Edradour near Pitlochry and Tomatin in Inverness-shire; tartans, tweeds and knitted sweaters from Aran and Shetland; Ulster linen, Belleek china and Tyrone crystal.

In Britain photo competition, with prizes including holidays in Edinburgh and the Lake District.

The Ulster Way, a 5-page feature on walking tours in Northern Ireland.

Travel Club, featuring the Jewish Museum of London, and a Clansman Monarch coach tour of Scotland.

Two pages of advertising for the National Trust of Scotland, and 1 of advertising for Cornish hotels.

A 4-page feature on the Minack Theatre in Cornwall, and its creator, Rowena Cade.

A 5-page feature on monster-spotting in Great Britain, including the Loch Ness monster.

A 4-page feature on an Edwardian country garden in Essex.

A single page of advertising for hotels in Sussex and Hertfordshire.

Twelve brochure offers, of which one is for the Isle of Man, one for Derry in Northern Ireland, and one for Snowdonia in Wales.

A 5-page feature on traditional Morris dancing.

A single page of advertising for Welsh attractions, including an exhibition called Celtica at Machynlleth, with the following printed at the head of the page: *Cyfle i Brofi Byd Hud a Lledrith y Celtiaid* ('Experience the Mysterious and Magical World of the Celts').

My Bit of Britain: a 5-page feature in which the actor Edward Petherbridge reminisces about his birthplace, West Yorkshire.

At least some part of the admiration for the Celtic world is derived from admiration for the Celtic philosophy and practice of monarchy. That ancient belief that the king or the queen is an inevitable visitor from outside our present world, someone predestined to bring us and our nation to peace, prosperity and fruitfulness, is immensely appealing, especially when such cynicism about governance is all around us. The appeal even transcends the normal political spectrum, because it is not about left or right, radical or conservative, abolishing or strengthening the establishment, which are topics frequently raised in political discussions about modern monarchies in general, and the present British House of Windsor in particular. The appeal is centred in a much more ancient need, a need which the ancient Celts understood very deeply indeed: the need to be represented, shielded, championed and inspired by a divine spirit, which is what a Celtic king or queen always was – the god or the goddess, whose ultimate mysteries were ineffable, temporarily acting through the person of the anointed monarch. When Diana, Princess of Wales, was killed in a car crash in Paris in 1997, the world was astonished at the tremendous outpouring of grief which the supposedly cold British expressed at her death. A total of 11 200 tonnes of flowers and gifts were deposited on the pavements outside her Kensington Palace home. Nor was this merely a reaction sponsored by the media: it took them just as greatly by surprise. Diana, far more successfully than the other members of the British royal family, had managed to tap into that ancient need of the people, to be a 'Queen of Hearts', as she expressed it herself. Living in America, I was struck by how many Americans also experienced and expressed a similar deep sense of grief and loss, and this in a nation where the general idea of monarchy does not even appear within the political spectrum. A letter to a local Vermont newspaper expressed the point well:

> Since her untimely death, the media has been wondering about the
> Lady Di phenomenon. The grieving of the British public is connected
> to the mythical link of people in England to their monarchy which has
> been in existence for more than 1200 years. Lady Diana defied an
> institution out of touch with the realities of modern life today and all
> its pitfalls for mortals. She also unmasked the ruthlessness of an insti-
> tution in dealing with people no longer of use to them. Diana Spencer,
> through birth into a twenty-generation British dynasty, was connected
> to the age of Camelot and Avalon, and this made her more of a truly
> British royal than any of the Windsors ever were. Their ancestry is
> mostly German and that is also part of their temperament. It made
> Lady Di an additional threat in a subconscious way to the ruling
> House of Windsor, and this is what the grieving public responded to.
> Diana truly was chosen to be their future queen sixteen years ago.
> The inability of her husband, Prince Charles, to deal with her immense
> popularity from the start is what ultimately cost her her position. . . .
> Diana triumphed in a way unintended, unimaginable to anyone before

her death. The events during the week of mourning in England demonstrated clearly that she was the chosen future queen because that had been her destiny from birth – even if it took her death to drive the message home for ever.[10]

This is a very insightful letter. While it was Charles who learned his few phrases of Welsh for his investiture as Prince of Wales at Caernarfon, it was Diana, the 'English Rose', who actually fulfilled the Celtic ideal of a monarch far more effectively. Even her alleged infidelities were relatively unimportant. The qualities she had, as the writer says, were Camelot qualities, Avalon qualities: physical beauty without blemish; commanding stature and presence, despite the shyness of her youth; an aura of destiny fulfilled, of having been brought to her place by fate, and snatched from it just as inevitably.

The Celtic kings and queens of antiquity harboured brutes and idiots in their midst, no doubt, as well as great warriors and sages. Some of their names – Caradog, Vercingetorix, Vortigern, Boudica, Cartimandua, Arthur, Brian Boru, Rhodri Mawr and Hywel Dda and Owain Glyn Dwr – will roll echoing through the corridors of history for ever, good and bad, strong and weak alike. The collective royal Celtic legacy which they left behind, however, includes these things: a love and respect for truth; a sense of harmony with nature, and a deep reverence for those forces in nature which reproduce life and bring us the fruits of the harvest; respect for women and for men alike, and for women leaders and men leaders alike; respect for true and correct utterance, and sound judgment given openly and publicly; respect for good law, founded in common sense and an understanding of the 'fitness of things'; admiration for 'fair play' and equitable treatment; chivalrous behaviour, and the pursuit of noble ideals; respect for physical courage and steadfastness in adversity; joy in the quest and the journey, as much as in the finding and the arrival; and finally, a profound awe in the face of the living spirit manifest in the universe, which writes our destiny, and which may lead us, we hope and believe, to a Tir na'n Og, or Land of the Ever Young, or to the sweet summer orchard of Avallon in the happy Isles of the Blessed. It is an impressive legacy.

Notes

1 Alwyn Rees and Brinley Rees, *Celtic Heritage*, p. 314.
2 *Celtic Heritage*, p. 317.
3 The *Journal of the New England Antiquities Research Association* is published from 305 Academy Road, Pembroke, New Hampshire 03275, USA.
4 *Ecclesiastical History of the English Nation*, Dent Everyman edition, p. 6.
5 Quoted in the Introduction to Alexander Mackenzie, *History of the Highland Clearances*, Inverness, 1883, reprinted by Melven Press, Perth, 1979.

6 *History of the Highland Clearances*, pp. 1–2.
7 Clan information is taken from *The Scottish Tartans*, Johnston and Bacon, Edinburgh and London, 1945, several reprints.
8 Introduction to *The Secret Rose*, Dublin, 1897.
9 Published by Premier Magazines Ltd., Haymarket House, 1 Oxenden Street, London SW1Y 4EE.
10 Amanda May, of Williston, Vermont, USA, letter published in *The Burlington Free Press*, 20 September 1997.

APPENDIX

✳

THE PRINCIPAL SCOTTISH CLANS

Chief: head and leader of the clan
Clan seat: ancestral territory or castle
Memorials: site of memorials or testimonials
Patronymic: personal name if different to title, usually in Gaelic spelling
Plant: plant emblem of clan
Slogan: public motto or legend
Tartan: plaid pattern identifying clan
Tryst: secret meeting place, or greeting, originally used as password or
   introduction

BRODIE Chief: Brodie of Brodie; clan seat: Brodie Castle, Forres, Morayshire;
   plant: periwinkle; memorials: Kirk of Dyke, Moray; tartan: green and black
   ground, blue crosshatch, red and yellow piping.
BRUCE Chief: Earl of Elgin; patronymic: The Bruce; clan seats: Clackmannan
   Tower, Alloa and Broomhall, Fife; tryst: Lochmabenstone, Annandale;
   plant: rosemary; tartan: grey and red, green crosshatch, white piping.
BUCHANAN Chief: Buchanan of that Ilk; clan seat: Buchanan Castle, Drymen;
   slogan: Clare Innis; plant: bilberry; memorials: Clare Innis, in Loch
   Lomond; tartan: red, green and yellow crosshatch, black and white piping.
CAMERON Chief: Cameron of Lochiel; patronymic: Mac Dhomnuil Duibh;
   clan seat: Achnacarry, Spean Bridge; slogan: Chlanna nan Con; plant: oak;
   pipe music: The Camerons' Gathering and Pibroch of Donnuil Dubh;
   tartan: red ground, grey and green crosshatch, white piping.
CAMPBELL OF LOCHOW Chief: Duke of Argyll; patronymic: Mac Cailein
   Mor; clan seats: Inveraray Castle, Argyll and Ardchonnel Castle, Loch
   Awe; slogan: Cruachan; plant: wild myrtle; memorials: Kilmun Kirk; pipe
   music: Argyll's Salute and The Campbells Are Coming; tartan: green and
   black ground, blue horizontal hatch, white piping.
CAMPBELL OF BREADALBANE Chief: Earl of Breadalbane; patronymic:

Mac Chailein 'ic Dhonnachaidh; clan seat: Kilchurn Castle, Loch Awe; slogan: Cruachan; plant: wild myrtle; tartan: green and black ground, yellow and black piping.

CAMPBELL OF CAWDOR Chief: Earl of Cawdor; clan seat: Cawdor Castle, Nairnshire; plant: wild myrtle; memorials: Barevon Kirk; tartan: green, sky blue and blue crosshatching, red and sky blue piping.

CHISHOLM Chief: Chisholm of Chisholm; patronymic: An Siosalach (The Chisholm); clan seats: Erchless Castle, and Comer, Strathglass; plant: fern; pipe music: The Chisholm's Salute and Chisholm's March; tartan: red ground, blue and yellow crosshatching, double white piping.

COLQUHOUN Chief: Colquhoun of Luss; clan seats: Rossdhu, Luss, Dunbartonshire and Luss Barony, Dunbartonshire; tryst and slogan: Cnoc Ealachan; plant: hazel; pipe music: The Colquhouns' March and The Colquhouns' Gathering; tartan: blue and green ground, white, red and double black piping.

CRAWFURD Chief: Crawfurd of Auchinames; clan seat: Auchinames, Lanarkshire; plant: boxwood; tartan: green and mulberry red ground, mulberry red and double white piping.

CUMMING Chief: Cumming of Altyre; clan seats: Altyre, Forres; Durdargue Castle and Inverallochy Castle, both by Fraserburgh; plant: cummin; tartan: red and green fine crosshatch, black and sky blue piping.

CUNNINGHAM Chief: Cunningham of Kilmaurs; clan seat: Kilmaurs, Ayrshire; tartan: red and black crosshatch, white and double red piping.

DAVIDSON Chief: Davidson of that Ilk or Tulloch; clan seats: Tulloch Castle, Dingwall and Cantray, Inverness; plant: cranberry; pipe music: Tulloch's Salute; tartan: light green and dark green ground, red and black piping.

DOUGLAS Chief: Douglas of Douglas; patronymic: The Douglas; clan seats: Douglas Castle, Lanarkshire and Tantallon Castle, East Lothian; memorials: St. Bryde's Kirk, Douglas; music: Dumbarton's Drums; tartan: green ground, navy blue crosshatching, white and double white piping.

DRUMMOND Chief: Earl of Perth; clan seats: Castle Drummond, Crieff and Stobhall, Perthshire; slogan: Gang Warily; plant: holly; pipe music: The Duke of Perth's March; tartan: red ground, fine blue and grey crosshatch, white piping.

DUNDAS Chief: Dundas of Dundas; clan seats: Dundas Castle, South Queensferry and Inchgarvie, Firth of Forth; plant: bilberry; tartan: blue and green ground, double yellow piping.

ELLIOT Chief: Elliot of Stobs; clan seats: Redheugh, Roxburghshire; Larriston Tower; and Gilnockie Tower; tartan: sky blue ground, narrow black crosshatch, red piping.

ERSKINE Chief: Earl of Mar and Kellie; clan seats: Alloa Tower, Clackmannan and Erskine, Renfrewshire; plant: red rose; tartan: red and green crosshatch, double red piping.

FARQUHARSON Chief: Farquharson of Invercauld; patronymic: Mac Fhionnlaidh; clan seats: Invercauld House and Braemar Castle, Aberdeenshire; slogan: Carn na Cuimhne; plant: scots fir; tartan: green and sky blue crosshatch, yellow and red piping, fine double black piping.

FERGUSSON Chief: Fergusson of Kilkerran; patronymic: Clan Fhearghuis Stra' Churra; clan seats: Kilkerran Tower, Ayrshire and Glenshellich in Strachur, Argyll; tryst: The Bloody Stone; slogan: Clan Fhearghuis Gu Brath; tartan: light green and dark green crosshatch, blue and black squares, white and double red piping.

FORBES Chief: Lord Forbes; clan seats: Castle Forbes and Drumminor Castle, Aberdeenshire; tryst: Culquhonny Castle; slogan: Lonach; plant: broom; pipe music: Cath Glinn Eurainn (The Battle of Glen Eurann) and The Forbes' Gathering; tartan: light green and dark green crosshatch, blue and black squares, white and black piping.

FRASER Chief: Lord Fraser; patronymic: Mac Shimidh; clan seat: Castle Fraser, Sauchen; Caernbulg Castle, Philorth, Aberdeenshire; and Beaufort Castle, Beauly; slogan: A' Mhor Fhaich; plant: yew; memorials: Rathen Kirk; pipe music: The Frasers' Salute; tartan: red ground, brown crosshatch, green and blue squares, white piping.

GORDON Chief: Marquis of Huntly; patronymic: The Gordon; clan seats: Huntly Castle, Huntly and Aboyne Castle, Aboyne, Aberdeenshire; tryst: Standing Stone of Strathbogie; slogan: An Gordonach; plant: rock ivy; memorials: Elgin Cathedral; pipe music: The Cock o' the North and Marquis of Huntly's Farewell; tartan: blue and dark green ground, light green crosshatch, yellow and double black piping.

GRAHAM OF MONTROSE Chief: Duke of Montrose; patronymic: An Greumach Mor (The Graham); clan seats: Mugdock Castle, Stirlingshire and Dundaff Hills, West Stirlingshire; plant: spurge laurel; memorials: Inchmahome Priory; pipe music: Raon Ruraidh; tartan: fine green and blue crosshatch, narrow black crosshatch, white and black piping.

GRAHAM OF MENTEITH Chief: Graham of Gartmore; clan seat: Inchtalla Castle, Lake of Menteith; plant: spurge laurel; memorials: Inchmahome Priory; tartan: blue and light green crosshatch, narrow white crosshatch, black piping and squares.

GRANT Chief: Lord Strathspey; patronymic: An Granntach; clan seat: Castle Grant, Grantown-on-Spey; tryst: Upper Craigellachie; slogan: Stand Fast, Craigellachie; plant: scots fir; memorials: Duthil Kirk; pipe music: The Grants' Gathering and Stand Fast Craigellachie March; tartan: red ground, light green and dark green crosshatch, very narrow sky blue cross hatch, red double piping.

HAMILTON Chief: Duke of Hamilton; clan seat: Cadzow Castle, Lanarkshire; plant: bay; memorials: Hamilton Ducal Mausoleum; tartan: red ground, narrow triple blue crosshatch, white piping.

HOME (pronounced Hume); Chief: Earl of Home; clan seat: Home Castle, Berwickshire; plant: broom; tartan: purple-blue ground, black squares, very narrow red crosshatch, double sky blue piping.

INNES Chief: Innes of that Ilk; clan seats: Innes, by Elgin, Moray; Motte of Innes, Moray; and Edder Innes, Garmouth; tryst: Loch Hill of Innes; plant: great bulrush; memorials: Elgin Cathedral; pipe music: Duke of Roxburghe's March and Balvenie Castle Strathspey; tartan: red ground, very narrow light green and dark green crosshatch, light green piping.

JOHNSTON Chief: Johnston of that Ilk and Annandale; clan seat: Lochwood Tower, Dumfries; plant: red hawthorn; tartan: green ground, dark green crosshatch, small blue squares, yellow and triple black piping.

KENNEDY Chief: Marquess of Ailsa; clan seats: Cassilis House, Maybole and Culzean Castle, Ayrshire; plant: oak; tartan: green ground, narrow blue crosshatch, red, yellow and triple black piping.

LAMONT Chief: Lamont of that Ilk; patronymic: Mac Laomuinn; clan seats: Ardlamont, Argyll and Castle Toward; plant: crab apple; pipe music: Lamont's Welcome; tartan: dark blue ground, dark green crosshatch, small light green squares, white and double black piping.

LESLIE Chief: Earl of Rothies; clan seats: Leslie Castle, Aberdeenshire; Rothes Castle, Moray; Ballinbreich Castle, Fife; and Leslie-on-Leven, Fife; plant: rue; tartan: green ground, blue squares, narrow black crosshatch, red and white piping.

LINDSAY Chief: Earl of Crawford; patronymic: Le Lindesay; clan seats: Balcarres, Colinsburgh; Ochteruterstruther Castle, Fife; and Finhaven Castle, Angus; plant: linden; memorials: Crawford Priory, Fife; tartan: green and blue ground, red and mulberry red crosshatch, double black piping.

MACALISTAIR Chief: Mac Alistair of the Loup; patronymic: Mac Iain Duibh; clan seat: Menstrie Castle, Stirling; plant: ling heather; tartan: red ground, very narrow green crosshatch, white piping.

MACARTHUR Chief: Mac Arthur of Tirrcladdich; patronymic: Mac ic Artair; clan seat: Tirracladdich on Loch Awe, Argyll; slogan: Eisd! O Eisd; plant: wild thyme; tartan: green ground, black crosshatch, yellow and black piping.

MACAULAY Chief: Macaulay of Ardincaple; clan seat: Ardincaple Castle, Row, Dunbartonshire; plant: scots fir; tartan: red ground, quadruple grey crosshatch, green squares, white and black piping.

MACBAIN Chief: Mac Bain of that Ilk; clan seat: Kinchyle, Inverness; tryst: Kinchyle; plant: boxwood; memorials: Dunlichity Kirk; tartan: red ground, narrow purple crosshatch, green, white and black piping.

MACCALLUM (MALCOLM) Chief: Malcolm of Poltalloch; clan seat: Poltalloch, Argyll; plant: rowan; tartan: light green and dark green crosshatch, purple squares, black and white piping.

MACDONALD Chief: Lord Macdonald; patronymic: Mac Dhomnuill; clan seats: Dunscaith Castle, Skye; Armadale Castle, Skye; and Ostaig House, Skye; tryst: Dun Donald; slogan: Fraoch Eilean; plant: heather; memorials: Iona; pipe music: Macdonald's Salute and March of the Macdonalds; tartan: light green and dark green crosshatch, dark blue squares, black and double red piping.

MACDOUGALL Chief: MacDougall of MacDougall and Dunollie; patronymic: Mac Dhughaill; clan seats: Dunollie Castle, Oban and Gylen Castle, Kerrera, Argyll; slogan: Buaidh no bas; plant: bell heather; pipe music: Dunollie Castle and MacDougall's Salute; tartan: red ground, narrow green and purple crosshatch, green squares, double white piping.

MACFARLANE Chief: Macfarlane of that Ilk; patronymic: Mac Pharlain; clan seat: Arrochar; slogan: Loch Sloy; plant: cranberry; pipe music: Macfarlane's Gathering; tartan: red ground, blue quadruple crosshatch, white piping.

MACFIE (DUFFIE) (Gaelic Dubhsithe, 'Dark Face') Chief: Macduffie of Colonsay; patronymic: Mac a Phie; clan seat: Isle of Colonsay; plant: pine; tartan: red ground, narrow green crosshatch, white and green piping.

MACGILLIVRAY Chief: Macgillivray of Dunmaglass; clan seat: Dunmaglass, Inverness; slogan: Dunmaghlas; plant: boxwood; memorials: Dunlochity Kirk; pipe music: The Macgillivrays' March; tartan: red ground, narrow purple and green crosshatch, double blue piping.

MACGREGOR Chief: Macgregor of Macgregor; patronymic: Ant' Ailpeanach; clan seats: Edinchip, Balquhidder and Glenstrae; tryst: Ard Coille; slogan: Gregalach!; plant: scots fir; memorials: Balquhidder Kirk; pipe music: The Macgregors' Gathering and Macgregors' Salute; tartan: red ground, very narrow green crosshatch, white piping.

MACKAY Chief: Lord Reay; patronymic: Morair Maghrath; clan seat: House of Tongue, Sutherland; slogan: Bratach bhan mhic Aoidh; plant: great bulrush; memorials: Kirk of Tongue; pipe music: Mackay's White Banner and Mackay's March; tartan: green ground, narrow black crosshatch, purple squares, black and white piping.

MACKENZIE Chief: Mackenzie of Kintail; patronymic: Caberfeidh; clan seats: Brahan Castle, Urray, Ross, and Eilean Donan Castle, Lochalsh; slogan: Tulach Ard; plant: deer's grass; memorials: Rosemarkie in Ross; pipe music: Mackenzie's Salute and The Mackenzie Highlanders; tartan: dark blue ground, narrow green crosshatch, blue squares, red, white and double black piping.

MACKINNON Chief: Mackinnon of Mackinnon; patronymic: Mac Fhionghuin; clan seat Strathardal in Skye; slogan: Cuimhnich bas Ailpein; plant: St. John's Wort; memorials: Iona; tartan: red ground, very narrow green crosshatch, white piping.

MACKINTOSH Chief: Mackintosh of Mackintosh; patronymic: Mac an Toisich; clan seats: Moy Hall, Inverness and Dunauchton; tryst: Loch Moy; slogan: Loch Moigh; plant: red whortleberry; memorials: Kirk of Petty, Moray; pipe music: The Mackintosh's Banner; tartan: red ground, green and purple double crosshatch, purple piping.

MACLACHLAN Chief: Maclachlan of Maclachlan; clan seat: Castle Lachlan, Strathlachlan, Argyll; plant: rowan; pipe music: Moladh Mairi; tartan: purple ground, red and narrow black crosshatch, white and double black piping.

MACLAINE Chief: Maclaine of Lochbuie; patronymic: Mac ill Eathain Lochabuidhe; clan seat: Lochbuie Castle, Mull, Argyll; plant: bilberry; tartan: red ground, narrow green crosshatch, white piping.

MACLAREN Chief: Maclaren of Maclaren; patronymic: Mac aub's Labhran; clan seats: Auchleskine and Achtow in Balquhidder, Perthshire; tryst: Creag an Tuirc, Balquhidder; slogan: Creag an Tuirc; plant: laurel; memorials: Balquhidder Kirk; tartan: light green and dark green crosshatch, dark blue narrow crosshatch, blue squares, yellow and red piping.

MACLEAN Chief: Maclean of Duart; patronymic: Mac ill Eathain; clan seat: Duart Castle, Mull; slogan: Fear eile airson Eachuinn; plant: crowberry; tartan: red ground, green and purple crosshatch, black, double sky blue and double white piping.

MACLENNAN (LOGAN) Chief: Logan of Drumderfit; patronymic: Ghilinnein; clan seat: Drumderfit, Ross; tryst: Druic na Claven, Kintail; slogan: Druim nan deur; plant: furze; tartan: green ground, narrow black crosshatch, purple squares, white and quadruple red piping.

MACLEOD Chief: MacLeod of MacLeod; patronymic: MacLeoid; clan seat: Dunvegan Castle, Skye; plant: juniper; memorials: Rodill, in Harris; pipe music: MacLeod's Salute and MacLeod's Rowing Salute; tartan: green ground, narrow black crosshatch, blue squares, yellow and red piping.

MACLEOD OF LEWIS Clan seat: Stornoway Castle, Lewis and Assynt, Ross; plant: red whortleberry; tartan: yellow ground, triple grey crosshatch, black squares, red and double yellow piping.

MACMILLAN Chief: Macmillan of Macmillan; patronymic: Mac Mhaoilean Mor a Cnaip; clan seat: Knapdale, Argyllshire; tryst: Macmillan's Cross, Knapdale; plant: holly; memorials: Resby Cnaip; tartan: dark green ground, light green, yellow and red crosshatch, black piping.

MACNEIL Chief: The MacNeil of Barra; patronymic: Mac Neill; clan seat: Kismull Castle, Isle of Barra; slogan: Buaidh no Bas; plant: dryas; tartan: green ground, grey, dark blue and narrow black crosshatch, white and yellow piping.

MACPHERSON Chief: Macpherson of Cluny; patronymic: Mac Mhuirich; clan seat: Cluny-in-Badenoch, Kingussie; tryst: Lochan Ovie, Creag Dhu; slogan: Creag Dhubh; plant: white heather; pipe music: Cluny Macpherson's Salute and Macpherson's March; tartan: red and blue crosshatch, black and white piping.

MACRAE Chief: Macrae; patronymic: Mac Rath; clan seat: Inverinate, Inverness; slogan: Sgur Urain; plant: club moss; memorials: Kintail, Auld Kirk; pipe music: The Macraes' March; tartan: red ground, narrow triple green and double blue crosshatch. white and double blue piping.

MENZIES (pronounced Men-ghees) Chief: Menzies of that Ilk; patronymic: Am Meinnearach; clan seat: Castle Menzies, Weem, Aberfeldy; tryst: The Rock of Weem; slogan: Geal is Dearg a Suas; plant: Menzies heath; memorials: Auld Kirk, Weem; pipe music: The Menzies' Salute and Menzies' March; tartan: salmon red ground, narrow white crosshatch and white double piping.

MORRISON Chief: Morrison of Barvas and Duneystein; patronymic: Mac Hulle Mhoire; clan seats: Dunetstein Castle, Isle of Lewis and Dun of Pabbay of Tarbert in Harris; tryst: Duneystein; slogan: Duneystein; plant: driftweed; tartan: green ground, blue and narrow black crosshatch, red and black piping.

MUNRO Chief: Munro of Foulis; patronymic: Tighearna Folais; clan seat: Foulis Castle, Evanton, Ross; tryst: Foulis Castle; slogan: Caisteal Folais na Theine; plant: common club moss; pipe music: Munro's Salute and Munro's March; tartan: red ground, narrow green and blue crosshatch, blue and white piping.

MURRAY Chief: Duke of Atholl; patronymic: Am Moireach Mor; clan seats: Blair Castle, Blair Atholl, Perthshire; Tullibardine, Perthshire; and Duffus Castle, by Elgin; plant: juniper; memorials: Tullibardine Old Kirk; pipe music: Duke of Atholl's Salute; tartan: green ground, blue and narrow black crosshatch, red piping.

OGILVY Chief: Earl of Airlie; clan seats: Airlie Castle and Cortachy Castle, Angus; plant: white thorn; tartan: green ground, black crosshatch, small blue squares, white and red piping.

RAMSAY Chief: Earl of Dalhousie; clan seat: Dalhousie Castle, Midlothian; plant: harebell; tartan: red ground, mulberry red crosshatch, narrow double white and double blue piping.

ROBERTSON (DONACHY) (derived from Robert of Clann Donnachaidh) Chief: Robertson of Struan; patronymic: Struan Robertson; clan seats: Dunalastair, Perthshire and Rannoch Barracks, Perthshire; slogan: Garg'n uair dhuisgear; plant: bracken; pipe music: The Robertsons' Gathering; tartan: red ground, light green crosshatch, very small blue, dark green and black squares, double blue piping.

ROSS Chief: Ross of that Ilk; patronymic: Mac Gillanreas; clan seats: Balnagowan Castle, Ross; Delny, Ross; and Pitcalnie, by Tain; tryst: St. Duithac's, Tain, Ross; plant: juniper; memorials: Fearn Abbey, Edderton; pipe music: The Earl of Ross's March; tartan: red ground, green and blue triple crosshatch, triple blue piping.

SCOTT Chief: Duke and Earl of Buccleuch; patronymic: Scott of Buccleuch; clan seat: Branxholm Castle, by Hawick; tryst and slogan: Bellendaine; plant: blaeberry; memorials: Buccleuch Old Kirkyard; tartan: red ground, very narrow green crosshatch, double white piping.

SINCLAIR Chief: Earl of Caithness; patronymic: Morair Ghallaobh; clan seats: Girnigoe Castle, Wick; Brawl Castle, Caithness; Roslin Castle, Midlothian; and Ravensheugh Castle, Dysart, Fife; slogan: Roslin, Roslin; plant: furze; memorials: Roslin Chapel; pipe music: The Sinclairs' March; tartan: red ground, very narrow green crosshatch, sky blue and mulberry red piping.

STEWART Chief: Stewart of Appin; patronymic: Mac Iain Stiubhart na h'Apunn; clan seat: Castle Stalcaire, by Appin, Argyll; tryst: The Cormorant's Rock; slogan: Creag an Sgairbh; plant: oak; tartan: green ground, very narrow double black crosshatch, red and yellow piping.

SUTHERLAND Chief: Sutherland of that Ilk, Countess of Sutherland; patronymic: Morair Chat; clan seat: Dunrobin Castle, Sutherland; tryst: The Brig o' Dunrobin; slogan: Ceann na Drochaide Bige; plant: cotton sedge; memorials: Dornoch Cathedral; pipe music: The Earl of Sutherland's March; tartan: light green ground, very narrow black crosshatch, dark blue squares, double red and double white piping.

URQUHART Chief: Urquhart of that Ilk; clan seat: Castle Craig of Urquhart, Black Isle, Ross; plant: wallflower; memorials: Cullicudden Old Kirkyard; tartan: dark green and narrow light green crosshatch, blue squares, red and black piping.

BIBLIOGRAPHY

CLASSICAL TEXTS AND TRANSLATIONS

Grant, M., *Tacitus: The Annals of Imperial Rome*, Harmondsworth: Penguin, 1956

Grant, M., *Readings in the Classical Historians*, New York: Macmillan, 1992

Graves, R., *Suetonius: The Twelve Caesars*, Harmondsworth: Penguin, 1957

Handford, S.A., *Caesar: The Conquest of Gaul*, Harmondsworth: Penguin, 1951

Lempriere, J., *A Classical Dictionary*, London: Routledge, n.d.

Mattingly, H., *Tacitus: The Agricola and The Germania*, revised S.A. Handford, Harmondsworth: Penguin, 1948, 1970

Scott-Kilvert, I., *Plutarch: The Makers of Rome, Nine Lives by Plutarch*, Harmondsworth: Penguin, 1965

Selincourt, A. de, *Livy: The History of Rome from its Foundation, Books I–V*, Harmondsworth: Penguin, 1960

Selincourt, A. de, *Livy, The History of Rome from its Foundation, Books XXI–XXX*, Harmondsworth: Penguin, 1965

Stevenson, J., *Bede's Ecclesiastical History of the English Nation*, revised L.C. Jane, 1903, London and New York: Dent, 1870, 1910, 1954

VERNACULAR TEXTS AND TRANSLATIONS, MEDIAEVAL TEXTS

Baines, K., *Sir Thomas Malory: Le Morte d'Arthur*, New York, Bramhall House, 1961

Bromwich, R., *Trioedd Ynys Prydein: The Welsh Triads*, Cardiff: Llanilltud, 1961

Gantz, J.,*The Mabinogion*, Harmondsworth: Penguin, 1976
Gantz, J., *Early Irish Myths and Sagas*, Harmondsworth: Penguin, 1981
Gantz, J., *Tales of Cu Chulaind: Irish Heroic Myths*, Harmondsworth: Penguin, 1995
Jones, G. and Jones, T., *The Mabinogion*, London: Dent, 1948, revised 1974
Kibler, W.W., *Chrétien de Troyes: Arthurian Romances*, Harmondsworth: Penguin, 1991
Kinsella, T., *The Tain*, Dublin: Oxford University Press, 1969
Luzel, F.M., *Celtic Folk-Tales from Armorica*, trans. Bryce, D., Lampeter: Llanerch Enterprises, 1985
O'Faolain, E., *Irish Sagas and Folk Tales*, Oxford: Oxford University Press, 1954
Rhys, E., *Sir Thomas Malory: The Noble History of King Arthur*, London and Newcastle upon Tyne: Walter Scott, n.d.
Thorpe, L., *Geoffrey of Monmouth: The History of the Kings of Britain*, Harmondsworth: Penguin, 1966
Tolkien, J.R.R. and Gordon, E.V., *Sir Gawain and the Green Knight*, Oxford: Oxford University Press, 1967

CELTIC LANGUAGE

Anwyl, J.B., *Spurrell's English–Welsh, Welsh–English Dictionary,* Carmarthen: Spurrell, 1934
Bhaldraithe, T. de, *English–Irish Dictionary*, Dublin: Oifig an tSolathair / Office of Procurement, 1959
O Donaill, N. (ed.), *Gearrfhocloir Gaeilge-Bearla*, Dublin: An Roinn Oideachais / Department of Education, 1981
George, K. (Profus an Mortyd), *Gerlyver Kernewek Kemmyn*, Seaton: Kesva an Taves Kernewek / The Cornish Language Board, 1984
Gillies, H.C., *The Elements of Gaelic Grammar*, London: D. Nutt, 1902
Gregor, D.B., *Celtic – A Comparative Study,* Cambridge and New York: Oleander Press, 1980
Hemon, R., *Nouveau Dictionnaire Breton–Français*, Brest: Al Liamm, 1978
Lewis, H., *Welsh Dictionary,* London and Glasgow: Collins, 1960, re-edited 1969
MacFarlane, M., *Gaelic–English Dictionary*, Stirling: Eneas Mackay, 1953
Williams, R., *Llawlyfr Gramadeg Cymraeg, Gyda Gwersi,* Wrexham: Hughes a'i Fab / Hughes & Son, 1923

GENERAL

Ashe, G., *The Quest for Arthur's Britain*, London: Pall Mall Press, 1968

Bain, G., *Celtic Art – the Methods of Construction*, London: William Maclellan, 1951

Berleth, R., *The Twilight Lords: An Irish Chronicle*, New York: Knopf, 1978

Berresford Ellis, P., *A Dictionary of Irish Mythology*, London: Routledge and Kegan Paul, 1987

Bord, J. and C., *A Guide to Ancient Sites in Britain*, London: Latimer New Dimensions, 1978

Breffny, B. de (ed.), *The Irish World*, London and New York: Harry N. Abrams, 1978

Burl, A., *The Stone Circles of the British Isles*, London and New Haven: Yale University Press, 1976

Campbell, J., *The Hero with a Thousand Faces*, Princeton: Princeton University Press, 1949

Campbell, N., *Pageant of Saints*, Oxford: Mowbray, 1963

Cavendish, R., *King Arthur and the Grail*, London: Weidenfeld and Nicolson, 1978

Churchill, W., *A History of the English Speaking Peoples (Vol. 1)*, New York: Dodd, Mead, 1956

Clark, G. and Piggott, S., *Prehistoric Societies*, New York: Knopf, 1965

Clayton, P., *Archaeological Sites of Britain*, London: Weidenfeld and Nicolson, 1976

Cone, P. (ed.), *Treasures of Early Irish Art*, New York: Metropolitan Museum of Art, 1977

Cornell, T.J., *The Beginnings of Rome*, London and New York: Routledge, 1995

Davies, J., *Hanes Cymru / A History of Wales*, London: Allen Lane Penguin, 1990, 1993

Dillon, M. and Chadwick, N., *The Celtic Realms*, London: Weidenfeld and Nicolson, 1967

Duckett, E., *The Wandering Saints of the Early Middle Ages*, London and Glasgow: Norton, 1959

Evans, J.G., *The Environment of Early Man in the British Isles*, Cardiff: Paul Elek, 1975

Falkus, M. and Gillingham, J. (eds.), *Historical Atlas of Britain*, London: Kingfisher, 1981

Gimbutas, M., *The Language of the Goddess*, London: Thames and Hudson, 1990

Graves, R., *The White Goddess*, London: Faber, 1948, revised 1961

Green, M.J., *Dictionary of Celtic Myth and Legend*, London: Thames and Hudson, 1992

Green, M.J., *Celtic Goddesses*, New York: George Braziller, 1996

Herm, G., *The Celts*, London: Weidenfeld and Nicolson, 1976

Hole, C., *Saints in Folklore*, New York: Barrows, 1965

Jenkins, E., *The Mystery of King Arthur*, London: Michael Joseph, 1975

Jones, K., *The Ancient British Goddess*, Glastonbury: Ariadne, 1991

Keller, W., *The Etruscans*, trans. A. Henderson and E. Henderson, London: Jonathan Cape, 1974

King, J., *The Celtic Druids' Year*, London: Blandford Press, 1994

Lansdale, M., *Scotland*, Edinburgh: Henry T. Coates, 1901

Mackenzie, A., *A History of the Highland Clearances*, Inverness and Perth: 1883, Melven Press 1979

MacManus, S., *The Story of the Irish Race*, New York: Devin-Adair, 1921

Masson, G., *A Concise History of Republican Rome*, London: Thames and Hudson, 1973

Matthews, J., *Taliesin, Shamanism and the Bardic Mysteries in Britain and Ireland*, London: Aquarian, 1991

Moran, Cardinal, *Irish Saints in Great Britain*, Callan: Sisters of Mercy, 1903

Nordenfolk, C., *Celtic and Anglo-Saxon Painting*, New York: George Braziller, 1977

Piggott, S., *Ancient Europe*, Edinburgh: Edinburgh University Press, 1965

Powell, T.G.E., *The Celts*, London: Thames and Hudson, 1958

Rees, A. and Rees, B., *Celtic Heritage – Ancient Tradition in Ireland and Wales*, London: Thames and Hudson, 1961

Ross, A., *Everyday Life of the Pagan Celts*, London: Batsford, 1970

Scullard, H.H., *Roman Britain – Outpost of the Empire*, London: Thames and Hudson, 1979

Squire, C., *Celtic Myth and Legend, Poetry and Romance*, New York: Bell, 1979

Thom, A., *Megalithic Sites in Britain*, Oxford: Oxford University Press, 1967

Tolstoy, N., *The Quest for Merlin*, London: Hodder and Stoughton, 1985

Treharne, R.F. (ed., posthumously) and Fullard, H. (ed.), *Muir's Historical Atlas, Ancient and Classical,* London: Muir, 1938

Webster, G., *The Roman Imperial Army*, New York: Barnes and Noble, 1994

Young, C.R., *The Royal Forests of Medieval England*, Philadelphia: University of Pennsylvania Press, 1979

INDEX